C000292900

PROSTITUTE LAUNDRY

PROSTITUTE LAUNDRY

CHARLOTTE SHANE

SERPENT'S TAIL

First published in Great Britain in 2023 by
Serpent's Tail,
an imprint of Profile Books Ltd
29 Cloth Fair
London
EC1A 7JQ
www.serpentstail.com

First published in the United States of America in 2015 by TigerBee Press

10 9 8 7 6 5 4 3 2 1

Printed and bound in Great Britain by Clays Ltd, Elcograf S.p.A.

A CIP catalogue record for this book is available from the British Library.

ISBN 978 1 80081 583 4
eISBN 978 1 80081 584 1

Because everything is for Sam, this is for Sam.

But only the parts he likes.

CONTENTS

Introduction by Katherine Angel   xi

Preface by Jo Livingston   xvii

SEARCHING
February 8—June 9

Bleak Week   3

The Splurge   7

Nick   9

Lights Out   13

When I Was In Trouble   19

First Quarter   25

Long-Term Relationship   27

Got This Body   31

More Than One Chop   35

Breasts   39

The Importance of Escape   43

FINDING

June 11—August 25

Nine Years   *49*

All The Mess   *53*

Girls On Stage   *59*

To Be Discovered   *63*

Practice   *67*

Breasts Again   *73*

His Face   *81*

Breasts For The Last Time   *87*

Normal People   *93*

Rushing   *101*

All Men   *107*

Some Guy   *111*

Imaginary   *117*

Orbit and Shine   *123*

RELEASING

September 2—December 23

Blushing in London	*137*
Why Love	*141*
Go Into It	*149*
Secret Life	*155*
The Game	*161*
Head Shop	*167*
Long Lost	*173*
Interlude	*179*
Post game	*183*
Gave Freely	*187*
Work Sex	*195*
Glamour	*199*
Everything I Wanted	*205*
The Urge System	*213*
In The Past	*219*
Pursuits	*225*

BEGINNING

January 6—September 28

The Ink In His Nail Beds   *235*

Indigo   *243*

A Good One   *249*

Wife   *261*

These Feelings   *267*

Jackpot   *279*

Do You Want Me Now   *285*

The Cord   *291*

Past Lives   *307*

Poison   *315*

Other Life   *321*

Committed   *331*

The Ones Who Can Pay   *339*

Forever Beginning   *349*

INTRODUCTION

by Katherine Angel

The 'best egress I have into any idea or inquiry is the pinhole of my own life, and my life is full of sex', writes Charlotte Shane in *Prostitute Laundry*. Sex, she states, '[is] my setting'. It's her setting, and it's her subject. I remember first reading Shane on Twitter, sometime between 2012 and 2015, when the platform still felt like a curiously intimate space, and a particularly playful and generative one for writers. It was also, for me, a way to discover – to listen to – smart, savvy and brilliant American writers.

I first remember Shane's voice from this era. It stood out: startlingly lucid, often very funny, and utterly itself. She initially disseminated the pieces that make up this book in newsletter form in 2014, and later published the entirety through TigerBee Press in 2015. This is *Prostitute Laundry*'s first UK edition. Over the years, Shane has written for many publications, as a reviewer and essayist, on topics including abortion, OnlyFans, incest, rape and video games. Across her writing, autonomy and self-determination are enduring concerns, though she is never glib about when these are possible, for her or anyone else. Her writing has always displayed something quite rare, I think: an immersion in debates both contemporary and historical, while writing in a voice that is entirely hers, and that speaks on its own terms. In *Prostitute Laundry*, she writes beautifully, precisely and achingly, about sex, love, money and work.

One of the questions to which Shane returns again and again in the book is that of the boundary between 'home sex' and 'work sex'. She writes about this against the background of a fractious public conversation about sex work: about its inevitability, its legitimacy, its legal status, its place in feminist discourse and activism. This background features as a condition of *Prostitute Laundry*, but is not often explicitly addressed in it. Shane refers to it briefly, however, when she writes that the 'refrain used to be that we'd die before giving away that which we could charge for'. Eva Pendleton put it this way a 1998 anthology called *Whores and Other Feminists*, edited by Jill Nagle: when women are 'paid to perform heterosexuality, that is to say, to play a role of sexual availability and feminine receptivity', they can become 'less willing to play that role for free'.*

The idea is that once one has sold sex, one has seen laid bare the contractual exchange of heterosexual relations. How does that change one? Shane obliquely ruminates on these questions without placing them centre stage. She conveys the value, the interest, the pleasure and excitement – and the pitfalls and pains – of sex, unpaid or paid. Sex with clients informs sex with other men, and, inevitably, vice versa – the boundary between the two is not rigid. On the one hand, delight, pleasure, care and love are not simply a delusional effect of labour sublimated as romance. But nor is it easy to understand – whether in paid sex or unpaid sex – when love is substantial, when a transaction is just that, or when fantasy and projection have got the upper hand. What's more, the traffic between sex at work and sex at home is productive. 'Now I believe', Shane writes, 'the antidote to work sex isn't no sex. The antidote is at least as much sex as I have at work but on my terms, with people I choose. I think I realized this, strangely enough, because of something that happened at work.'

Prostitute Laundry is an investigation of sorts. Shane puts her experiences under the microscope, and relaxes into their examination. She is not in a hurry. Nor, thankfully, does she feel the need to justify her examination. There has been, over the past decade, an impressive and growing literature – both first-person narrative and critical argument – from the perspective and expertise of sex workers. Publishers are more willing, it seems, to make space for sex workers to write about their lives and work, and about the questions of safety, (de)criminalisation and policing that frame them. But *Prostitute Laundry* is unique in refusing to define for itself, or for its readers,

---

* Eva Pendleton, 'Love For Sale', in Jill Nagle (ed.) *Whores and Other Feminists* (Routledge, 1998), p. 76

what exactly Shane is doing, or whether she is writing about sex, or about sex work. The certainty and usefulness of the slogan 'sex work is work' doesn't help capture the dynamics and quandaries which Shane evokes in granular texture, in such a singular voice.

In her review of the reissued Nagle anthology in 2017, Shane writes of the 'dissonance between the way I experienced sex work and the way most authorities (prominent feminists among them) said a woman should experience it'.* Shane knows this terrain – the debates, the legal and political discourses around sex work – better than anyone, I'd bet. But she turns sideways from it, and gets on with the business of writing without capitulation, without hand-wringing, without gestures of exculpation. Shane's writing is not governed by the rubric of shame or its refusal; she's not defiant – she's too good a writer for that. This writing is a rare accomplishment: knowledgeable yet hermetic, in-the-world yet decisively oriented to what it alone is doing. It's as refreshing as spring water.

Sex is the frame through which Shane examines the world. She looks at men – really looks at them – and feels all kinds of things for clients: tenderness, contempt, hatred, love, patience, generosity, boredom. She thinks about writing an essay on the idea that 'All men are johns. Meaning there is no identifying characteristic that fingers purchasers of sex from the ones who finagle it for free. The entitlement, the capacity to commit abuse, the cruelty, the kindness, the sincerity; it's always all there.' She examines men forensically, but not unkindly, and she knows that her engagements with them, whether clients or not, are worth detailing.

Shane falls in love, and she conveys the alarming disorientation of this joy. She wonders if she should quit sex work, and the question becomes compelling and puzzling to her. She has a 'startlingly basic thought' – that 'I could have a life where I never have to endure someone touching me when I don't want them to'. But she knows about her attachment to the work – the pull of money and independence, the aura of glamour and power – 'I felt like a colossus of capital, of men, of the city.' What the work enables in her is complex: walking into hotels, 'I turn off more, I turn on more. I dim and

---

* Charlotte Shane, 'Saying it for themselves', *Bookforum*, June–August 2017,

shine at the same time.' I loved to think of Shane 'believing my own hype. Getting high off my own hooker fumes,' even as I knew her endlessly alive reflection makes every experience rich and ambiguous. Shane knows better than most that sex work is one of the many forms of labour that thrives in conditions of precarity. But she knows too, and conveys so beautifully, that sex work is not just work – that it is not exhausted by its conditions, by the practical reasons anyone has for undertaking it. 'I couldn't apologize for my sex work', she writes, 'without apologizing for myself, and I liked who I was. Sex work was an important part of my adult development.' This is the work of 'providing warm mystery, intimacy with enough boundaries to stay interesting'.

Therapy and psychoanalysis have sometimes been denigrated as a form of sex work – you're just ears for hire! – while sex work is often justified as a form of therapeutic service. Justifications and denigrations aside, the real point Shane makes here is about this work as a kind of curated intimacy. The frame, as a therapist might say, is important. The boundaries of the encounter are what make it possible, and what can make it generative. But Shane makes us think about the frame that surrounds all sex. Unpaid sex, too, is a negotiation of intimacy and distance, a space of real contact and of immense projection.

The book is also a musing on the pull of sex, all sex. A friend says to her that '[y]ou talk about sex in a car with a stranger like it were a feng shui consultation or something'. There is sublime joy in the book, giddy glee; she tells one man 'I was so happy the whole time you were in me. I was just thinking, "Thank you for fucking me!" over and over in a loop.' Shane's descriptions of sex are precise, factual, yet often soaringly lovely and funny too. And Shane's lucidity extends too to the pain from which she doesn't turn away; she is bleakly clear-eyed about doing 'what almost every woman knows how to do when a man has violated her in some way: placate, affirm, reassure'. She is heartbroken, though stoical, when a man she loves humiliates her – when she is painfully reminded of her status as a 'whore'. Saddened by her own self-hatred, and bruised by encounters with clumsy, insulting doctors when she is considering breast surgery, she tells us that she loves men for 'not hating our bodies as much as most of us hated our bodies'.

The writer Juliet Jacques once said, advising other writers: 'Never humiliate or sensationalise yourself or others.' This is phenomenally difficult advice to follow, and only some writers can pull it off. What Shane does so beautifully in *Prostitute Laundry* is allow us to see what she sees, as if we too had her perspicacity, her ferocious intelligence, her drive to live her bodily life through the prism of her exacting thought. This is a book about the pleasure and pain of it all. I'm so glad more readers can now have their own encounter with it.

PREFACE

by Jo Livingstone

The book in your hands bears an intricate relation to the period of time it records. In its original form, Charlotte Shane published its sections as diary entries, via an email newsletter service. Once published, these messages, which are structured as essays and concern Shane's relationships—with her memory, her body, her primary partner, and other men, whom she pursues for reasons both private and commercial—were not available to readers in an archive.

That meant, as Shane explained on her Kickstarter page (which in 2015 raised triple the amount she'd asked for to fund her press, TigerBee, which has now printed three editions of *Prostitute Laundry*), that "only those subscribed could read the most recent letter."

The letter's readership grew to around 5,000. "The blog," she told a *New York Times* journalist covering the shift to newsletters in 2016, when they were newfangled, "was too public." People reading her previous blog, Shane explained, "took advantage of my self-disclosure," and sent her crazy emails. "TinyLetter did a good job mitigating that. There's a sense of intimacy that's reciprocal with delivering an email direct to your inbox." Better for security, too, to know exactly what email address—a kind of parallel identity used for guaranteeing us on the internet, a little bit like a professional alter ego—signed up. The mid-2010s were an interesting time, shall we say, for women writing online in the first person, and the strict boundaries that Shane placed around the *Prostitute Laundry* project seem, in retrospect, to match well with the themes of autonomy which her diaries examined.

Because it was serialized and then collected, *Prostitute Laundry* is imbued with a sense of real time, the same way certain Dickens novels bear the stamp of serialization; the reader joins the author as she moves through time, innocent of what lies ahead and on the cusp of the big revelation, which is always out of reach.

Subscribers were trapped in the present moment along with her. When she republished it in book form, the number of intimate acts remembered (reading an email at one's work desk on a Monday morning; a kiss with a person one no longer speaks to) seemed to double, then triple, then spiral into infinity. The result of this tightly controlled and maximally autonomous publishing practice "was a meditative serial memoir," she wrote on Kickstarter, "in which each entry stood alone but meant more to those who'd read what came before."

"Every moment," the English essayist Walter Pater wrote, "some form grows perfect in hand or face; some tone on the hills or the sea is choicer than the rest; some mood of passion or insight or intellectual excitement is irresistibly real and attractive for us,—for that moment only." For him, the critic's obligation is to know when they are occurring. To "burn always with this hard, gemlike flame, to maintain this ecstasy," he wrote, "is success in life."

Shane has said that the central project of her life is "to understand heterosexuality," which would certainly seem to fall into Pater's remit of "some mood of passion." Pater never wrote about sex, but his interest in the minutiae of the passing moment is as erotic as Shane's. "I lavish attention over one moment like a gem," she writes of her practice of revision and refinement. "I polish it in my head, then I set it down and clean it even more, until I'm satisfied with the shine."

A lot of the moments Shane polishes are between men and herself; often she notes transformational moments not in her own understanding but in those of the men she meets. For example, Shane recalls that one guy on AOL who, when she was 14, "cursed me out violently when I couldn't tell him my pantyhose size to prove that I was a girl." Another asked "if I could wear bikini tops, which was something I'd never thought about before . . . I remember this particularly because I've always been fascinated to learn how men imagine women interacting with the artifacts of femininity."

She uses this approach, of observing a moment from many different angles, to consider her own effect on the spaces she moves through, like a narrator undercover as herself, which in some ways she is. In a strip club she wears "a severe black and white number with a long hemline," she writes. "With the heels I was well over six feet and I knew I looked slim as a knife when I walked through the tables of single men to the restroom." If reading *Prostitute Laundry* today is an act of remembering past intimacy with an email, this passage is Shane remembering past intimacies with a space.

I asked one subscriber from the newsletter's earliest days what effect reading such intense analysis under such particular publishing conditions had on her. She said that reading *Prostitute Laundry* has felt, to her, like dropping pennies into one of those arcade machines that move coins forward. It happens in increments, with the maddening inexorability of one's own heartbeat, then all at once comes the crash, with all the magic of an ordinary law of gravity accomplishing a miracle.

PROSTITUTE LAUNDRY

The following 55 entries constitute the bulk of the letters sent out on the Prostitute Laundry mailing list since its inception. They've been edited for clarity but are otherwise true to their original form.

Part of me wanted to leave out more of the early letters, which have less narrative propulsion than the later ones. But my ability to anticipate what readers connect with is not very good. Sometimes a letter I was particularly proud of elicited almost no response while another that I worried was unsatisfying won a barrage of feedback.

The greatest compliment was that most subscribers kept reading no matter what I sent. In the spirit of their (your) continued attention, I tried to err on the side of generosity.

SEARCHING

February 8—June 9

BLEAK WEEK

February 8, 2014

This week, my most frequent regular said he'd come up with an idea. One of us would give the other explicit sexual instructions (that the other was free to refuse) but the one being instructed couldn't do anything spontaneously. They simply had to obey. He said I could choose who took which role and that was easy—I said he should be in charge. It's no secret that many sex workers hate the ubiquitous "tell me what you want to do" client line.

But I wasn't off the hook yet. Because he added that whoever obeyed this time would have to instruct next time, and then he proceeded to cheat. "Put your hand on my hand and guide me," he said with his fingers between my legs. "Put your hands on my head and guide me," he said later. He asked for 69 by prefacing it with, "I know you don't like this"—or "I know this isn't your favorite," maybe, which is so mildly stated that it's almost a lie—"but since I'm the one deciding . . ."

I thought about this for days. Normally he is someone I like and feel warmly toward, but the fond regards now felt poisoned by reality: he hires me, I do what he wants. Why did he preface the request with admission of his knowledge? Why not pretend he forgot? Why announce the irrelevancy of my pleasure or desires when it comes to his own enjoyment? This is a man who has said he loves me, with whom I've spent copious amounts of time since we met three years ago.

I tried to think of an instance when I'd done something like that to someone else, and I succeeded. Years ago, when my boyfriend and I were still relatively new, I asked him to let me go down on him for a while even though I knew he didn't really like it. I wanted to convince him to like it and I thought I had a decent chance of pulling it off. But I couldn't, so I didn't ask it of him again. I wish I knew then what I know now, which is to trust another person's knowledge of their body enough to not force sensation, no matter how much you might like stimulating them that way. I was in my early 20s at the time.

There are lots of examples of men ignoring what I tell them I don't like, and those men are not all clients. But they are men in their 30s, 40s, 50s, beyond. They should have learned better a long time ago. It happens with anal penetration, with receiving oral. Normally I endure more than I deny at work. But if I see an opportunity for discussion or just can't take it anymore, I'll say, "I don't really like that" or "That doesn't feel good." It's very rare that this makes anyone stop. Even outside of work, when I immediately tell guys not to go down on me, they'll try to dive between my legs and change my mind. *If only they knew how many other mouths have tried,* I think, forgetting that even then they wouldn't be dissuaded.

My boyfriend has a habit of pinching or sucking on my nipples whenever I'm topless around him. I sleep naked, and I change clothes in front of him. We shower together. I know, without fail, that in these circumstances he's going to reach for my nipples in spite of the fact that I've told him many times not to do it and that I don't like it, in spite of me crossing my arms over my chest, actively resisting him, moving away, whining "no" while it happens. This is from someone I've been with for many years. He knows what I do for work, but perhaps makes no connection between what I tolerate there and what I tolerate at home. Or, the more probable option—feels entitled because of what I allow at work.

I don't like being this pessimistic and cynical and angry about sex, especially when I used to sincerely love it, but I don't have many moments of sexual joy. The ones I try to create can backfire and seem not worth the risk, leaving me more disenchanted than I was before. A few months ago I managed the mundane rape attempts of a very large, condom-less man who didn't even pay me for my troubles. It wasn't traumatic, but it was a frustrating, stupid waste of time and energy that deepened my bitterness.

The way I feel about sex corresponds with the way I feel about (straight) men in general, and vice versa, which makes it all the more fatiguing. I hate dwelling on this evidence, but it keeps accumulating. Fairly frequently, a man says he loves me, but then communicates that his urge to use my body in a certain way is more important than any displeasure it brings me, more important than my right to say no. "Why don't you care when I say I don't like it?" I should ask. "Why does my unhappiness enhance your pleasure, or impact it so negligibly that it's still worth it?" But I don't think I would ever get an honest answer. At least not one I couldn't already arrive at on my own.

THE SPLURGE
February 19, 2014

January was a slow month. I saw no new clients and barely worked at all but I still made enough in one month to keep most U.S. households above the poverty line for a year. I checked. The threshold is really low.

I haven't thought it all out yet but keep returning to the idea that those who sell sex are probably experiencing the same stratification as those who sell or make or do anything else, meaning the eradication of the middle, meaning some people drowning in money and most simply drowning. This month I met a man who only wanted to take me shopping, so that's what we did, with one salesman dabbing his profuse forehead sweat (I think he was sick) as he chased us around the shoe department stacking up boxes of heels.

"Everywhere we go, everyone stares at you," the buying man murmured to me. He was one of those harried, submissive business types who seems to melt from the intense blend of barely-there humiliation and arousal and delight of being in public together. "Do you like that?"

"I'm used to it," I said. Because when I go out into the world as an escort, I wear the air of a celebrity. Because his worshipful energy lends me that credibility. Because obviously they're going to stare as the man in the suit tails an imperious young woman, the intent to spend wafting off of us like an odor. I was in Las Vegas on a double once, and as we both changed in adjacent dressing rooms, the man outside said to the Agent Provocateur saleswoman, "Bet you don't see many guys my age come in like this!" I could hear the suppressed eye roll in her voice as she replied, "Vegas is a pretty wild place." She wasn't being paid to nurse his notion that he's a god among men for being 30 years older than the two shapely women on his arms. That's our job, the ones who wear the lingerie she fits us for.

During last month's de facto vacation, I mostly read. I felt ready to confront my conviction that I'm literally worth as much, as a human being, as the money I make in a year. I wasn't ready to believe I've hit my earning ceiling though, I'm not yet ready for that. I need to believe there's more ahead. But at least I'm ready to admit that last year was maybe a little too much, too much travel and too many overnights. That after a certain point, the money is worthless and I forget what it's supposed to mean or what I'm supposed to do with it.

Years ago, I told a fellow yoga teacher what I did, and that I had the urge to give away what I made. "Yeah," she said. "But I think maybe you should keep it." This was delivered with so much understated sincerity that I still remember the otherwise forgettable moment. I wonder now if she might have been afraid for my future. It's a place I'm incapable of thinking about.

After he settled the bill, the man and I went to the café and he asked me about the most outrageous or impressive gesture any man has ever made for me.

"Chartering a plane when I missed my flight," I said and then thought of another. "Taking me to Europe for a month."

He asked how much it would require for me to be exclusive and I told him, honestly, that I'd turned down an offer for half a million before. He asked why, so I gave a variety of true explanations though the main reason is that it just wasn't enough. I've never wanted to be exclusive so it's not something I dwell on, but after this conversation I tried to guess how high the number would have to be to make me consider it instead of rejecting it out of hand.

Part of me never gets tired of thinking about money but it's usually a lonely and shameful endeavor. Sometimes I miss the old days when it was more about physicality, high volume, a string of messy bodies, and I felt like a titan for having $600 at the end of the day.

NICK
February 25, 2014

In December of last year, after spending the day with a client, I got in my rental car to meet a man I'd exchanged about 300 words with through Craigslist. It took us all of 20 minutes to set it up. I spent half the nighttime drive with only my parking lights on, confused about why people kept flashing me. I thought it was my usual aggressive maneuvering.

While I was walking to his house from where I'd parked, I felt an unfamiliar trepidation. The suburbs make me uncomfortable; I'm used to hotels in the city or vacation homes in the country. There was something vaguely ominous in the darkness surrounding the other cars and single-story buildings, but the sense of unease was as brief as two heartbeats.

He opened the door and we said hello to each other. I apologized for being in a rush and asked him if quick was ok, my hands on my own zipper as soon as he said yes. He seemed a little suspicious, unbelieving maybe, but not in an awed or boyish way. He was observing at a remove, almost as if he wasn't entirely on board yet but willing to go along with it.

I don't remember much about the fucking except that it was exactly what I wanted. He wouldn't let me keep my mouth on him for more than a moment because he wouldn't have been able to control it, and once he was inside me he had to stop periodically and tell me not to move. Unless I'm thinking of someone else. He was maybe the seventh man I'd met that month under similar circumstances and my memories might be blurred. But I'm pretty sure it was he who barked "No, stay still" if I shifted my hips against him after he'd told me not to, and eventually pulled out entirely rather than trust me to obey.

He was hard and filled me up fully. He put his fingers on my clit sometimes but didn't force it, didn't press too hard. He'd turned the lights off and closed the blinds but kept the muted TV on, and it was very dark. Afterward I kept swiping my hand over the sheets as I squinted at them, trying to see if I'd bled at all and wondering if I could hide it if I had. "What is it?" he said warily. Maybe he thought I was implying his bed was dirty.

While I was pulling my clothes back on I brought up his name. I couldn't remember if he'd mentioned it in the emails or not, but I cut myself off with "It doesn't matter" before I actually asked.

"It's Nick," I think he said, and I wished he hadn't. I said we could meet again next time I was in town if he wanted, and he said that was fine. He was laconic but not cold. He didn't seem to give a shit about me, but not in a mean way.

The second time we met it was he who bled, the friction from the sheets opening a wound on his knee that he said was from his martial arts practice. He has a muscular, compact body with a wholesome, blandly handsome face. He looks like an athlete, it's in his haircut and his demeanor, too. Like he was popular in high school, kind of dickish but mostly quiet, not as cruel as some of his friends.

His compliments were reflexive.

"Your body is amazing," I'd say, undressing him.

"So's yours," he'd say, taking over. Or at least they were until he was inside me, and then he'd say, "You're so hot," now and then, and I would smile or rather I kept smiling, so grateful for how good everything felt and for how he didn't try to force my orgasm or obsess over it or have a conversation with me about it, how he seemed to both defer to me and yet not make the sex about me.

I imagine him fairly often now when I'm close and want to finish. I can come from any imagined scenario, I don't need real people filing the roles, but he's the perfect placeholder. Me holding my cheeks apart for him as he slides into my ass. Him ejaculating on my face while I come from touching myself. His cock is just how I like it, and his body, and I know that, without comment, he'd let me choreograph whatever scenario I wanted and his erection would be perfect and he'd hold off for as long as he could and then he'd ask if he could come before he did it.

The last time we saw each other he said something that surprised me. We were talking about work in the moments while we dressed—I wasn't being honest about mine—and he mentioned that he spent a lot of time sitting around at home. I could have been imagining it, but it felt like a test, or a challenge, like he was making a confession about himself in order to see what I would do it with it. Because he looked right into my eyes while saying it, and there was no self-pity or apology in his tone. The thought that he should try to impress me or that I should try to impress him doesn't seem to cross his mind. That's what I like most.

He sends me occasional emails between the times when I'm in town but they're like text messages. "Hey." "Hey (my fake name)." "When are you back in town?" Etc. I don't reply or even look at them very closely because they're all the same. But the other night, when I was checking that account again for the first time in a week, I noticed that in his last message he'd said, "It's Noah btw" and nothing more. I don't know if he'd lied to me before or if I just didn't remember what he said, and he wanted to remind me.

LIGHTS OUT

March 13, 2014

I realized I'm most effective and focused when I give myself a project, so the project of this year is to become single. I've tried to end my primary relationship many times. I've had the Talk with him. I've been resigned and relieved, even convinced myself it was really over. But he pretends it's a meaningless psychodrama without consequence and I, incredulous, let him. He won't leave after we've resolved to end it. He'll start talking about what we should eat for dinner.

I've been with my boyfriend for a long time. Because of our strange beginning it's hard to pinpoint when exactly we got "together," but the general estimate is that it's lasted about eight years. I've been trying to figure out a way of describing us that doesn't feed into old narratives, like how fucked up I am for letting it last for so long, how weak, how ashamed I am or should be for not "being true to myself" sooner, or differently, or more firmly.

There's no good way to talk about it from the inside. It doesn't seem fair to say that it's never been what I needed or that we've always been dysfunctional, though from the outside I imagine it's impossible to see those statements as anything other than fact. My mother won't listen to me talk about it anymore. She'll change the subject or simply bark out a non sequitur in her too loud, "I'm uncomfortable" voice. And I don't even talk to her about the sex.

What I can say without feeling like I'm disrespecting or distorting our history is that I've spent the last few years repeatedly asking for his attention and not getting it. While I think I've patched over the hole it made in my self-esteem, I still don't want to be with someone who doesn't really want to be *with* me. Reading Thich Nhat Hanh on this is like lancing a puss-filled wound. "To be loved is to be recognized for existing," he writes.

We're terrible at making each other feel loved so the only fuel we have to go on is habit, hard-headedness, desperation, hope. Which are qualities I would like to transcend, not rely upon.

I found some pages handwritten from late last year: half journaling, half writing for real. I don't know what's going on with the verb tenses. I think I was trying to write like everything was far behind me. This is part of what I said:

The best sex of my life was initiated on Craigslist. A former military single father posted an ad showing his thin abdomen and considerable dick, and I replied. His name was Ethan. It took us a while to actually meet, but once we did he picked me up and we fucked near the monuments at night with tourists passing by. The windows were fogged. In the backseat, above me, he drove himself in and then pulled out to come on my stomach. The condom either broke or he pulled it off. There was blood, which baffled me, but he was used to it because of his size. He dropped me off afterward. That was it.

That was the first time, I mean, which wasn't the best time but I can get to that later. Years after, when I began a fresh Craigslist mission, the first man I met responded to my ad suggesting we fuck in his car. We drove for half an hour before we found a place free of cops. It was a small parking lot bordering a park outside of the city and someone had beaten us there, their windows fogged, the engine and lights off. We joked about partner swapping as we crawled in the back. He came quickly and I was glad when it was over because the sex came nowhere close to justifying how intensely wet I'd been in anticipation. But, as I told a friend once I was alone, it was somehow so soothing and reassuring. "You talk about sex in a car with a stranger like it were a feng shui consultation or something," she texted.

Getting back on Craigslist woke everything up for me. Suddenly I was always alert for possible partners: in the airport, on the street, no matter what I was wearing, no matter how makeup-less my face, how inconvenient the timing. I felt like men were even more aware of me than they'd been before but that might have been my imagination or my new willingness to look at them. I told myself I would limit my hookups to 10 and if I hadn't found anyone I wanted to see regularly, I'd stop looking online and only try in person. I regularly had to remind myself that 10 was a limit, not an imperative. I was crushed if someone with particularly promising pictures turned out to be flaky or mean. I was constantly mourning the loss of what I assumed was out there: another Ethan.

The second time I met him where he worked. We fucked—no, he fucked me while I stood up, bent over in a bathroom. We didn't use a condom and blood stubbornly flecked the base of his cock. It wouldn't come off with a wet paper towel but he didn't care. I'd worn a sleeveless gray wool dress, which I still own, and crotchless pantyhose, no underwear. Dark gray heels. If I can choose only one sexual memory to have for the rest of my life, it would be this one. It wouldn't even be a choice.

The sex probably only lasted five minutes. I wasn't close to coming but my body shook. His cock filled me up completely and beyond. I would start thinking, "It's so big," and there would still be more to go. He was tall and thin with some silver in his hair though he was still in his 30s. I was 26.

You understand it wasn't really about sex as genital experience. It was about sex as revelation, illumination of connection amid chaos. Is it good or bad to have sex like that early in life? There's lots more to say about how it happened and the eventual end but the point is that whenever I went on Craigslist, no matter how many years had passed, what I was really looking for was him.

I couldn't remain loyal to him forever though. He joined the ranks of other men who redefined chemistry for me and were gone. The list is short. I'd put it at four and at least two of those might only have earned their positions by not remaining in my life for long enough for the magic to fail, to falter in familiarity or some misunderstanding. Learning too much about someone regularly ruins or at least dampens whatever lust I have. These were men I felt intensely turned on by for a while but the spell wore off in the long term. It never wore off with Ethan.

Other urges arose around this time. A disinterest in writing anything for publication. A general predilection for drugs and a willingness to drink, which I otherwise never did. I didn't exactly seek it out so much as I stayed open to the possibility. I felt the desire to be outside, to see the stars without contamination from city lights. I recognized this as an impulse to return to my teenage years, which were spent in a rural town with many male friends and plentiful aids to alter the monotonous nights we spent together. I had no male friends now, though I did have a strong community of intelligent, supportive, funny women and I felt confused as to why they weren't enough for me.

I also had no idea how to attract male friends without having sex with them first—an almost exact reversal of my situation in high school. But I liked sex with new men, I wanted it and the diversion it offered. I also wanted someone to go to the movies and to concerts with, someone to be out with me on the few nights I had free from work. My boyfriend and I had no converging interests. The vast majority of our time consisted of him sleeping or being on his laptop or on his phone, or eating.

For the first few weeks I told myself I would only meet other men during the time when he and I couldn't be together, but how that time was designated was unclear, and I started claiming more space for my own non sex activities (a yoga class, a long movie on a Saturday afternoon) in the hope that I would establish a pattern of not recognizing any time as "our time."

It was harder for me to do than I thought it should be. From our behavior, it seemed we wanted it to be the way it was. He would escape to the gym for long stretches of the day, go out with friends without me, work constantly and at hours too demanding for us to see each other during the week. And I worked on weekends, which I used not to do, took work trips whenever work warranted it. I gave up trying to get a straight answer about what hours were set aside for us on any given week.

I considered telling him that the wild instinct was awake in me again. But I'd been taught he valued stability, peace, and quiet, and was profoundly relieved to be spared discussions about my natural unhappiness, and my restlessness, and especially about how our relationship may or may not have contributed to that. After years of asking him to talk to me, to start conversations, to express some interest in who I was and what I thought and how I spent my time, I realized it was not in his nature to do that.

I loved him anyway, or thought I did, although what that meant to either of us was ever more a mystery to me. For him, I think, caring for me translated into letting me do whatever I wanted. I believed that caring for him meant caring for myself in the ways I most needed so as to absolve him from responsibility: weathering my own boredoms, disappointments, rages, etc. as unobtrusively as *possible. And I knew he wanted semiregular sex, at least three times a week, initiated by me when I would be sure to come during it. But I found that component more of a challenge.*

WHEN I WAS IN TROUBLE
March 26, 2014

It hurts to come home and not give him the affection he so palpably wants and expects. He is wounded by not receiving it yet resilient; I see him make an effort to stay cheerful, authentically cheerful, to rationalize or excuse me so he can let go of the anger in the same moment it arises. It feels false to act happy to see him; I'm already hyperconscious of every term of endearment I use, tense like a woman on the phone with a kidnapper. ("No, there's no one else here," she says, making eye contact with the police around her.) Because I believe I have information he doesn't have. That I'm the one who knows it will soon, finally, be done.

Withholding warmth feels false in a way too, though, because there's still love. It hurts me to see him hurt by me. It's weird to be part of a sick and stagnant couple. Even if you think your participation is already halfhearted or caged because of how it developed in the boundaries of the relationship, it can always become odder, unfamiliar to the other, more constricted, more punishing. He's been sweeter lately, which makes me think I'm doing something to give myself away, and which means there's no right way to be around him.

I made up a list of rules to start breaking myself of the habits of our life. They basically all boil down to "don't spend time together." The sense of facing a slow ending makes it easier to feel tender but also easier to commit to distance. I still wash and fold his laundry. I buy him toothpaste. I take his phone to get fixed. Not as a matter of habit but as a conscious decision.

Sometimes I feel despair. Mostly I feel normal. It's been such a long time in the making.

~

It's hard to assemble all the feelings in a way that makes sense. They're not even that preoccupying. More like a murmur underneath the rest of my life that briefly spikes to a clamor and then dies back down. Last year I realized a lot of his behaviors that cause me confusion or anger or pain aren't designed to, maybe aren't even intentional in the sense of being the result of thoughtful decisions. I might have insights he doesn't have. For instance, I am not sure he realizes he's waiting to find another woman to replace me before our relationship ends. But I have never been more sure that he is hoping, or perhaps expecting, to recreate what happened for us while he was married.

He may still be married. I've never seen any proof of the divorce—why would I?—and our living arrangement has never graduated beyond man visiting his mistress. He lies constantly, whenever it's expedient and often even when it's not. It makes no sense to me. He told me once that a friend's wife was a blonde cheerleader who would probably want to go salsa dancing after dinner when in fact she was a warm and heavyset brunette who gave a confused laugh when I mentioned I'd heard she liked dancing. It wasn't a joke on his part; I don't know where it came from. Maybe he assumed those things about her and somehow forgot that they were just his ideas, not facts. If I'm out with his friends and ask if another of them has set their wedding date, I'll find out there's not an engagement. He will make up entire conversations and eventually be forced to admit he hasn't even spoken to the person.

Thinking about all this more, synthesizing various understandings and intimations from the past, means finally seeing possibilities that are more plausible than I previously believed. Years ago, we went to Paris for my birthday. I wept at one point and admitted to him that I was terribly sad and felt alone all the time, and he got so angry with me for being selfish and bad company and whatever other complaints one can make about a depressed person. He's always maintained he was going to propose to me on that trip, that he had a ring and everything, but I ruined it with my attitude.

And I believed him. Now I feel certain that it is untrue. In eight years, I've never met his parents. Usually when I'm anguished he yells at me.

You're only hearing one side, or rather a small slice of one side. I'm telling the truth when I say there's still love there. He's not a bad person.

$\sim$

I started having more Nick fantasies, almost always summoned as opposed to spontaneously occurring. I found thinking about him comforting, the same type of comforting as sex in car with someone I don't have to see again or whose name I'll never know. Him jerking off on my face. Him fucking me from behind while plunging a toy in my ass. I liked this last idea enough to pack the toy I had in mind when I traveled to his city recently. It's black and has a ridged handle and resembles a baton. I thought it was called the Anal Invader, but then I looked it up, and it's called the Anal Probe. That makes it sound less intimidating than it appears but it also feels less intimidating than it appears so maybe that works out.

It was my favorite anal toy when I worked on webcam because it was smooth and comfortable and dramatic—much better than the hard string of anal beads, which almost always came out with a bright lace of blood, or the incomprehensible swizzle stick, too skinny to do much of anything if I was warmed enough to be pushing things in there at all. When I used to work on webcam, I would try to fist my own ass if I was feeling charitable enough or needy enough. Heel fucking was a thing for some reason, a common request most of us obliged with our stripper stilettos. If I had to describe how it felt in a word, I'd say, "scrape-y."

There was no transcendent chemistry with Nick. In some ways I almost want to call the sex we had workmanlike. It was so straightforwardly, quintessentially heterosexual, so predictable, so unimaginative. Yet it always felt right and satisfying, like drinking water when your throat is dry. Like ur-sex. Like plainly pleasurable, physically directed, functional sex. The way some people seem to think sex, by definition, is or should be.

And what appealed to me about him beyond that was his blankness. I could lay anything I liked over my mental image of him because he was so taciturn and unexpressive. He'd never done anything to offend me. When

I first wrote about him, on paper, in a college-ruled notebook, I named him "the dud" because there was no distinguishing aspect of his personality except for its indistinguishableness. What made Nick stay in my mind was simply that I had no grudge against him. He'd never tried to go down on me, never pried for personal details, never confessed some overwhelming love for me. The things he'd not done to me mattered as much if not more than the things he had. It's all past tense for a reason, as you'll see.

The latest news on the Nick front, in the time since I'd last seen him, was that he was about to move to a city I never visit. About three days after I visited his current town, actually. And also that he has the same real name as a French guy I was screwing in another city. Which is funny, because Nick is the least French person I've met, and of the two of them, I'd only ever come with the French guy though I found him much less compelling. They both lived in homes that repulsed me a little bit, with their solitary, damp towels in the bathroom, their apartments uniformly disheveled like they'd been rummaged through by disappointed burglars.

The night before I was to leave, I thought I should take the probe out of my luggage. I so clearly wouldn't use it. I didn't know why this seemed important or worth doing—it didn't take up much space—but I forgot about it in the morning until I'd already left home. With an air of definitiveness if not quite urgency, I threw it out in the airport bathroom's trash before I went through security. I think what seized me was shame not about the sexual nature of the thing but about the daydreaming that occasioned its inclusion. Admitting to any type of planning or anticipation feels like vulnerability. Because it is. Hope is vulnerability. And I'd hoped there would be some moment between Nick and me that I could cling to as proof of connection or richer possibilities, some bittersweet swell to float on after there was no chance of ever seeing him again. Not because it was him but because of how he existed outside the regular boundaries of my life. Because he was a hook to hang these desires on.

I want adventure, potential. The only thing that's ever sustained me, that's ever made up for the degree to which everything otherwise seems pointless and mean and wrong, are intense and mysterious emotional experiences that stick in my soul until I can work them into something beautiful. Without that irritant, there's nothing—no activity. The wind stops blowing, the sails go slack. I hoped Nick's placidity was a choice that would be revealed as interesting. That something more would happen between us.

But he'd gotten back together with his girlfriend or at least "sorta" had, and so he wasn't free anymore when I got done with work. He complained a little. He made it sound like she was his mom and he was helpless to leave without her permission. I hadn't been sure how I felt about seeing him again anyway. I was more harassed than horny as I ran errands before the car service came, dragging my roller bag around the streets full of tourists. But when he said he couldn't meet me, I thought I might cry. No more potential and no more blankness. Now I knew he was as passive and uninspiring as all the rest. The rustling sails entirely stilled and the nothingness left over felt unbearable.

Whenever I'm disappointed, I turn on myself rabidly. Because how stupid, how irrational, to not live by what I know. That's become the refrain in my relationship, if we ever speak about things going wrong. "I'm just angry with myself," I'll say, wearily. Why can't I get better at being immune? Why aren't I stronger? Why can't I live like I should, making choices informed by my history instead of by my wishes? I'm tired of knowing what I don't want to know and having no better coping mechanism than to pretend it's not true. Tired of being right about all the saddest things.

"I'm sorry you're mad," Nick texted me.

"I'm not mad," I replied.

I hated myself for hours.

FIRST QUARTER

April 8, 2014

I slept with Nick again. That may not be a surprise. The morning after he abandoned our plan to meet, jet lag woke me earlier than I wanted, and I texted him to come over. Not horny but restless. I threw the latch on my hotel door so he could let himself in and I could stay in bed naked. He undressed in the dark and slid in next to me, warm and smooth. I still wasn't sure how interested I was in what was about to happen but when he reached between my legs he found wetness that seemed to impress us both. It was the worst sex we'd ever had and presumably the last sex we ever will have, but afterwards I felt redeemed, satisfied, smug. Probably because I'd told him to come to me and he did, like a dog deciding to obey on the second command.

The reasons for why it was disappointing are mundane. (The client I'd seen the day before was hugely endowed, and fucked me roughly, so I was in pain. Nick was distracted by and anxious about his upcoming move, so much so he even told me to visit him there. We rushed, because he had to get to work soon and so did I.) But even not-as-good sex with him was better than most sex I have. There was still a pause in my brain when I held his arms and felt the muscles under my hands and admired his body as sincerely as I admire a beautiful sentence or a song. Men say that type of thing about women all the time but I don't think I'd ever experienced it before, that sort of pleasant, distanced approval of a human body interacting so closely with mine. Usually I'm too bound up in reacting to the man as a whole to have some separate thought about his casing. And too busy working.

Either a man's form induces rapturous worship because I am devoted to him and everything about him seems miraculous, or I am repulsed by an otherwise impressive body because I dislike something about the man in it, or—most commonly—I ignore his body because it's largely irrelevant to me. A man's body almost never dictates what type of relationship I'll have with him. I guess that's what's unfamiliar.

LONG-TERM
RELATIONSHIP
May 5, 2014

For a long time now, sex with my boyfriend almost always ends with me lying flat on my stomach and him behind. This is almost the only way he comes with me. There used to be more doggie style involved, but the shape would often descend gradually until, again, I was prone.

This came up once during one of our sex fights, a year or more ago. He accused me of only lying there and not doing anything, which was unfair to me on two counts. One, my boyfriend is shorter than me but weighs at least 50 pounds more, so he is compact and presents a physical obstacle to much movement when I'm on my stomach. Two, it's not true that I don't do anything. I reach my arms behind my back to play with his nipples, which is something a lot of people can't do because of shoulder mobility issues. He can't even scratch his own back. If he were in my position, he wouldn't be able to reach his nipples.

And furthermore, when I thought our sex life was still worth trying to improve or save, when I still felt some obligation to make sex "good" for him or wanted him to find me sexy and "good" at sex, I used to try moving as much as the limited position would allow. I'd arch up into him, or lift up and down, and squeeze myself around his cock with one constant, strong exertion or break it up into pulses. Sometimes my motions would screw up the angle and he'd slip out. But even when he stayed inside, he couldn't finish if I were doing anything with my lower body. I noticed that through a lot of studious observation. The only way he would come is if I were totally inert from the waist down.

We don't talk about sex anymore unless we're joking, in the not particularly funny way, about how much we have it with each other or how much we have it with other people. A month or so ago I ventured one sharp question about our sexual dynamic, and I admit I felt a little gratified by the amount of anger it evoked in him. He rolled away from me and lay awake on his side in palpable irritation while I, smugly, felt sleepy and not as disturbed, but excited enough to stay alert to the possibility that he might actually respond, albeit in a pissy way that provoked a fight. In all the romantic ("") relationships I've had, I've spent too many nights lying awake next to the man, hoping he would start a conversation about what was on my mind. It's never once happened. It didn't happen this time either.

The next morning we had sex and I was sore from a cosmetic procedure I'd recently had done around my hips, so it hurt when he gripped me there, but I just ignored it and reminded myself it isn't a big deal anymore to feel like home sex is like work sex, and it isn't. It used to distress me, but I've gotten to a place where it truly doesn't matter and this is healthy. Any arguments to the contrary are sentimental and cruel.

I've mentioned this before, but I'm still bemused by the fact that around the time I decided to give up on improving my experience of being with him, he seemed to think we're getting along better than ever—arguably, we are, if superficially—and seems even more fond of the idea that our relationship is a permanent one. Here are the adjustments I made:

I stopped trying to plan anything with him, ever.

I stopped expecting him to show up at any particular time, or to show up at all.

I stopped fantasizing about the future, aloud to him or privately in my mind.

I stopped asking him what he was doing, where he was, and when he would be done.

I committed myself to various things during the weekend, which
    was once informally designated as "our" time.

I stopped trying to have conversations with him.

I abnegated any responsibility to initiate or enliven sex with him.

I started having unpaid sex with other people, which I hadn't done
    in years.

Basically, I stopped trying to live my life with him, which had never really worked anyway, and started trying to live it around him. Like I am single but not single, or maybe single but not interested in dating. In giving up on trying to improve our relationship, I improved it for myself as well. But not in the way I was hoping for. It started to hurt less because it mattered so much less.

Between he and I, the sex part of this is the most confusing aspect, maybe because I want it to mean something different or more than what it does, which is—possibly, probably, who even knows about these things, who even cares, human beings themselves usually don't understand why they do the things they do—a sporadic act that serves as practical release for him; confirms his ideas of what should at least be marginally present in a romantic ("") relationship; and perhaps confirms something else more distasteful, like a notion of ownership of me or my sense of responsibility to him; or acts as a denial of the fact that we both ultimately don't get a lot out of being sexual with each other.

    That very last part—us not getting anything out of it—has been explicitly affirmed. We haven't fought in a long time and we haven't talked about sex in as long, but in the past, when we did, he inevitably complained that we never had sex and the sex we had was crap. I inevitably asked why he wanted more of something so awful. The bad food and such small portions dilemma was never resolved. But sometimes I would say, not looking for ego confirmation but looking to figure it out, what about this specific time, when this and that happened? Was that time also irredeemably awful? Not that I thought it was spectacular or unforgettable or the best either of us had ever had, but I thought it was pleasant and fun and we both felt nicer about each other afterwards. He would communicate, no, it's all awful and it's never once been good. That was more a calibrating of opinions than it was me trying to flex my sexual power, which I am not sure is a thing I have or want anymore anyway.

Throughout all of this, I believe my boyfriend genuinely likes me. But I think he likes me more when I engage with him in a very limited way and we don't spend much time together. Our relationship has been one of the most humbling things I can recall participating in. I'm grateful for it in that respect.

GOT THIS BODY

May 12, 2014

A lot of current and former expensive escorts are involved with fitness competing or modeling, at a fairly intense level, and that makes sense to me. It's an outlet where you can channel an obsession with appearance, and it's most available to people with disposable income and lots of time on their hands. Most of those escorts don't have kids. And, as one of them pointed out to me, bodybuilding is a realm kinder to older women, by which I mean women who are still young—you know how that goes. From what I can tell, a lot of stars in that world are in their late 30s or even 40s. It would be tough to make any other modeling career take off at that age. I think the tan and low body fat has an aging effect on most of the competitors anyway, so maybe that's why. Not that I mean any disrespect; increasingly, I contemplate going off the weighlifting deep end myself. I'm thin but I wish I were trimmer and had better definition.

I found out one of the guys I hooked up with late last year competes. He keeps sending me pictures of himself on stage. I never thought I would be the type of woman who fucks a bodybuilder, probably in part because my mental image of a bodybuilder is someone squat and cartoonish instead of lean and cut, like him. I imagined having to explain this to any of my (inevitably mystified) friends, and saying, "He's probably just lonely and insecure," as to why he's into it. That's my main motivator, anyway. The same way animals in cages pace or chew themselves. When all other resources except time are gone, as one of my favorite yoga teachers once said, you can always say, "Well, got this body."

I laid awake last night full of anxiety. That's not a usual state for me, so it took a little effort to realize I was panicking. I've been looking at a lot of before-and-after pictures of cosmetic breast work, and though I usually find the "after" pictures totally underwhelming, I'm becoming increasingly convinced I will be paying someone to do the same to me in the immediate future. It's starting to feel inevitable. I can't tell if I want to do it or not.

I've been unhappy with my breasts my entire life, but looking at other people's makes me realize most breasts look odd and quirky, whether they've had doctor intervention or not, so I feel a little less judgmental of my own. Still, the idea of what my breasts *should* look like is there. Just like when I'm at a crowded pool or beach, I can look at the bodies of other women and realize that most are nice but not spectacular, that mine might be more pleasing or as pleasing, but I still have my ideal body in my head and the fact that my body doesn't look like that makes me ashamed.

A decade ago, when I worked on webcam, I was talking with a newish girl named Kelly about how I wanted to have work done on my breasts because I didn't think they were perky enough.

"No," she said, "Yours are great. Mine are really saggy."

"I'm sure they're not," I said.

Standard girl talk. Then she took off her bra and showed me. I was fully prepared to say, "They're fine, you're crazy!" but I couldn't. Kelly had those long, flattish boobs in most of the "before" pictures of breast lifts. I'd never seen any like that before, and I'm sure I managed something complimentary in response, but I couldn't blame her for wanting that changed.

I assumed for years I could do a breast lift to get them where I want them, but after research, I know they already look like the "after" pictures, except without the substantial scars. The thing is, when I first started in-person sex work, men flipped out for my boobs. And Kelly made as much money as any of us on cam, once she had some experience and knew how to work. When I used to encounter lots of clients instead of only a few, I was more aware that men are enthusiastic about all types of bodies, and often love all types of breasts. I'd heard it before, that women's magazine line about how you shouldn't turn the lights off during sex because your boyfriend doesn't mind your cellulite, but I experienced it directly for myself over and over with a lot of different men. I loved them for that, for not hating our bodies as much as most of us hated our bodies.

But the pressure to make my body better is always tied to making it look better for men. Even if I quit sex work today, that would still be true. No women in my life do or say anything to make me feel bad about my body. But I can't even watch a TV show with my boyfriend without him constantly commenting about which women on it he thinks are hot.

All my emotion goes into my stomach now, so if I get extremely upset I walk around holding my belly like an alien is about to burst from it. I'm going off hormonal birth control because I've been on it almost nonstop for 10 years, and I hope that stopping will improve my libido and make me better at work and overall a happier person. I haven't told my boyfriend yet. Our attempts to use condoms in the past were disastrous but he uses them successfully with other women, so why can't he use them with me?

When I asked him how his weekend was he said "fine" and faked a yawn, which is his awful, ridiculous tell for being uncomfortable and hiding something. That made me so angry. I know he has sex with other women and he should know I know, and the suggestion that I'm in the dark about it feels so disrespectful. I feel sick thinking about having a fight about my not being on birth control, or just not having sex and then having a fight about that, or him trying to fuck me without a condom, which is how I got pregnant before. I was about to tell him this morning instead of waiting for it to come up at a worse time, but then I realized my skirt felt wet because he hugged me when he came out of the bathroom, and he left behind some semen on it.

He spends hours in the bathroom. I know he's masturbating in there, among other things, possibly just to porn or with someone he paid on webcam. It's always very quiet though. It's his business. I don't report to him every time I masturbate. But the man I was with before him used to masturbate in bed next to me. I would help him, or not, but it was always companionable and pleasant. I suggested that to my boyfriend years ago, and he acted appalled.

Somehow the semen on the skirt made it impossible for me to speak. I dialed my gynecologist's number to talk to her about getting a nonhormonal IUD but then I made myself hang up before it went through, and put the phone down and held my stomach.

Everything feels wrong right now. I started setting up random sex again. It's almost all I can think about; arranging it, finding it, etc. I know I reach for sex the way some people reach for food, because I'm bored, lonely, insecure. It's either that or chew my own arm off.

MORE THAN
ONE CHOP
May 19, 2014

I sent Nick a text telling him to come to my city. He replied telling me to come to his. It made me stupidly happy, to feel connected to this man I don't know and like because of it. He'd told me he had family near me once, but apparently they'd moved, so the odds of our paths spontaneously crossing are low.

The definition of insanity is not doing the same thing over and over again and expecting a different result. Repetition can pay off. It takes an axe more than one chop to fell a tree. The definition of insanity is probably closer to occasionally thinking about how funny it would be to seriously date a man I met for sex through Craigslist when the man in question is Nick. At least 10 times I've thought about visiting his city just to fuck him. I'm not even that into him. But Nick is so uncomplicated. Thank god I have a presence like that in my life.

I visited the bodybuilder again, since he lives in my city, and is nice and sane, and had sent me some new shirtless selfies. He gives great hugs and is easy to be with. I think we're a fit that way because I'm pretty good to fuck—direct but mellow, undemanding, permissive, kind. Sort of maternal and affirming after the guy comes, by which I mean I let him stay plugged deep inside of me with us wrapped up together, talking and touching while the condom risks slipping off. The after moment is sometimes the best: that sense of pure peace, the relaxation of the body that was working so hard, the way a guy sinks his weight down gradually, with care but with relief.

He fucks like a man with a lot of stamina who hasn't had sex in a long time. His style is the right mix of forceful and tender, controlled and urgent, and he doesn't mind taking the lead. There are moments when I worry it might be too much—his hand on my throat or whatever it is—but I never become alarmed, because I trust he won't hurt me and I can make him stop if I need to.

That's unspoken. I trust my own body, too, to respond in ways that protect me. I probably shouldn't take for granted how nice it is to have found someone I can say that about and feel that way with, but the vast majority of sex feels common to me. So familiar. It's easy to have sex and it's not a big deal. Or rather, it kind of is but not the way people usually make it out to be. It takes special circumstances for me not to feel like, "Oh, this again."

He wouldn't keep his cock out of my throat and finally kneeled over my face with one hand at the back of my skull, in my hair, plunging himself in, holding my face against him and narrating with his moans. I wish he were bigger when he's inside my pussy but I could feel the tight ring of tissue in the back of my mouth sawed raw by his shaft. The extra thick saliva started to come up, the pre-vomit saliva, so I had to be careful with my breathing and how I swallowed.

If I can't be entirely consumed by my body, I'd like to be entirely consumed by my mind, but in the place where it's intimately observing my body. Both ways create space through focus and can give the illusion of obliteration, liberation. It's what yoga does. I wasn't overcome by what was happening with him over me—not in sexual rapture—but nor was I upset or put upon. I felt fascinated, impressed by how he maneuvered himself and me at the same time, and also by how accommodating I was. Physically, I mean. We worked so well together. I couldn't remember the last time a blow job felt so collaborative. And it was hot, the way he moved, what he said. It was energizing to use my throat again that way.

When I worked on webcam, I had one regular client who liked me to deep throat a double-sided dildo until I threw up on myself. That may sound horrifying but I liked him. He had me tell him stories throughout the sucking, stories about dogs and broom handles, which turned me on too. The subject matter was always up to me, but the intensity was not. "NASTIER!!!" he would type, or probably a misspelled version of that. He was so enthusiastic.

The biggest relief for me during the second time with the bodybuilder was that I never felt like I was working, like I had to be the sex manager. Last year, when I started having unpaid sex with nonboyfriend men, I had the hardest time escaping work headspace. I'd let them do things I didn't like, and I wouldn't tell them to leave even though they'd worn out their welcome long ago. Placating, placating. Acting like I cared about what they had to say or that I was enjoying something that didn't feel good. Not reserving the right to meet someone, find them unattractive, and end it right then. I wanted to train myself out of that, so I made it a project, to keep finding and fucking people, to relearn how to have sex for free. I didn't shave for Nick. I showed up at the bodybuilder's home in workout clothes with no makeup.

He has a funny, old-fashioned name, like Harold, though not quite that bad. It seems unfair to call him the bodybuilder since competing is only a hobby, and he has a job that's not related at all. Not that I know him well enough to say definitively but I'm pretty sure he has a truly sweet heart. Back when he and I met, I sent his picture to a few of my friends to brag, and they all asked about his ethnicity. He volunteered this information, apropos of nothing, while we lay together after our first time. He's probably used to being asked, so he preempts it. Maybe I'm weird for not having been curious.

The men I sleep with, clients and otherwise, ask me about my background all the time. I'm not sure why it's so standard; I look like a generic white girl. People usually guess I'm Irish-German though I'm neither. They could be hoping for something unusual, and when I tell them about my mom's side, they usually say they can see it. Which is a lie. Only one man ever said, "Of course, your eyes," and then I believed him. The school I attended until eighth grade used to have yearly "global awareness" days when one country was celebrated, and in my fifth grade they chose my grandfather's country (because they'd have someone to go to for guests and props.) My mother tried to surprise me with the news by telling me to look at her eyes to guess. I stared into them, clueless, convinced she was trying to communicate with me through telepathy or pure expression alone.

I don't get to claim her heritage as my own no matter how many men might want me to be exotic. A quarter something is a lot different than half something. But I grew up with my grandfather, just like my mother grew up with that same brusque man as her father, and my great grandmother was in my life, too, the woman who prayed five times a day and never learned English. I only know two words of her language. All I can say is, "very good. Very, very good."

BREASTS
May 26, 2014

The first doctor communicated to me that my boobs were trash, which I can't imagine was ethical. The first thing he commented on while I stood topless before him was my unusual breastbone and ribcage, which is old news to me but seemed to offend him. It's genetic, from my father's side, and my brother has it too. I can't even imagine what a "normal" chest looks like, I'm so used to seeing my own. And anyway, there's no surgery to fix the way my bones display against my skin. Not yet. Maybe that's a new cosmetic field to pioneer.

He asked if I noticed a discrepancy between the hang of the left breast and the hang of the right. I wanted to request the word "hang" be stricken from the record, but instead I said I only ever thought the left was slightly bigger and he confirmed that much for me: "That's why it's lower, because gravity has more to work against there." He announced some numbers, which were written down by the apathetic woman in the corner, then paused, and added severely, for her notes, "Breasts have stretch marks."

He asked how long I'd had the stretch marks and I said since I was a young teenager; coincidentally, as long as I've had my boobs. All my stretch marks are from a massive growth spurt I had when I was 11 or 12. Surgery can't fix those either.

He glanced at the pictures I'd collected on my phone and commented that I wanted to look like someone who had implants. Or more specifically, that I wanted to look like someone who had virtually no breast tissue at all, then got reasonably sized implants. Just as I feared. Mine are of a respectable size currently, and at various times in my life have been heralded as large or even "huge" by various men who'd seen them naked. This doctor characterized them as "narrow" and "rocketlike."

"You should know that I don't like big breasts," he said meanly just before I tried on some different sizes. He was so weird and hostile the whole time, like I and my inferior breasts were keeping him from his important business of saving the lives of babies. Cosmetic surgery is all he does! The materials I was given to take home all had a Greco-Roman statue of a woman on them, that trite, ubiquitous branding strategy that is apparently mandated by law for vanity surgeons. Like there's some timeless ideal they're honoring, or that they make women look like they're supposed to, as evidenced in ancient statues. Like the stone figure in question, if alive now, wouldn't go to him for liposuction and implants and a tummy tuck.

I tried 275 ccs and looked at myself in profile in the white t-shirt I'd been instructed to bring. I looked . . . pneumatic. I hated it. I asked for a smaller size and the nice nurse suggested I put them in my sports bra, which made them look a lot better. I have a thing about lifting my boobs up as high as they can go and then mashing them against my chest—always have. I just like them more that way. In the sports bra, as compressive as it was, I didn't really look that much bigger than I am now.

The doctor came back in and was angry about the sports bra. "Questions?" he demanded.

I asked him how much my postimplant breasts would look like the breasts in the pictures I'd brought, and he said they would look like they look, still my boobs, just fuller at the top and sides. Like a bomb instead of a rocket, maybe. I'm only speculating there, that's not a quote.

I wanted more description but all he would give me was a curt "They can look better." When I'd asked him about a lift, he said he didn't think I would like it now but I would "need" one when I got older. A medical professional telling anyone they "need" an entirely cosmetic procedure has got to break some type of code, no?

What I'd really wanted was for someone who looks at natural breasts all the time, day in and day out, to tell me that mine were fine, because that's the conclusion I myself reached after looking extensively through before-and-after pictures on a slew of plastic surgeons' websites. I would still get something done; "fine" doesn't mean they can't be improved. But I wanted the brief relief of a professional opinion that mine were good enough just as they were, and in fact possibly pretty good, period, for being crafted by haphazard genes and not (yet) by human aesthetic preference. But I didn't get it.

I texted my friend Emma and told her I thought I was going to get implants. Emma is one of the more unusual women I know, because she has never once said a nice thing about how I look. That's standard issue bonding among women, for casual acquaintances and most definitely for friends who occasionally worked together nude. But that meant I trusted her to be honest. I thought she might act like implants were a sort of goofy move, but instead she replied, "Really? Did I tell you I got implants last year?"

This was astonishing news, not least of all because I'd seen Emma not that long ago, more than once since she'd gotten them, probably, and never noticed they were bigger. She was happy about that because she didn't want the change to be dramatic. She said her recovery was so easy she'd driven a car the day after surgery, though she wasn't supposed to.

The entire world felt a little different after this discovery. Nonchalant, affectless, proudly-didn't-brush-her-hair Emma had implants. She hadn't mentioned it to me, and the man she's most often naked around and with whom she spends copious amounts of clothed time, too, didn't notice. I wasn't sure what this news meant for me, only that maybe it opened up my idea about women who get implants versus those who don't. The divide between implant me and "natural" me felt thinner now, perhaps even as narrow as one of my rocket-like breasts. I would meditate on this for weeks, not really pondering with any scrutiny but just floating in it. Then I would go to see another doctor.

THE IMPORTANCE OF ESCAPE
June 9, 2014

After I saw the bodybuilder again, my boyfriend confronted me about me having sex with other people outside of work, which apparently I was not supposed to do. He knew about it because I was tweeting about cock size, I guess. I'll never grow out of wanting something more once I'm denied it, so while I didn't make any promises to him and he didn't issue any orders, I wondered if my thinking about George in the following days intensified because of a sense of obstacle. I was a little uncomfortable with how dreamy I'd started to feel about him. It reminded me of how it happened with Ethan, the military man from Craigslist. We met, fucked, and then didn't talk or see each other again for a few months. After the second time, the acceleration was immediate.

With Ethan, our dynamic mutated under pressure of separation until the sense of emotional connection was almost too much to bear. He wanted us to really be together. I didn't—I try not to remember this part wrong and make us into mutually invested star-crossed lovers. I wanted to keep him at a distance while still having access to him. He said he wanted to marry me; I was struggling to handle the jagged fragments of my own life without getting cut.

The idea of moving into a new relationship was overwhelming. I wasn't even sure I could or should end the one I was in. And I couldn't imagine being with him that way, probably because ardency pushes me away. But how I felt around him was real, the most urgent physical attraction I've felt to anyone before or since. When I think about that time, it feels so desperate and intense. Like I was holding my breath for months. Soon we were both coming back to each other for the suffering as much as we were for the pleasure. There was no way to distinguish between the two.

My boyfriend said all his best sex memories of the past few years were with people other than me and that makes him sad. Then he had to give me an example of this, even though I've told him many times I don't want to hear about him and other women. For as long as I've known him, he described his sexual history as one of constant exuberance, one in which everyone comes and is happy and satisfied and it's all easy and hot.

That's how he depicts more recent episodes as well. The women are initiators, they know exactly what they want (spanking, pure fucking, etc.) and love every second. It occurred to me that it's how a lot of clients talk about their time with escorts. Or even how some of my clients probably feel with me. I spent a disgruntled weekend with someone new not long ago, after which I swore I didn't care if I ever saw him again and even thought about quitting work entirely. But during our days together, he told me he had the strongest orgasm of his life, and when I emailed him recently he proposed another long date.

I don't think that disconnect is unique to me. I think it's how a lot of guys feel about sex in general. If they're having it, it's great. There's barely a measure of better or worse, it's just sex or not sex. Personally, I have tiers. Tier One is the swallowed-up sex, when I feel willing to pay virtually any price to keep having it, in any form, with one particular man. It's rare. Tier Two is really good, easy, undemanding, natural. It's also rare. Tier Three is pleasant and ok. Definitely tolerable. Probably short, probably not worth going out of my way to have again. Tier Four is bad. Tier Five is really bad. Tier Six is . . . unbearable.

I've never come with George or Nick and part of why I like them both so much is that they don't pressure me to, or ask if I did, or make a big deal out of it. But I don't know if that's because they assume I have, or if they don't care. It's unusual to find a guy who believes a woman might only want to be fucked and that alone is enough. Does my boyfriend assume these more recent women come? Do they tell him they have? Does he care? For at least a year of our relationship, he and I had copious amounts of sex and

I never got off. Eventually I asked him directly what he was thinking when he constantly initiated sex that wasn't making me come, and then things only got worse.

Most of my questions now are bigger than him and me. He disclosed some other things that moved me and yet felt like distractions. After our most recent talk, I went outside while he slept, and sat on the steps of my building. It was 2 a.m., not as quiet as I wanted it to be. I wished I smoked. I wondered if I would spend my entire life tortured by this sense of being not beautiful enough. These days it feels like the biggest burden I wake up with. A permanent sense of failure and inadequacy.

After telling me about his best sex memory, he fell asleep before I could say that he and I would never have the type of sex he wants. Which he thinks should be so easy. He made a point of saying he never flirts in front of friends or hits on women in front of friends, but fucking a woman from the gym that is his entire social universe, in his car in a well-lit parking garage, does not strike me as particularly discreet. None of the men I fuck for free know my job or my friends or even my name. So I will take the mantle of the nobler one.

All my best sex memories would be Tier One stuff, and they're marked by pain and confusion. I would say the best sex of my life was with Ethan, but I can't think about it without thinking of all the sadness that went along with it.

There's a young couple I barely know who are engaged, and I spent a few minutes one day feeling touched and baffled by that fact. By all appearances they are both attractive, successful, smart, incredibly cool people. Young, but not so young as to make the decision seem impulsive. I like trying to imagine what other people's relationships are like but I can't imagine theirs. Or I can, and it's so much like my younger self's idea of what finding my soul mate would be that I can't take it seriously. I can bestow upon them a sympathy and honesty so powerful that it made them already united for life.

But as charmed as I am by their public faces, I believe their marriage will be full of anger and sexual deception because I can't imagine a marriage that isn't. I'm so distant from them, my ideas and opinions don't matter even a little, but it's a mental exercise. Somewhere along the way I've given up on the idea of loving a man deeply or being in a true partnership. For a while I fantasized I might achieve it with my boyfriend, then I held onto the idea of finding it in another guy, and now it's gone entirely. I told a friend this, a former escort who now is basically the kept woman of one client, and she said without hesitation, "I know exactly what you mean."

I'm getting better at shedding some of the blinders, recognizing how my friends are partners in important ways. Since high school, my female friends have been my soul mates. But it still feels sad and wrong to have successfully erased the desire to have that intimacy with a man. It feels sad to let go of hope, even if I know it's right.

The first time I read a Buddhist say something against hope, I got so mad. Now I know the groundedness that comes with giving it up. It can feel like freedom or like death, depending on your mood. Now I believe that if I understand my life as a series of projects, learning how to live without hope is probably the most challenging and vital one. Hope is insidious.

FINDING

June 11—August 25

NINE YEARS
June 11, 2014

I was tired of being sad and in my head so I took some molly and went to see George. It was slow coming on and I even worried I'd made a mistake at first but when it hit, it was amazing. He fucks for so long, it's much easier to take on drugs. I was on my stomach with him inside, telling him how much I wanted a cock in my mouth while he was behind me and that did it.

He pulled out and pulled off the condom, cursing as he came on me. "Goddammit. Shit. Goddammit."

"Yeah goddammit, you came after fucking me for, like, 60 minutes straight," I said. "What a loser."

"I know," he said. He lay down next to me and I kissed his chest.

"Back to Craigslist with me!" I said. We laughed.

He leisurely rubbed it into my neck and shoulders, saying, "Come massage."

"Mm, so good for the skin," I said, fine with it. Definitely high.

"Your body is perfect."

"No, yours is! I was going to ask you how it feels to have such a perfect body. Do you walk around feeling better than everybody else?" We laughed again.

"I remember in your ad you were really specific like, 'I'm fit and you need to be too.'"

"Well, I'm not the female equivalent of you. I wish I were more defined but I think it's good to be a little soft."

It was so nice and communal lying there together that I confessed I was high, so he should tell me to shut up if I got obnoxious. I could tell a rush of chatter was about to come on. I was so delighted by everything. He said he'd never taken molly and we talked about smoking crack. I said I thought everyone should have to try it at least once, so they would never judge or be mean to anyone addicted ever again. I also admitted, when he asked, that the name I'd been using wasn't really mine. His name wasn't really George either, which I learned the first time I met him because the doorman called him by his real name. But I'd forgotten that through sheer will, like I would want a client to if he had found out my real name.

I noticed he has two phones too, like I do.

"You're both fucking liars and you deserve each other," my friend Beatrice said when I was texting her about it, with George reading on. I'd been telling him how much I loved her and how no man has a chance as long as she's in my life. I wanted to take a picture of us together for her but it was too dark even near the candles, and I shouted at him not to turn the lights on every time he offered to.

I kept running my mouth, telling sex story after sex story, with a few drugs tales thrown in. I'd periodically ask if I was boring him and he said "No, I love it! It's turning me on."

I asked him how many women he had in rotation right now and he paused.

"I like knowing about other people's sex lives," I said, but I could tell he still didn't want to answer. I'd said before he shouldn't be monogamous, that he should spread himself around so lots of women could enjoy him and he said he knew I really meant it. But he was still shy until I told him about escorting. ("That makes sense. I noticed you don't like kissing.")

"Ok," he said, "since we're sharing secrets, I'll tell you one. My ex-wife and I used to run an agency."

I asked him if he was always nice to the girls and he said, "Oh, yeah." He talked about coming home to find six women eating pizza at his house and knowing that meant new recruits. They found people through his wife's circle of friends and word of mouth. That was in the 90s, so they took out ads in phone books and papers. He said he carried a gun and was crazy back then.

"I used to go along on calls as protection, and I figured if anything ever went wrong I could just shoot the door and get in." But then something did go wrong, and he realized how nuts it would be to shoot a hotel door. Hotel security finally came and one of the guards said he saw this type of thing all the time.

"You didn't look like a hotel guest at all, did you?" I said.

"No, I was all thugged out . . . That was how I dressed at the time. And I had a gun on me! I can't even own a gun anymore. It's for the best because I would have killed someone. I mean, I stabbed people, but it was because I had a knife. I was really messed up, I wasn't thinking right back then. I was doing drugs . . ."

It didn't come out right away, but later that night he told me he'd spent nine years in prison. He explained some of the story around it, not denying anything or even sounding bitter. I was curled up between his legs, lying against his chest.

"I'm sorry," I said, reaching up to hold his face while I kissed his stomach.

Early in the night, before he told me that, I said how sweet he seemed, and he made a noise like that was not good. "I know, I know, men don't like being called sweet but you just seem you have a real good heart. It's so rare in this city." And he said something to the effect of having to be careful when he was with women, because he didn't want to be in a committed relationship right now. I don't know if he meant he had to be careful for their sake or his own. I couldn't imagine this tenderness kept alive for almost a decade in prison.

He said he and his wife were like Bonnie and Clyde, though she didn't face any charges.

"She thought I was invincible," he said. "I was being led away in handcuffs and she was like, 'He's not going to jail.' And I was like, 'No, this is real!'" He said he missed her so much and was so tortured by the idea of her still escorting, fucking all these men while he was away, that for a long time he didn't eat or leave his cell, just stayed in bed with the pillow over his head. But eventually he got really into working out there. So that explains that.

He said in prison, everything was about respect. And you had to treat everyone with respect because you never knew who could stab you or who might have a lock in a sock. He said he saw someone get hit in the head with one while they were eating in lunch, but the scariest thingthat happened was a stabbing because someone cut in line.

"But you've stabbed people!" I said.

"It was scary when I did it, too!" he said.

I sort of don't understand where George came from, how he exists. He told me he'd been in a long-term relationship with a woman a few years older than him, who now wanted kids but was in her early 40s and it wasn't happening naturally. He said he'd paid for IVF once before for her and it didn't work, and she wanted to try it again but it was $15,000—which he was willing to pay, but starting to have reservations about.

When I told him I thought I was going to get implants he said, "Wow, really? I love your boobs now. I can't wait to see what they look like with implants." Which is a response so perfect I couldn't have conceived of it on my own.

I asked him more than once if he was still involved in anything shady and he said no, his time convinced him he never wanted to go back. But I don't really understand what his job is. Not that it's my business. He told me I look a little like his ex-wife, and that she was Native American, and he asked me about my heritage again. When I asked him if he had a type, genuinely curious, he said me. There's a lot of evidence he's just smooth, but I believe there's sincerity there. Sincerity and diplomacy maybe. Like how I am when I want something from a man.

Every time I come over, he lights candles and opens a bedroom window. That night we could hear the rain outside, coming and going in fits. Sometimes I felt his gauzy curtain billow against my calves. I lay against his perfect naked body and just buzzed. It was happiest I'd been all year.

ALL THE MESS
June 16, 2014

The night after I took molly, I went to see George again. I worked beforehand, so I couldn't come by until late, and I knew he was tired because when I woke up very early, still high, he texted me back right away.

He left the door unlocked and I let myself in. His body was so sunken into the bed that I could barely make him out at first. "Are you asleep?" I asked, teasing, and then I saw he really was. I peed in his bathroom and didn't flush. I wondered about how best to wake a sleeping felon. I took off my clothes and climbed on to the bed next to him. I watched him for a moment and then he woke with a start.

"You're stinky," he said, immediately gathering me into his arms, slurring his words from grogginess.

"Stinky?!"

"Yeah, sneaky. I didn't even hear you come in."

I came that night with him. After I did, he was taking a long time and I started to feel sore—in my hips, not my pussy, which he assiduously keeps wet with outrageous amounts of saliva and lube. He wadded me up in a ball to fuck me missionary, with my knees in my armpits and my calves on his shoulders. Finally I asked him if he was too tired to come and he said he thought he could do it if he had his fingers in my ass during, which was what he'd just been doing. We did that again, and he finished.

~

Sometimes I start feeling paranoid and panicked that George is going to stop having sex with me. Once, after 36 hours of missing each other's windows for fucking, he didn't reply to my text at all, which was unusual, and I thought, "He's punishing me."

"Don't withhold sex from me, I'll die!" I texted him. But then I remembered how early he'd gotten up, and I guessed he'd fallen asleep.

He told me that's what happened when I saw him the next day, cursing that he'd missed me when he texted back that morning. I told him what I'd thought about him punishing me, and how I corrected myself almost as soon as I thought it, because that's not who he is, or at least not how he's ever shown himself to be.

"It's funny how much we make up about the world around us, you know. How wrong our perceptions can be about what motivates someone, but we'll be so convinced," I said.

"Yeah. When I was in the military—well, wait, I can be honest with you," and he smiled at himself. "When I was in prison, I met this guy who told me he treated everyone like they were shit until they proved themselves to be otherwise. And I was like, 'Wow, I'm the exact opposite. I treat everyone like they're good until they prove different.' And he was like, 'George, man, that's no way to get ahead. That's no way to be in the world.' I thought about that for years but I still think my way is better, because what if I miss out on being friends with someone I wouldn't have otherwise?"

We pulled apart and I started getting dressed. We'd given up on him getting off again. I slipped back into a silk dress I'd only ever worn for work before. It wasn't fancy in spite of the fabric; it had a girlish cut that made me feel young and skinny. I'd thought about wearing it when I'd fallen asleep the night before, fantasizing about coming over in the morning to be with him. It was how I wanted him to see me: pretty, fresh.

It was 9 a.m. and I'd been there since 6. I'd rolled out of my bed and went straight into his courtesy of an UberX. I left my work phone next to my bed with the ringer on, which I've never done before.

While zipping up, I glanced over next to his stereo and saw two phones charging on top of an iPad. "Oh my god, you have FOUR phones! You were trying to get my real number like, 'Now you can have my real number, too' and you've got two other phones?!" He was laughing. "You're so fucking shady!"

He grabbed me. "Let me fuck you again," he said. I'd tossed some condoms I like for work on his bed, suggesting that he could try them and let me know what he thought. I'd pulled them out because I'd called another Uber and they were loose in my purse. "Let me try one of these," he said.

"Fine," I said, "but I have to go soon."

"Oh, I love you," he said as I leaned over his bed and he flipped the skirt of the dress up over my back. "I love you."

When he came, he pulled out and I kneeled in front of him. I'd never tasted his come before, and I told him I wanted to, but most of it fell on the dress. What remained on my lips, I liked.

"I'm sorry," he said. "Wow, it's everywhere. I'm sorry. I couldn't stop thinking about Monica Lewinsky, and you in this blue dress."

What's most remarkable to me is how accepting I am of the mess. He sweats all over me but I don't mind. He can come anywhere and I'm ok with it. I'm ok with everything. Once when he was above me and our parted lips were hovering over each other, he closed his mouth and I knew what was happening from the way his throat moved, and he released his spit right into my mouth, not forcefully but purposefully. He almost pushed it out. Snowballing without the snow, as I said later. I don't think he knew what I meant.

I paused for a beat. (Paused what? Paused everything. It was a totally suspended moment. It tasted like water.)

Then, "You're a freak," I said. And he started laughing.

No one had ever done that to me. Do you know how few sexual firsts I thought I had left?

~

I lie awake at night sometimes, in my own bed, in a hotel, with a client next to me, and think about fucking George. I imagine him sitting on his couch and me kneeling between his legs and keeping my mouth on him forever while he puts his hands behind his head and melts into it. He said he'd never been on the receiving end of any ass play and I told him we should try it, that I would be very gentle and usually it felt better for guys than for girls. He described a porn clip he liked of two girls going down on a guy while fucking him with a dildo, and how the guy came so hard that he grabbed a pillow and put it over his face afterward, embarrassed.

That's what started the idea of the sex agenda, my mental list of things I want to do with him or to him. Go to a strip club with him and take molly there, go back to his place and fuck until it wears off. Be with him and another man at the same time, and then maybe him and a woman as well but I imagine us both focusing on her, as a team, not she and I competing over making him feel good, like it would be at work. I imagine just kneeling in front of him while he's dressed with my face pressed against his crotch, whatever fabric is over it—cotton, denim—and feeling myself getting wetter and wetter just from knowing how near I am to what I want. Going down on him in an alley at night.

There were a few times when I imagined him surprising me with a second man when I don't want it, and me being too afraid to say no, me suddenly realizing he's the type of man who likes to be intimidating, who wants to get me in a position where I'm not receptive and enthusiastic because he likes it better that way. Or him forcing anal even after I tell him no, turning into someone he's never given any indication he is but that I might be expecting anyway.

These thoughts started because he seemed eager to be with me while I was high again. That could be for any reason—because I'm less edgy, more affectionate, more forthcoming, more fun. But for some reason I worried it was to do something cruel to me, to find out my home address and come steal my cash—whatever.

New clients always ask if I'm not afraid when I go to meet someone for the first time, and I never am. Maybe it's starting to catch up with me, or I just feel like I've had too much good luck for too long. But then he does something, like calling me "honey buns" in a text, and I know it's pure paranoia to imagine that someone so playful and kind would want to damage me.

I used to love making money but now I don't care about that anymore.

I only want to fuck George. Not caring about something I used to care about more than anything else is both intimidating and marvelous. During work sex, I think about him. It's a good strategy in a way, because it makes me happy and distracts me from whatever whiny rant might otherwise be going on in my head. But it can turn me on, which I then resent and feel weird about—I hope I never get used to feeling physically aroused by sex I wouldn't engage in if I had a good way to avoid it.

And sometimes I start to feel a little panicked, like I can't abide by any more unwanted sex ever again, never, no matter how much money is involved or how brief and not that bad it is. After a certain point, the fantasies and memories of him exacerbate my irritation and impatience. I start thinking emphatically, "No, I don't want to do this," like someone backing out of zip-lining or chickening out on a high dive. More and more often I also feel this pointless sense of unfairness: I've already put in so much time having sex I didn't want. I spent my entire 20s having sex with old or middle-aged men I had no connection to or sexual interest in. The whole idea of having free sex with strangers was to reclaim my sexuality for myself. But I don't know if it's possible to do that and to work at the same time.

∿

My best regular bought a condo in my city and on our date, he took me to see it. He's a placid man, stoic on the outside, but I knew he was excited, not least of all because he told me so. He couldn't help but think of the space as our love nest, and he was eager for us to have sex in it before his son brought some girl over. It was unfurnished, smaller than I imagined but not small. We walked through the empty rooms and he told me what would go where, laying out the scene of an inhabited space. His wife already bought some basics: utensils, towels, soap.

"This is nice," I said, as I picked up a pan still in its packaging.

We went to the rooftop and were alone in the wind. It was a beautiful, quiet night. If my client and I had a different relationship, I would have proposed sex on the roof. I could have and maybe should have, but I didn't. I was thinking about my casual sex project and how I'd describe it to someone else or even to myself. I was thinking that it felt so good to not be the sex manager, to not be responsible for initiating, then feigning wild desire and pleasure throughout, suggesting kinky things, etc. But in some ways it felt like being in charge was exactly the point, that I'm the one choosing when and with whom and even where, and I got to a point where I would just say in advance, "Don't go down on me, I don't like it, but feel me up, grope me everywhere, I love that." Which is of course the position the client is normally in. It's like the difference between being the person who winds up a toy and being the toy itself.

Sometimes my home is so familiar to me it doesn't feel like a real city, but that night in a different neighborhood, amid flashes of neon, I felt a sense of affection and admiration for it, for its urbanity and activity. Across from our rooftop, a couple moved around in their condo from the couch to the kitchen and back again. I felt curious about their lives and connected to them at the same time.

It was like being a teenage girl again, in awe of the busy city world, as separate from my slow and sedate rural one, and eager to be a part of it. I still have the urge to project glamor onto everyone who lives in a high-rise with nice furniture and clean floors. What fascinating things they must get up to. How complex and full their days must be. I bet they live just like I'd live, if I could. How I'd want to live if I could conceive of something different.

GIRLS ON STAGE

June 23, 2014

Drunk client was getting slightly drunker than usual at one of our lunches when he decided we had to go to the city's ritziest strip club. As the client goes, so goes the hooker, and we got into a cab with under two hours left in our date.

The taxi stopped a few doors from the club itself, and my right foot slipped out of my heel while we walked toward the door. Several men loitered outside, the bouncer and two guys smoking, someone else doing who knows what. They watched as I struggled to leverage my foot back in. I gave up and told DC, "You'll have to kneel down and fix it for me." Gamely, he did so.

"Shoe trouble?" the bouncer said as we passed.

We were seated near the rail, but to the side, at a cramped table. There were maybe 15 customers total, including DC and I, and an elderly man who was the only one bothering to clap (pointedly) after each dancer left the stage. I'd been thinking about strip clubs recently because I wanted to go with George, but I wouldn't have chosen this one. The one I liked was rowdy, with multiple platforms in a row. There, strippers on stage shouted at customers in enthusiasm or derision or both.

DC's choice was supposed to be "upscale," with less physical variety among its dancers and a more refined clientele. The last part might have been true, comparatively. At the rowdy club, several years ago, a customer did something horrific that resulted in the long, protracted death of an employee.

DC immediately ordered more drinks, which worried me, but he complained about how watered down they were. I trusted he was getting blitzed enough for me to start speaking to him a little differently, and I asked if I could tell him something I hadn't yet told any other client.

"Of course," he said.

"I'm going to get implants," I said.

"What? No. No, don't do that. It's because you're getting older." He shook his head and I felt a stab of anger but also recognition. I know him well enough now. What did I expect.

"Lisa has implants," he said. "During one of our threesomes, it came up and I had to pretend I didn't know. But really I did." He imitated his look of surprise and then gave a simpering grin, finishing witheringly: "I knew."

"That was very gallant of you," I said. "But look, Lisa has implants and you still like her."

Lisa is his London-based escort, the one he's been seeing for even longer than me. I once referred to her as "affordable and available" and he's never forgotten it; he brings it up regularly and comments on how catty I am. But my frustration wasn't with her, it was with him. For at least a year he's badgered me to come to Paris with him at a steep discount. During one of our lunches, I finally told him to write a number down on a piece of paper and slide it across the table for me. I overturned the napkin to see a third of what it would have been according to my rates. I was impressed by the crassness, even for him.

"Here's my counteroffer," I'd said. I slid it back to him with a number double my rates.

"She has implants," I pointed out for almost every dancer who got on stage after our conversation. Most had great boob jobs. They weren't too huge and the placement was nice. I goaded him to get up and tip them all while I sat back in what I'd dubbed my Rachel Duncan dress, a severe black and white number with a long hemline and a neckline too plunging to accommodate any bra I owned. With the heels I was well over six feet and I knew I looked slim as a knife when I walked through the tables of single men to the restroom.

I kept thinking about aging and how my other clients would take my post surgery scars. Most of the men I see are regulars I've known for years, and part of how they see me rests on the conviction that I'm not a vain or shallow person, that whatever beauty I have is "natural," and they enjoy the prestige that confers on them. They like thinking of themselves as men who appreciate women for more than their looks and even actively reject the "fake," the ostentatious, the desperate and calculated.

I'd talked about this with an escort friend who has implants, and who asked if I wasn't worried I would lose business from getting them. She said she had a friend who wanted them for herself, but was too afraid to tamper with the "all-natural" marketing stance that was an important part of her business. I said I couldn't imagine anyone not seeing me anymore because of it, but I wasn't looking forward to the conversations that would ensue, the hurt and baffled looks I anticipate when they struggle to readjust their ideas of me to accommodate the possibility that I might be Machiavellian, greedy, willing to shape my body to whatever I think the market might reward, or self-hating and neurotic, anxious about "getting older," stricken in my own skin.

I've wondered if my decision is about those things, too, but I don't feel anymore insecure or self-hating than usual and I'd be surprised if the change had a big impact on my income one way or another. I've talked about getting cosmetic surgery on my breasts since I was 12. I never pursued it before because I didn't want them bigger and didn't know much about the options beyond that, and in some sense it simply hadn't occurred to me, like it doesn't occur to me to skydive or take up tennis.

When I worked at the in-call and on webcam, clients always insisted to me that I should never get a boob job, though most clients who talk (apropos of nothing) about how they hate implants regularly see an escort with undeniably man-made, massive breasts. I wasn't tempted back then; I had other things on my mind and I fixated on weight loss above all else. But I wish I'd done it before. I wish I'd done it years ago.

"I think your clients know you're the type of person who wouldn't not do something because she was worried about other people's opinions," my friend said, sagely. My boyfriend said the same thing to me when I recounted DC's comment to him: "It would be unlike you to make this decision based on what other people might think."

I second-guessed myself in this environment, though. The look I'd gone for that morning had been intended to suit the restaurant and hotel we'd be in, and to amuse DC with something different. He had a great appreciation for style. I assumed it was ok that red lipstick is aging, because it would be sexy in the context of our afternoon. Now my cold, cock-teasing businesswoman costume clashed with the bikini-clad barely legals and I didn't like the dissonance. I bet most non-sex-working women are used to this feeling, too. Aren't we all trained in the subconscious work of recognizing what's hottest in a particular environment, and analyzing how we do or don't measure up?

One of the dancers with implants was a young blonde with a few tattoos and a full body. She had the type of roundness I'll never have and never have had because my height gives me too many angles, even when I'm chubby. Here and there she made a concession to her audience by bending at the waist and shaking her ass, but in the mirror she made eye contact only with herself. Of all the women we saw that day, she alone did tricks, sporadically flinging her body around the pole, levitating or upside down, mouthing along to Jhene Aiko ("I don't need you, I don't need you, I don't need you") as she slid down the metal to the floor.

TO BE
DISCOVERED

June 30, 2014

I had a few hours in between flights, so I used one of them to visit George.

"I've never seen your door latched before," I said when he let me in. "Why are you so suspicious? Who were you expecting?"

"I was just about to leave it open!" he said. Wearing a polo. I hardly ever see him in clothes. He normally greets me naked from the bathroom, wet towel still in hand. We matched this time, both of us in red and white.

I still haven't gotten used to feeling his body upright, how wide it is in some parts, how tapered it is in others, how dense and carved. "Your arms are so hard," I said, squeezing his triceps. I felt him flex against the pressure. "Are arms supposed to be that hard?"

We hadn't seen in each other in two weeks, possibly more. Possibly less. After we first met each other, he said he was looking for a weekly thing, and it was so funny to me then, this man trying to negotiate regular hookups when I wasn't convinced I wanted to see him again at all. Now I think, *Of course once a week. At least.* It was the middle of the afternoon. We'd never been together during that time of day.

I went down on him until I was a mess of tears and snot, wiped away as much as I could and brought my head up to his chest.

"You smell good," I said.

"So do you," he said. Up by his armpit I thought I caught the faintest whiff of sour sweat underneath the clean, but I couldn't tell if it was from him or from me. I wondered if he could smell it, and hoped if he did, he couldn't tell either. I wiggled up a little more so he could reach over my ass crack between my legs like I knew he wanted to. He slid his fingers in and out while I rested my head near his.

And then he kissed me deeply, and it felt like it had some importance for him or he thought it had importance for me. I'm sure he still remembered what he himself had said—that I don't like kissing. I wondered if he was overcome, wanting me to believe he was overcome, if he thought this might be a profound moment for me or . . . It's hard to stop speculating, even at times like that. He rolled me over onto my back and reached for a condom.

Eventually he said, "We're almost out of time. And neither of us came." I had been in too much pain—not pain, maybe, but discomfort—and wanted it to be over. I thought it was a mistake to come by. He'd destroyed my hair like he always does—pulled it and matted it and sweated into it until the fresh, clean curls I'd arrived with were a shapeless mess. His fingers dug into my scalp and flexed across the hairline on my forehead as he clutched and pulled, clutched and pulled, digging in hard. I thought of how meticulously I'd shaved before coming over and felt foolish. I'd never fussed like that for him before.

"You should come," I said in spite of that, coyly. There'd been a moment with my calves next to both of our faces, and he'd licked one and kept going, and after I thought I was smelling something sweet that he'd eaten but then I realized it was my lotion, not food, on his breath.

"If you come I'll come," he said.

"Oh really? Flip me over again."

"Look at all your drool," he said when I was face down next to a wet spot on the edge of his bed.

"You were gagging me with your hand!" And he had been, muttering something about me being a "dirty fucking liar." But I don't lie to him. Maybe he wanted to say "whore" but was worried I'd be angry. I don't know if he likes it rough or thinks I like it rough. Maybe both. Maybe maybe maybe.

I came and it lasted a long time and I was noisy, probably stupid sounding. I was aware and a little self-conscious but unable to stop it. He started moving so fast he pulled out completely. "I'm sorry. Were you still coming? Did I ruin it for you?"

"No . . ." I only wanted stillness while I came, but I'd never told him that.

He went back in and bore down with his hands around my head and throat and in my mouth. "It's so good," he said. "It's so good it makes me want to share you." But before that he'd said something about my pussy being all his. Not that they're incompatible. I like all of it. Anything that makes me feel like I'm learning something about him that might be true, I like.

In the shower, I spat out some heavy saliva and watched it slide down the side of his tub. It was bloody. I spat again into my hand and studied the traces. From his fingernails in my throat. For the rest of the night I could taste a faint metallic tinge and when I looked at my face in the airport bathroom, after five hours and $600 lost to a missed flight, I saw dark flecks of red under my eyes and at the top of my cheeks, blood vessels broken from choking.

"I'm coming in, too," he said. "Bend over."

"I forget how tall you are," I said as he loomed next to me. "Because we're always lying down."

Then I said, "'I'll come if you come,'" and shook my head. "That's extortion."

He said, "I'm learning from the best."

When I stepped out of the shower, my gaze fell into his almost entirely empty trash can. I started smiling.

"Ohhhh, my little boy is growing up," I said. "Finally using tampons."

"What?! Oh my god, and I emptied it right before you came over!" He shouted while I went searching for my clothes.

I laughed. "No wonder you weren't coming. What am I, number eight today?" It's fun to be able to give someone a hard time this way, instead of being on the other end of it. A former client would always gripe that he felt like he was on an assembly line, that he was at McDonald's. He kept seeing me, though. He tried to set me up with his son on a normal person date.

"Who does that? That's so rude." George fumed.

"It was only the wrapper," I said.

Once I was finally dressed, we held each other for a moment by his door. I'd caught a glimpse of family photos when I first came in. They weren't new, but I'd never noticed them before. I'd been thinking about how when he first told me about going away, I emphatically said, "The prison industrial complex is bullshit." I was high at the time, but that's no excuse. I wanted to apologize to him for that but I was too embarrassed to bring it up. I felt stupid and not good enough.

When he hugged me I pressed my nose into his chest. I don't look at his face if I can help it. His face is too cute. My hair looked like such shit. I'll never tell him my real name.

He texted me a contrite apology later, saying he was so embarrassed. I loved that he cared. I loved that he thought I cared.

I texted back, "I don't care how much tail you get. I find it endearing." He takes so many showers. I know what that's like.

That he and I found each other, that our lives could look so different in circumstance but be so alike in one way . . . It doesn't feel meaningful but it does feel like a happy coincidence that deserves to be enjoyed. It's given me a sense of symmetry and calm.

"I missed you," George said while he was inside me, more than once. I know better but I still believe him. He pays attention to me. He remembers things about my friends that I mentioned in passing. Maybe he's trained himself to do it. I remember developing that skill in high school. All it takes is you paying attention and people will think you're psychic, uncannily connected to them. It makes them value you more.

Lately I don't know what's going on but it all feels ok. Even my boyfriend says I'm the happiest he's seen me in a long time. He's started talking again about us getting married.

PRACTICE
July 6, 2014

When my boyfriend found out that I'd been having unpaid for sex for months without telling him, something strange happened. Not right away, but eventually.

At first, he blew up in a typical way: confrontation, accusation, etc. But all that burnt off relatively quickly because I knew, and he knew, several things. One, that we'd been together for too long and through too many bad stretches to finally end it over something as pedestrian as nonmonogamy. Two, that I cannot be told what to do and if he tried to stop me, he would fail. And three, which we did not discuss until a week or more after, that he really, really, really likes it when I fuck other men.

It's not a cuckolding scenario. He simply gets off on watching me with other men, thinking about me with other men, hearing about me being with other men, being with me while I'm with other men. All of it. I don't remember when I learned this about him but in some ways it may be our primary point of compatibility. I've never understood sexual fidelity and it's a relief to know, deep down, that I don't have to abide by it.

I'm not being hyperbolic when I say "never." One of my more vivid high school memories is of several girl friends and I going to eat at the Chinese restaurant where the boy who had a crush on me worked. It was summertime. We were barely clothed and all giggly with the news that I'd given my first blowjob to Mike, a boy outside our usual social circle.

Mike and I went to school together but we weren't friends in school. We didn't have any classes together and our respective groups of friends didn't intersect at many points, but for some reason he struck up a conversation with me over instant messenger. It eventually progressed to phone calls, which eventually progressed to him coming to my home during the day while my younger brother, oblivious, I hope, played video games in the living room.

Mike was not at all attractive to me in terms of his appearance but he made me laugh, sang me made-up songs, and was more popular than I was. Plus, I was on a mission to teach myself how to be good at sex. That had to start with engaging in the main components: hand job, blow job, intercourse.

In my bedroom, I maneuvered my braces around his penis for what was probably only 30 seconds. As far as I can remember, he was hard from the start. I didn't take off my clothes and he only pulled down his pants, and perhaps because he started out hard, I expected an immediate result from my efforts, so I stopped and asked him if it was alright/ok/good.

"I think if you let me rub against you . . ." he said, and we laid down and dry humped for what may have been even less than 30 seconds before he hurriedly stuffed himself back into my mouth. After he came, he went on his way, and the phone calls continued though we never had a sexual encounter again.

I knew that Caleb, the restaurant waiter, liked me. I don't remember if he told me directly or if it was relayed through mutual friends. And because I was otherwise boyfriend-less and we were already around each other all the time, I think part of me assumed we'd end up "going out." But nothing official was in place at the moment, and I hadn't considered that I shouldn't give another guy a blow job out of respect for Caleb's random crush, nor that it would be bad form to tell him about it. I learned pretty quickly, though, that he did not find this recent development nearly as amusing or charming as I presumed he would.

It was my first experience with a man reproaching me because of my sexual behavior with another and it didn't feel good. More accurately, it felt searingly awful and totally confusing. I was willing to believe I'd done something wrong because I knew Caleb was a good person. But I hadn't intended to hurt him and I didn't feel guilty.

In my mind, men wanted to have sex, so it was good to know a certain girl would be sexual. And it was a good thing if the girl you were with was sexually appealing to other guys. The more people wanted her, the hotter she was; that was just math. And the more sex a girl had, the better a girl would be at sex.

This was all basic and self-evident, so much so that at the start of that same summer, I shamelessly enlisted my best friend on a quest: we'd practice sex now with whoever who would offer himself up as fodder, and then we'd be good at it when we met men who really mattered to us. These ideas came from somewhere or else I was born with them.

Later, close to graduation, I found out Mike had told everyone at his lunch table about our two minutes, and therefore probably 90 percent of the people I took classes with knew and had known for years. I cannot recall feeling hurt or embarrassed by this, though I was struck by his general immaturity and tackiness. He had more social cache than I did, so maybe I'd banked on class embarrassment to keep him from telling all the assholes he hung out with, which is probably a little hypocritical since I told my own gang of beloved assholes, though, in my defense, most of them went to another school.

Even later, Mike and I went to the same college and ended up on a lame date that involved wandering around campus at night and eventually going back to his room. Sitting next to him on his bed, fully clothed, and declaring it was time for me to go is still one of my proudest moments. And perhaps it only became so in retrospect, but I believe his lack of discretion and the resulting lack of respect I had for him was the main reason why I left.

When my boyfriend and I are getting along, I don't like writing or talking about our relationship because it seems disrespectful to him. There are plenty of things I won't share when we're not getting along, too, because it is too great a violation. But getting along in particular feels exclusive and more private than pretty much anything else in my life ever feels. It feels like an alliance with many secret components that wouldn't be intelligible to anyone else but the two of us, and you can laugh when I say that I'm loyal but it's the truth. So trying to explain what evolution took place will not be easy, not to a friend and definitely not to strangers.

The odd thing is, he apologized. He apologized thoroughly and more than once. In some ways it was like a moment in a fairytale when a human emerges from some nonhuman form. He seemed to transform but out of his own will. He then pledged his continued transformation to me.

I have my theories: that I was shaking him out of complacency, reminding him he doesn't control me, or that it was evidence of my being ready to move on. I know he'd been telling himself our sex was unsatisfying and sporadic because I didn't have a sex drive, but now here was proof that I did. He'd told himself he knew everything there was to know about me, but it shocked him that I would take any drug before fucking someone I barely knew. I think he saw me in that big-picture, real way of seeing someone, and some of what he saw he didn't recognize but that obscurity was itself recognizable, and why he responded to me in the first place so many years ago.

The following months were somewhat astounding. Not without emotional flares on his part or wariness on mine. But he seemed dedicated to this newness. He impressed me.

Caleb and I did end up "going out." He made me an elaborately hand-drawn poster that read "Ass of the Land" after I said I had no idea how butts were supposed to look, and couldn't believe mine was any good. ("Ass of the Land" was his drunken attempt at conveying my superiority in this department.) He was very handsome—beautiful bones in his face, dark hair, blue eyes. He was even confirmed penis-length champion out of our social circle of eight or so core guys, who all measured together one day. I never saw it myself, though we made out extensively and often in his basement bedroom. I know I felt it once or twice through his jeans.

His affirmations never meant much to me because I could tell he liked me for my personality, not my (negligible) looks, and he was observant enough to know I didn't make the space for him that he made for me, so we didn't stay together for long.

I went on to give my second blow job to a guy equally entrenched in our clique, and this news came out at a group meal at Applebee's, and Caleb and I didn't really talk much for the rest of high school, though I'd trust him to call me by my nickname from then if he saw me now, with sweetness in his voice.

Since adolescence, I've mainly attracted a certain type of guy: intelligent, likable and funny, a bit nerdy, outgoing, with a kind but shy heart. Brave enough to tell me how they felt in some quiet patch outside a noisy, drunken party while their friends shouted taunts at them and I listened with my arms crossed, not meeting their eyes. Good enough to not treat me meanly even if I didn't extend the same care.

I never liked them back. I shot them down quickly and badly. I was not a pretty girl as an adolescent. I was awkward, self-hating, with the same bad hair I have now and a crumpled, closed-lip smile that stuck around for a year after the braces were gone. I didn't want declarations of love or respect or admiration; I wanted to feel physically attractive, so I was only interested in finding men who pursued me explicitly because of sex.

What I mean about their hearts being shy is, they were expansive and generous people, enthusiastic and high energy while still being gentle. They had a tender space they wanted to share with someone else. They had connections but they wanted intimacy, and they were looking for the right person to help create it.

We're not perfect, and he's done some bad things, but my boyfriend might be the only man I've been with who keeps trying to make space for the shaded-in parts of me, the places in my heart that are dark to him either because dark is what they are or because they're simply not yet in the light. It doesn't solve everything but it's a start. So we keep starting again and again.

BREASTS AGAIN

July 9, 2014

After the consultation with the mean doctor, I became even more certain I would have surgery. I was filled with incredible tenderness for my breasts because of this conviction. I held them more while I walked around the house naked. I studied them more in mirrors. I wanted to throw them a farewell party and invite all my friends. What had they done that was so wrong, after all?

I was completely willing to part with them but I didn't want the goodbye to be cold. And in some ways I grew to like them more than I ever had in the past. I felt magnanimous, expansive, benevolent. *They're not really that bad,* I would think to myself. *They're actually even kind of nice.*

If you look at enough naked breasts for long enough, whether natural or enhanced, they become meaningless and silly. And you see that their largely standardized appearance in clothes, thanks to bras and fashion conventions, reflects almost nothing about their untamed states. I've looked at over 200 sets of before-and-after photos and in only two cases did I think the implants were a mistake, because the "before" breasts were my own ideal—not small, exactly, but compact, round, high, athletic, and girlish—and the enhancement wasn't bad per se but it made me sad in that it erased the lucky, genetic goodness that had been there before.

In most of the other cases, I thought the implants were irrelevant; the boobs looked goofy before and they still looked pretty goofy after, but bigger. The nipples splayed dramatically to the sides in both, for instance, or the shape remained odd. Cosmetic surgery is too expensive a procedure to not be picky about these things, so I studied the "after" breasts like any diligent consumer would, with an eye for the smallest flaws. I wasn't in the market for bigger boobs. I was in the market for nude boob excellence.

One of the biggest reasons I'd been hesitant to get implants was the ridiculously high rate of patient satisfaction. No matter how rock hard, strange, or downright unattractive a boob job is, in my experience, the woman who has it done is usually thrilled with the results. I was frightened to fall under the same spell, to become deliriously happy with my not-much-better-looking tits, the breast equivalent of the girl who's proud of her damaged, split-ended long hair. At least now I had the good sense to be ashamed of my boobs. God save me from ever being happy with my body if it's not aesthetically perfect.

It pains me to admit it, but I was willing to hire the mean doctor. Maybe that was just the heady rush of commitment to the idea of the procedure. Now that change felt within reach, there was no reason to wait. And since my boobs were even uglier than I thought they were—no matter how much more I liked them now, their inadequacy was conclusively established—surely they could only be improved upon. Screw my lofty ideas of traveling around North America checking out all the most talked-up doctors until I found the literal best one through the tenaciousness of my own investigation. As one of my doctor clients once said, "Anyone can do a breast augmentation. You can do them in your sleep."

But I had work appointments and travel ahead, and after talking with Beatrice I realized I would be doing myself, and possibly the universe, a huge disservice by giving that monster my money and my body. So I scoured my immediate area, spent an afternoon making calls, and set up some alternatives.

The second breast engineer was a woman who saw me on a day when she normally didn't do consultations. She and her staff had been so kind and accommodating, I had a good feeling that my experience this time would be far more encouraging than the first. Feminine empathy. Sisterhood.

Humility. Etc. She herself came to fetch me from the lobby, wearing a wrap dress with no white coat, and we went to her office, where I talked about what I had in mind. There were implants everywhere, piled around like gooey paperweights.

Then she took me to the examination room, which felt extra cold because it was so huge. She fitted with me some sizers and took pictures of me topless. My skin tone seemed pastier than usual under those lights, my areolas less pink than more like the brownish yellow of a very old bruise, and the nearly transparent hairs on my skin stood out wildly like overgrown weeds. *Just take them off, take it all off,* I've found myself thinking more than once during this long experience. Take my breasts. Take my whole corpse.

Back in her office, she pulled up the pictures and started in, like the first doctor had, on my unusual ribcage. I always thought the dent at the center of my chest where my cleavage is, or rather is under the right circumstances, was the weird thing about my breastbone. But apparently that's not all. We'd talked about it while she was using the sizers, too; she pointed out to me that she thought one side projected more than the other, and so we'd definitely have to use different size implants. All my post-pubescent life, I'd thought the left boob was the larger one and mean doctor had agreed, which meant the left would get a smaller implant. But now this woman was telling me the right side would get the skimpier implant because the right side had more rib issues.

It was hard to argue with her because while the mean doctor had commented on the general freakishness of my chest, he hadn't been as precise as she was. And the senseless cresting action of my breastbone on the right could not be denied. I'd never fully registered it before, but, particularly in the course of my newly thorough self-handling, I sometimes idly pushed against the lifted bone there while I was watching TV or reading, patting the surge of skeleton like it were a pet. Maybe it was my body making a cry for help: *Notice this fucked up bone thing, please. It's not functionally wrong but it looks stupid once you notice it and is impossible to correct and you should feel bad about it.*

The good news was, that wasn't all I should feel bad about.

"Do you see how the nipples are different?" the doctor asked.

"Oh, yeah," I said, kind of bullshitty, the verbal equivalent of a hand wave. But in my head I was thinking, *No.*

"You see, there's actually quite a large difference. This one's lower."

I looked more closely and decided it was true. In my decades of life I'd never noticed it, but my nipples are not the same. Or maybe the nipples are the same, but the areolas aren't, and so upon close inspection you might say that one was lower within the areola, or rather that the other was higher, or that the other areola was rounder and larger. I couldn't tell you what exactly I thought I was seeing in that moment and I'm frankly too afraid to check again now, but whatever I was looking at, it was not good.

I waited for her to say something about how everyone's asymmetrical because I know this is an uncontested fact about human bodies, but she didn't. She was not about to downplay a damn thing about this insufficient body of mine.

I was ready for us to change course. Ok, we'd spent some time assessing the garbage pile, but now it was time to talk strategy for cleaning it up. So I prompted her about my reluctance to get a lift in conjunction with my desire to have higher breasts. Mean doctor, to his minor credit, had vetoed the lift for now. You may or may not recall that he was staunch in his prescription that I get one in the future, post-40s or kids or whatever. And this doctor agreed that the scarring from a lift is considerable and that I was very young to take that on. She even said she suspected I'd want another lift later in life if I got one now, because lifts are a temporary fix and because my skin is so thin. But she seemed rather morose about all our available options.

So I brought up Dita Von Teese. I've seen Dita Von Teese perform live at relatively close proximity, and I was impressed most of all by how non-implant-looking her implants are. I asked the doctor if she knew who Dita was. She didn't, so she googled her. What I'd recently been hoping was that plumping up my breasts without a lift would give me the DvT effect of a lush teardrop shape. But we couldn't find many bare-breasted pictures of Dita with her arms down. It was all arms up, over her head or raised in some other way, which is a temporary lift.

"Everyone looks better with arms up," the doctor confirmed. "Hers definitely have some sag." (Mean doctor was also disapproving of Dita's "low" implant placement. He frowned at the picture of her I'd saved to my phone and pointed to the underside of her breast aka her "droop.") I guess

Dita's weren't so impressive after all.

"Let me show you a woman who should have gotten a lift but did implants instead," the doctor said, pulling up her practice's website. "The guys really didn't want this picture up, but I insisted, because people need to see what that looks like."

She shifted her monitor toward me a little to reveal a woman whose torso looked about mid-to-late 40s. Her breasts were low in the before and they stayed low after. I honestly didn't think they looked that much worse, and perhaps not even any worse, than some of the other before-and-afters I'd seen. But it was good to know that this doctor thought my implants would look like those of a woman who had a decade and a half on me, whose "after" pictures worked best as a cautionary tale, and were so hideous the male doctors worried making them public would negatively impact business.

I digested this for a moment in silence.

"And you have stretch marks," she added.

"I've had those since I was 12," I said. Did she think my boobs were picking up speed in their premature aging, like they were racing each other to my belly button?

"Oh, I'm sure you have. It's the result of any rapid growth. But it's another indication of your skin quality. It just depends on the individual. It's like fabric, you know? Some people have spandex and some people have . . . cotton." Then on the sketch in front of her, on the top of each breast, she made three squiggly, vertical lines.

What can I say? It's true. It's all true. My skin is cotton. Everyone always comments on how soft it is, but that's because it's thin like the membrane of a soap bubble. That's why I have such tenacious cellulite, and I bruise so easily. One of my biggest life rules is no cotton sweaters, and I'm living in one. One hundred percent cotton. Not even 2 percent spandex.

I could tell I was going to start crying and not in the sniffling, quiet way but in a full out face-collapsing bawl. I started to do the "yes, I realize you're still talking but I'm about to burst into tears" nod and then the tears were there.

"I'm sorry!" she said.

"It's ok."

"I used to have tissues in here . . . Let me get you some tissues."

"I can just go to the bathroom," I said. That would be preferable anyway so I could really wail.

She paused, probably thinking about how it would look to other patients to have me wandering around in the halls sobbing. "No, I'll go get some."

I had a lot of thoughts in my head, not fully articulated thoughts, but they had a general theme. The first was that I couldn't believe I'd let George see me naked. Glorious George, of all people. Just a day ago I'd stood fully naked in front of him in the daylight talking about whatever the hell and putting up my come-crusted, ruined hair in a clip while my uneven, stretched out, so-bad-even-modern-science-can't-fix-them breasts dangled around in front of him. He'd gotten hard from it!

And naked in front of clients. Topless in front of men who paid me thousands of dollars. That didn't even make any sense. My whole life up to this point felt ridiculous and confusing. How could I have been such a fool as to talk myself into liking my breasts at a time when they must be the worst they've ever been?

She brought back a box of tissues, and I tried to use less than I needed before giving in and continually pulling them out while she looked at me sadly.

"I'm sorry," she said again, making that vaudevillian, sympathetic "I'm almost crying too" face that women give each other.

"No, I'm sorry. I just . . . It's not your fault. I shouldn't be so upset. When I see the pictures of breast cancer survivors' before-and-afters, I feel like such a superficial little shit."

"No, no!" she said. "They get really overwhelmed when they're trying to make their decisions, because they have so little control in their treatments, and this is something they have total control over. I have to do a lot of expectation management. I was thinking to myself, 'Am I being too hard on her, because I'm used to that?'"

I didn't really understand what she was saying. I was still trying to clean my wet face. I was ready to give Jesus the breast wheel and just sign up for the soonest available appointment to get the whole ordeal over with. Do whatever you want, doctor, but don't even make me sit through a consultation ever again. I had only one last move.

"What about an areola reduction?" I said. One of my friends had one, and she mentioned it while we were working together late last year. I'd never heard of such a thing before, and I wouldn't have undergone it for its own sake, but if I was going under the knife anyway and my nipples were so uneven . . .

She brightened up considerably. "Yes, we could do that. It's a form of a lift, and you have the extra tissue. We could even them out and you'd get them a little higher without such extensive scarring . . ." Enthusiasm began to peek through. "We could do that. I think that's a great idea. Implants with the areolar mastopexy. I think we could make them look really good." It was the only time she'd seemed even remotely optimistic about the final effect.

I went into a different office room to get the estimate. The sweet woman who'd helped me set up the consultation talked me through pricing, and I wondered if the so-called discount was standard to make it seem like a good deal or if I'd cried my way into a cheaper procedure. I was sure she knew I'd started sobbing—inevitably, she handed off the box of tissues—so I just admitted I had and said I felt badly about it.

"It's an emotional issue!" she said. "You're talking about an insecurity. Dr. _____ came in asking for the tissues and said she was about to cry too." My boobs: officially bad enough to make strangers weep.

I left feeling a little shaky, like I'd given blood or been mildly sedated. I would always elect to give a woman money over a man, so maybe this doctor was The One. But I couldn't rush into surgery at the moment anyway because of the work I had coming up, and there was one last consultation on the horizon. Surely the third time couldn't get any worse than the previous two?

HIS FACE
July 14, 2014

We met in the afternoon again. It was the first time we'd been together since I missed my flight. I got there before him and waited in his condo lobby trying to arrange my thin cardigan to hide the bra strap in the back of my open dress without covering my shoulders. I saw him outside as he approached, several days of stubble on his neck. We hugged but I wouldn't meet his eyes for more than a moment. He was in work clothes, a white button-up shirt that wasn't tight but still gave away the broad planes underneath.

Upstairs I sat on the edge of his bed with one knee up and he moved away my skirt to see me bare below. "You're so sexy," he said, touching me there. We kissed and kept kissing even though his mouth is too much for me, plush and good, and I can't kiss. I try a little but then I stop because men's mouths are a changing puzzle I've had to solve almost every day for almost a decade and sometimes I just shut down, I hate it so much, I don't know how to respond to wanting to do it well. The next day I'd be off on a long date with an old man who leads with his hard, short tongue, his mouth open in a grimace around it, like an animal struggling to eat from a narrow jar.

He came on my face again. "I've been saving up for you," he said, which was what I'd told him to do in an email but with a wink, because I can barely imagine him going eight hours without coming let alone multiple days.

"Two days' worth," he said and I laughed at him: "You have not."

"You don't believe me? I have, I swear! You don't think so?" Mock surprise, mock innocence, mock honesty.

After he came, he said, "Ok maybe more like . . . half a day." He laughed.

"Probably more like three hours," I said, rolling my eyes.

"I don't know when it was. But it feels like two days." He got off the bed and made a move toward his bathroom to get me a towel.

"Wait wait wait, give me my phone, I need to take a picture." I tried to hold mostly still as I gestured to the chair where I'd put it, a chair on which he'd left a pair of gray sweatpants. When I saw that, before I sat on his bed, I had the vision of his body in them and I could hardly stand it, how sweet and boyish and sexy he is and those sweatpants struck me as the epitome. The idea that I might come over in the future and he'd be wearing them and nothing else made me want to wiggle like a puppy.

He passed me my phone and without being asked to, straddled my face.

"Yeah, get him in there," I said, looking at myself on the screen as he nudged the head of his cock against my cheek. "I don't know what expression to make."

I experimented quickly with three poses, then I stuck with the third one, a look of surprise, and showed it to him. He laughed.

"I'm going to put 'whoops' on it," I said. I'd shown him Snapchat when I was high and told him how my friends and I send each other platonic nudes. He seems to love the thought of me including him in an otherwise all-girl circle.

What's bad now is we know enough of each other to want to talk but we don't have time. When I first came in, I sat on his sofa and he stood in front of me as I traced my fingers up and down his upturned palms, and told him my best suggestion, if he really wanted to charge for it, was to link it to personal training and find clients on Craigslist. He said Craigslist isn't high-end and I agreed, but men can't charge as much as women anyway. And I told him about Andrew, the man who'd paid me $1,000 for one hour after he responded to a Casual Encounters post of mine. But that was a fluke in almost every way. I thought George wanted to experiment with Craigslist the way I did back when I was still new and would contemplate taking the train to the suburbs to give a $100 hand job in a parking lot just for the adventure of it.

George told me before, at a different time, that he first thought of charging when he wasn't sure he wanted to keep seeing some women he'd fucked in the past. I assumed it was mostly for couples because I know he meets a lot of them, but apparently there was one person he had in mind who'd told him, "You're so cute, I just want to take care of you." Then she was shocked when he suggested money. ("I can't believe you asked me to pay you.")

"But she brought it up!" I said. "That's not fair. What else is that supposed to mean? That's what it would mean if a man said it." In retrospect, maybe she wanted to cook for him or something.

He sees too many couples for me to keep them straight. He got stoned with one of them and dropped his phone off their balcony. He said they used some smoking device he'd never seen before; "I don't know, I'm not that experienced," were his exact words, and that someone who'd lost a decade of his life to drug charges would say that struck me as so absurd and terrible that I thought of it occasionally for weeks afterward.

I knew the two-day thing was a lie not just because of the obvious—who he is and his habits—but because he wasn't very hard and the sex felt distracted. Both of us were pressed for time. He'd rushed home from lunch and shown up sweaty when he seems to prefer being straight out of the shower. He had a meeting in the same area he'd left and he would inevitably be late returning. So he pulled my hair too hard again, wrenching my face to the side, and my head ached as he dug his fingers into the sensitive skin at the top of my forehead.

"Your ear is red," he said at one point.

"Yeah, because you've been chewing on it. You're like Mike Tyson," I said. I don't know if he realizes it, but he almost always does. My ear sometimes hurts for days after.

He even went down on me, which I despise, and my mouth was full of his cock so I didn't tell him to stop, but the whole thing was off. I realized that no matter how much either of us rubbed I wouldn't come. I got sad and suddenly wanted most in the world to go home and get a hug from my boyfriend. I couldn't think of why I was there anymore, why I'd shoehorned this into my day when there were so many other things I should have been doing.

In the car, I couldn't avoid looking at him straight on. We sat angled toward each other with our knees touching, and I laid my hand on his thigh, against the pants I'd admired him in when I'd seen him coming in his own front door. We talked about sex with only the slightest consideration for the driver; we were riding together because his meeting was near where I lived. I said that he was right about internet-arranged sex being addicting, which was something he'd mentioned in an email to me way back when we'd only seen each other once.

I said, "I can look at pictures of someone and know exactly what sex with them is going to be like. But then sometimes I'll just go do it anyway and then afterward I'm like, 'Yup, just what I thought.'" And he listened with amusement like he understood the feeling of "why not" even when the gamble isn't promising. The decision to take a lame adventure over no adventure at all.

I don't think it's about adrenaline, really, because for years I've met strangers for sex, and I rarely feel giddy or nervous though it often does turn me on. I think it's the potential that hooks me. The anticipation of something outside the familiar. The sense that anything could happen. It isn't scary and it's not a high level of excitement, but it's a low buzz, the way I imagine a dog feels when it's hunting for a scent. You're not on the trail yet, but you're looking for the trail. Something's about to begin. You're making it begin.

The only person I'd met for unpaid sex since regularly being with George was a man with a big dick, bald head, and slightly jowly face that made him look older than he claimed to be, which was early 30s. He met me on the street in a neighborhood I'm normally never in to take me up to his overheated bedroom with an inadequate ceiling fan. Meek, out of his element, just like I knew he'd be, particularly when he said he tended to be dominant.

When he pushed into me the size alone made it feel good but there was no hope of enjoying it. He was so turned on he was frantic and panicky. He yanked my hair too hard and sweated more than the heat or his effort warranted, trying desperately to get me off while he tried desperately not to come. Bucking the orgasm out of him as he struggled against it didn't even feel interesting or powerful—or maybe it did feel a little powerful, but it was a type of power I'm bored by. A queen on a throne who motions with one finger.

In the car, George said he wanted to ask me about something I'd said to him once when we parted, which was that I'd been feeling uncharacteristically paranoid recently. The only reason it stood out to me was because he said, "I didn't like that," in a way that suggested concern for me. And I knew for sure then, because of how I felt about this hint, that I don't see George anymore because of the sex or the distraction. I see him because I want him to care about me.

When my boyfriend prompted me to talk about what it's like, I said, "He's my friend."

"How do I look?" George asked when we first got into the car, both of us frazzled. Out of the shower, I'd put my dress on inside out and looked at him blankly to correct me because I had the vague sense something was wrong. He'd run back inside to grab his phone, then again to look for his watch. We hustled down his hall together to the elevator, co-conspirators.

"Do I look crazy?" he asked, as if his tight curls could betray anything. As if he'd been the one with come across his cheeks.

"You look perfect," I said, and I touched his face.

BREASTS FOR
THE LAST TIME
July 21, 2014

As I suspect is true for a lot of women, I've long related to my breasts primarily through the ways men respond to them. I got my period when I was 11 and had a growth spurt around the same time. I was the tallest person in class for all of junior high, with stretch marks around my knees and a rack larger than many grown women's, though with that soft, pokey newness of a kid's.

The first time I remember realizing a boy was staring at my chest was during a paired assignment in sixth grade. "Andy," I kept saying as he sat across from me. "Andy." He chewed furiously at a hangnail, unblinking, eyes on my tits. I always wore baggy clothes but it didn't help much.

That wasn't bad though; I wasn't bothered by things like that. Sometime before or after, two gooney older boys in my gym class trailed me while we ran outside. I was alone, near the back of the pack.

"Jiggle, jiggle," they said to each other loudly, snickering behind me. Mocking, like they'd caught me sucking my thumb or seen me sitting on the toilet. Like they had a weapon and the weapon was my body. "Bounce, bounce, bounce."

I tried to outrun their voices but I couldn't. I'd never experienced humiliation like that before, the embarrassment of simply being in a body. Or such shame. It was then that I started telling my parents I would have a breast reduction when I got older.

Those moments, or at least my memories of those moments, are blessedly few. The closest I ever came to feeling that helpless again was when I was in grad school and I came home from working on webcam around 2 or 3 a.m. It was warm, and I wore a tank top and skirt and my long, dark wig. I parked a few blocks from my rental and walked by a townhome porch brimming with kids my age. (I was a few months into 21.) They had the lazy, mean energy of people up too late, not sober, bored with each other and edgy with disappoints and anticipations. Meth was big in my neighborhood.

"Hey you," one of the boys yelled at me, a smirking girl on his lap. "Hey Tits. Come here. Why are you out so late? Come here. What are you going to do for me? I'll pay you." I passed so close by them all. I didn't turn my head and fought the urge to change my pace. My hands were empty. The laugher of the girls with the boys, the whole lot of them. It wasn't about what he said. It was the way he said it. Like he'd pinned me down and was lifting a knife.

I didn't realize I had big areolae until I worked on webcam and men would comment on that feature obsessively. One guy asked me if I could wear bikini tops, which was something I'd never thought about before. I wasn't the kind of girl who wore bikinis. I remember this particularly because I've always been fascinated to learn how men imagine women interacting with the artifacts of femininity. It reminded me of the man I chatted with on AOL when I was 14 and looking for cybersex, who cursed me out violently when I couldn't tell him my pantyhose size to prove that I was a girl.

In my first serious relationship, the man I was with told me that most women would kill to have my body, my breasts. He was much older than me and used his age and consequent experience as authority but it was hard for me to believe him in spite of other confirmation.

For the first few years of my sex work career, my breasts were, no pun intended, front and center in client commentary on my form. They were unusual because they were relatively large for my frame but un-augmented. I checked some of my old reviews from ages ago, when I worked at an in-call, and found a few typical quotes: "God, I love her breasts," "Her rack is fantastic," "Her big, natural breasts are SUCH a treat." That was the general, though not universal sentiment. I still hated them and possibly hated them more in spite/because of this. I wanted to be sylphlike. I wanted compact, pert B cups that would make my silhouette sleek and willowy. I did not want my breasts to be my defining feature.

As I got older and lost weight, I achieved a bit of this wish. My breasts lost mass but that did not translate to them becoming perky or supple. Increasingly, new clients never commented on their size or enthused about them much at all. I hadn't liked them when they were a selling point and drew attention. Now I still didn't like them and they offered me no financial benefit. They stayed as prominent as ever in my own mind.

I went to my third consultation with a sense of resignation and resolve. I was prepared to learn new details to hate about my breasts, as I had during the previous two, but I maintained high hopes that I wouldn't cry this time, or that if I did I could at least be blasé about it. ("Oh, this always happens.")

I had my spiel honed at this point, so when the doctor came in I could get straight to the point: I've always hated my breasts; to get the look I want it would be better if I'd been born with less mass than I have; I don't want the scars of a lift but I suspect I'll need a lift; etc. etc. He was warm and sedate, and laughed a little at my demeanor, at my demonstration of my ideal look that involved hefting my boobs up as high as possible to create what he called "a youthful show."

"But you *want* that natural teardrop shape," he added with gentle authority.

Then, as I released my boobs to his scrutiny, there suddenly came the affirmation I'd once hoped for but no longer expected.

"I think you're being a little hard on yourself. They've got a very nice shape." He touched my breasts gently with his fingertips, like he were holding a lightbulb. "Your nipple line is slightly lower than average. About half a centimeter against a baseline of about 100 women. So that, that doesn't really mean anything. But if you wanted to know: I think we could get a really nice look with implants alone, but the areola mastopexy could certainly help a little more if you're sure you want it. You could always decide about that later, after you see what the implants look like once they're in. And you have a bit of an excavatum but that's easy to fix with a fat graft, if you wanted. Or a silicone implant. That could help the entire area look a little fuller."

(My weird skeleton thing—it had a name! And it was, in fact, changeable! Modern science! The marvels of civilization!)

"That would be great," I said. "Let's do that."

"Normally we can just take a little fat from elsewhere and that fills it out really nicely," he said, lightly pinching at my belly and hips. "But you don't really have anything to take it from."

"Get it from my thighs," I practically screamed. Lose some outer thigh fat and get the good boobs I'd been dreaming of for years? I was in some type of pre-surgical heaven.

As he was leaving the room, amid the reiteration of his optimism, his calm confidence in the end result, his thanks that I came in, he paused for a moment and then squinted at me a little with a smile, "Don't be so hard on those little guys. They're going to make a lot of people very happy someday."

"They've already made a lot of people happy," I almost said, thinking of course of my clients, but luckily kept my mouth shut. Did he think I was a virgin? A virgin poised to become a wild slut?

"Well, at least one person happy," he corrected himself, with a faint chuckle. So now I would be a virgin until marriage? Then suddenly I realized he was referring to babies. He was talking about breastfeeding. A reminder that my breasts would never truly be my own and my own alone.

But fuck that. I have no intentions of bearing children, let alone nursing them. It was time for my boobs to make me happy, only me, and I'd found the doctor to do it. I scheduled the appointment for my surgery that day, with a woman who asked if I had a boyfriend, and then what he thought about me having them done.

"We've been together for years and he always made me swear to never get implants. But I think he's come to terms with it now because he knows I'm determined."

"He must not be a boob man," she said. It was so hard for me not to snap back that it was *because* he's a boob man that he didn't want me to get implants. He's lavished my tits with praise ever since we met.

"Isn't Dr. _____ so nice?" she then asked. "I've worked for a lot of plastic surgeons and there's no one else like him."

I confirmed that he was indeed disarmingly nice.

"He's Mormon," she added. "He has nine kids."

I saw my most devoted client a few days before my surgery. I didn't think he was particularly taken with my boobs but maybe I just don't pay attention.

"To say I'm fixated on your breasts . . ." he sighed as we were naked together in the dark. "Well, they dance in my dreams."

He'll have new breasts to dream about soon enough. Goodbye, original boobs. Thank you for your service.

NORMAL PEOPLE
July 28, 2014

The first time we had sex outside his home it was in a hotel room I'd rented to see a new client, an attractive, tall man with a huge dick who luckily didn't last too long. I thought of it as foreplay for George and was glad I could save my orgasm for him, though it was awkward to see him in that same space a few moments after I said goodbye to the guy who'd paid me. I'd booked a room with two beds so that George and I could have a clean one.

I've been working for so long but it's still hard to slip right back into my regular life after being with a client. For years, no matter how late it was when I got home or how late a client left my hotel, I'd have to watch TV for an hour, or read, or eat, or everything, before I felt at equilibrium.

I told George that Emma recently had sex with a guy who had a pierced dick and it was great, so now I was curious about what it felt like.

"You want to pierce yours?" I said, playing with it.

"Yeah. Let's go."

"Let's go! Tattoo parlor right now." Neither of us moved; I rested against his chest with his arms around me. We undressed and got into bed with no sense of urgency in spite of the fact that I had to leave soon for an overnight.

Emma had been on my mind recently because I wanted to have a threesome with her and George but I was anxious about him seeing me naked next to her. I worried he would like her body more and see new flaws in mine. When I mentioned this nervousness to her over text she replied with "Haha, why?" and then I dropped it. Emma is the only girl friend in my life who's never complimented my appearance, not even incidentally, and I long ago came to the conclusion that she finds me truly unappealing though I still sometimes can't resist trying to fish compliments out of her under the dictates of politeness. But we'd worked together before, so it wouldn't be weird for our threesome to look more like us taking turns with the same man in real time. I was pretty sure she'd be game particularly if there was some molly involved. And I thought she and George would like each other.

She said she wanted me to have sex with her fuckbuddy when I last visited her city, in order to find out if he knew or suspected she had implants. I told George as much because I wanted him to know how communal and generous we were with our men.

Seeing him somewhere other than his condo made me more aware of his larger life, which made me more curious about him, and so I asked if he got hit on a lot by guys at the gym. I knew he did. And it made me happy to think about all these people wanting my George. Like when I told him it makes me jealous to think of him coming on another girl's face, but jealous in the fun way.

"Oh, all the time. I don't mind, I just tell them I'm not gay. Like, one guy came up and said, 'I'm sorry but I think you're so hot.' And I said, 'That's cool, man, but I'm not gay.'"

"So what's the most aggressive come-on you've ever gotten from another man?"

"I don't know. That was pretty bold. On Craigslist, guys are crazy. But in person . . . I'm not sure."

He thought for a moment and said, "Actually, once, in prison, I was in the weight room and this big dude, like I mean a real big, black motherfucker, was arguing with a little guy half his size and he yelled, 'I'll knock you out and suck your dick.'"

"Wait, who yelled that? The big guy or the little guy?"

"The big guy."

"What did the little guy do?"

"We were all quiet. I don't think anyone even knew he was gay."

"After that, were you like, to your friends, 'Guys, if I ever get knocked out, make sure no one sucks my dick?'"

He laughed. "Yeah."

Then I said, "I don't know if that really counts as a come-on."

"Well you probably get some crazy stuff, right? I bet men say insane stuff to you just when you're out on the street."

"Maybe? I don't know, I try to ignore or forget most of it. Men don't really approach me that much. It's probably different for you because you're so friendly. You're the friendliest person in this city."

"Yeah. Me and you."

"Oh, no, not me. I'm a total bitch."

"What. Really?"

"A total bitch," I said, amused and surprised that he thought otherwise.

"That's so cool," he said. "It's like I'm getting all your niceness. I mean obviously, you have it in you."

Last time we saw each other it had been in his house and I'd asked him about the potential third man he'd mentioned to me in an email.

"Tell me more about this Greek guy," I said.

"Well, I fuck his wife while he watches on Skype, and he says he's somewhere else but I'm pretty sure he's just in the next room or something. I'm nosey like you, so I looked at their mail one day because it was on the table where I came in, and then I looked him up. The guy's got money. He owns a nightclub. That's why his wife is so hot."

I didn't care much about the nightclub owner but the nosey thing bothered me. I assumed he was saying that because of all the questions I'd asked about his sexual adventures, but that was out of genuine curiosity, not because I wanted to be controlling or invasive. Part of why George excites me is because I'm curious about him. He's the only person whose life I've been interested in for a long time. Normally I never want to know more about anyone. I remembered asking him something once and then dismissing it in the same breath, and saying aloud that he shouldn't bother responding since, like me, he was good at deflection and never had to answer a question he didn't want to.

I was gathering more insights into how George operated. He was a hustler for sure. That was obvious to me pretty early on. But his style is a little like mine; he disguises it with a charisma that feels trustworthy and probably *is* trustworthy, but edited for maximum effect. It's about disarming someone with your sincerity, which is legitimately sincere but also strategic, selective. Almost everyone does that—balances their personality to serve themselves given whatever the moment demands—but some people are really good at doing it and really good at hiding it.

"You're nosey, huh?" I said.

"Yeah . . . I didn't want to say anything because I didn't want to upset you but . . ."

"What, you went through my stuff?" I tried to act knowing instead of panicked. Just like with work, I never traveled with my ID if I could help it. Maybe he'd seen my real name on a phone notification, like when my Uber would arrive?

"No, nothing like that. Just googled some stuff."

"Because of what I showed you? That's not really snooping. I mean, I know you could find more with that." When I'd been high I'd shown him some things about my work persona online. It doesn't matter to me if he knows about all of that; that's not real me.

But it was because he said I was nosey that I noticed his business cards spread out on his desk. I'd never gone through his belongings or looked hard at anything adorning his home, even though I had plenty of opportunities. I can't help absorbing some details but I'm not hunting for them, and what I notice is personal but insubstantial, like his collection of sunglasses or some crumbs on his counter. I know how to put on the privacy blinders I would want someone to wear for me.

That time, however, I let myself take it in. I read his last name and I googled him when I got home, and there he was, on a real website, a nice website. He has a job at a trendy firm. His bio detailed things about him I never suspected—I even wondered if some of them were a lie, the way so much escort marketing isn't true—and he looked so normal in his picture, or better than normal; accomplished, successful, happy. You couldn't tell from looking at him that he was a fuck maniac arranging his life around boning women all over the city. Or that he'd lost so much time to his sentence.

I almost wished I hadn't found it, though I admired him all the more to know how completely he'd excelled after what he'd been through. But now he'd never have the chance to tell me those things about himself, with me learning about them for the first time from him. That was what scared me when he said he'd been looking into me. I didn't think he'd do anything bad with that information, or that it was objectively important. But it's supposed to mean something when you tell someone your real name. That's what I've always believed; it's supposed to be a gift. He'd never get to give it to me.

We left the hotel room together, both in our work clothes. Him in his business casual, me in a Narciso Rodriguez dress with Gucci booties. Out into the world like normal people. As I was about to get into the cab, I felt the spontaneous urge to kiss him goodbye, so I did, on the mouth. I immediately felt presumptuous and guilty and sent him an apology from the car in case it had somehow been weird or wrong.

"Was it wrong that I kissed you in public?" I said.

"No, it was good," he said. "Tell me how early I should be there tomorrow."

≈

The next morning, I woke up next to my client. We ate breakfast, I tended to his orgasm, and then I left his hotel for another. I was in a taxi when SCOTUS released their Hobby Lobby decision. I scrolled through Twitter while I waited in the room, standing with my ankle boots and jeans on. I'd chosen my outfit in part for George so I wanted him to see me upright in it, but he was late and I was angry, still raw from the news about the raid on Redbook, in a hurry as always because I had to leave for another city and another overnight later that day.

When he finally showed up, it felt like an in-call appointment right down to my irate "let's get this over with" vibe. He could tell I was cross but I made an effort. I hugged him in spite of how I was feeling. He told me that when he left yesterday he'd passed a girl he'd shared the elevator with and she said, "You're the guy from the elevator."

"Then what?" I said.

"She kept walking. She was with some Middle Eastern guy in a suit … I thought about telling them to come back and party with us. He looked like he had money."

"You're like me," I said. "I start plotting when I get a whiff of it." I told him about the investor meeting that was going on in the hotel I stayed in when I went to Germany recently, and how I couldn't concentrate on anything else amidst all the men in suits. "All I was thinking is, 'So much money . . . and it all should be mine.'"

He shook his head. "You're a bad influence on me. You make me want to get back into my old ways. That's what I was thinking with that Greek guy, about him having money and that maybe we could get some from him . . ."

"Did you tell him I was an escort?"

"No, I didn't say anything. I don't know what I thought I was going to do."

"I was thinking about you once and suddenly started imagining you sending me out to go fuck guys and bring the money back to you, and how I wanted to do it and that it would be really sexy . . . Then I was like, 'What the fuck. Where did that come from?'"

We were laughing about it and it felt good to tell him. But I couldn't mention some of my other fantasies, which seemed cruel to him because they made him into someone he isn't. They weren't really fantasies but just flashes of thoughts, like him hitting me or us having sex when we were angry with each other. I think my brain was going wild with possibilities because he was still a slightly mythic character to me then, a vessel. But the more time I spent with him, the harder it was to use him as a canvas.

We started undressing and a huge roar came from outside as he pulled off his shirt.

"We're playing Germany," he said.

"Oh, that's what's going on! I saw them setting up equipment in the park." I peeked out the window at the crowd below. "It's like they're cheering for us."

I kissed him and he seemed reluctant. Had he given up on me because of all the times before? Did he hate the way I did it? Maybe he was thinking about the client I'd seen before him.

When he got up from the bed to get a condom, the crowd went wild.

"They're like, 'Finally!'" I said, "They've been waiting all morning for this."

"Finally. They're doing it," he said.

I can't remember much about that encounter except that while he was inside me, everything else started to fall away and it wasn't because I was so overwhelmed with the physical sensations. I didn't even have an orgasm. It was something else. I felt like I started shining. I know I started smiling, grinning into the pillow. I remembered the day before, when he was encouraging me to come and I told him I already had, and he said lowly, "Ok, my turn," like he was talking to himself. I liked that so much, how he seemed to concentrate on letting himself go and I could hear the focus in his voice. The focus on release.

I started welling up with the purest gratitude. It felt like warm oil. It was totally insular and expansive at the same time. *Thank you for fucking me, George*, I heard in my own heart. *Thank you, thank you.* Childlike and completely ridiculous, like I was skipping in a field throwing flowers into the sky. *Thank you for fucking me, George!* I wanted to shout it out the window at the soccer fans. I was so happy, the happiest I'd been sober in a long time. Thank you, thank you.

"Oh shit, I didn't want to come," he said. It was one of the few times he'd come inside me instead of pulling out. "But you felt so tight."

I bumped my butt back against him as he rested in me, and flexed my ass cheeks one after another. I starting laughing while I wiggled. "I should have been born a man. All I like to do is flex and have sex," I teased. I felt drunk. I thought about what Beatrice said when I sent her the facial shot: *You look so happy.*

"Lucky for me you're not," he said, as we pressed ourselves together. I didn't know what he would make of it, but I had to tell him: "I was so happy the whole time you were in me. I was just thinking, 'Thank you for fucking me!' over and over in a loop." What I didn't say was how I'd also been thinking about how his cock makes me want so much more cock.

Sometimes I can hardly stand having him in me in one place and not everywhere else, too. Especially on my stomach, when he holds my neck in a way that makes it impossible not to fantasize about him forcing my mouth down on another. *He makes me want to have more holes*, I'd thought. But I didn't tell anyone about that, not even him. It sounded too made up.

We walked outside together and hugged goodbye.

"Oh, no kiss today!" he said.

"I don't want to mess it up for you if there's another girl-in-the-elevator situation," I said, happy that maybe I'd been wrong about how it felt when I kissed him in the room.

"I'll just tell her I only play with my other half," he said. I couldn't believe that was what he said, but it was.

It would be weeks before I'd stand in front of him again. In the meantime, everything between us went to shit.

RUSHING
August 5, 2014

Once I knew the name of George's firm, I saw it everywhere. It was plastered all over my most frequented neighborhoods, including the one I lived in. And as George (unprompted) shared more of his life with me, sending me messages and pictures throughout the day, I realized his presence saturated the places where I spent the most time. Whether he was working, eating, or at the gym, he circulated in the same space I did, and both of us were regularly on foot, walking the same sidewalks again and again. I became highly aware of the likelihood that George would see my boyfriend and me together when we were out taking a stroll or grocery shopping or getting a meal. He'd already seen me on the street once, ages ago, at night when I was walking home from my straight job, and he called out my fake name until I went to him out of concern that the exchange would get even more awkward, and people from my straight job would witness it. (It seemed surreal that I had any job during this time, let alone a straight one. But I did.)

The boundaries between George and I were slipping. After the incident when I missed my flight, he drunk texted me, calling me "BABYYY," and telling me he missed me and we should go back to his house right then so he could play music and fuck my throat. He sent me selfies from his bed, from the incline bench after he worked out, pictures from his lunch table, links to songs. I sent him selfies from work, complaining that I'd so much rather be with him than sitting through a boring dinner. I told him where I was that day—Boston, Denver, Houston—and he told me he was living vicariously through my travel.

Once I went four days without contacting him and he emailed: "We fell out of a touch for a few days but it doesn't mean I stopped thinking about you . . . I love getting little notes from you, let's not go so long without keeping in touch." It had been three days since we last saw each other, two days since I discovered my boyfriend and he worked together.

∾

My boyfriend struggled a lot with my free fucking, particularly in the beginning. He was moody, which was incredibly unlike him, and prone to fits of palpable sadness. Once, when I was on another coast for work and had just finished a beautiful day with one of my favorite clients, he started texting me, nearly hysterical, demanding to know if I was with some random guy at exactly that moment. At exactly that moment, I was standing amid piles of fruit with too many peaches in my hands, trying to discern which aisle had almonds and watching his texts become increasingly wild. Moments before I'd bought him an embarrassingly stupid card with two cats on the front, the interior of which read, "You're the one who makes me purr." I'd been wandering in the sun, blissful, thinking about how good my life was. It took only 10 minutes for me to turn into a smoldering coal.

Part of me had sympathy for his emotional volatility. But another part of me had my own mourning to contend with. By his insistence, I sat alone with my pain and disappointment and fear for years, whether those emotions were about us or not. How dare he expect me to help him manage his suffering when he'd abdicated helping with my own?

When he first confronted me about my sleeping with men outside of work, I said repeatedly that I never do anything to hurt him. Which was the truth. Hurting him does not motivate or interest me. He assured me of the same but in the anguished and angry conversations that sporadically followed, he admitted to regularly doing things designed to provoke me, intended to harm me. Mostly I absorbed that information and set it aside for later. But during our coast-to-coast meltdown, it hit me, the full extent of the tireless internal labor I performed to convince myself that a slew of his behaviors were his oblivious personality quirks and not swords he'd sharpened with my guts in mind. I struggled for years to convince myself of something that wasn't true. That seemed the worst part of all.

The ultimate effect of those years in my own head, methodically and patiently trying to believe a lie that might make me feel more loved, was that I never felt sad about our relationship anymore. I'd become inured to it. I could be exasperated or mad or compassionate, but I couldn't feel let down or scared or intimidated or guilty or any of those traditional pains. They'd peeled off of me like old skins. This emotionally clean body felt good to be in. And it seemed that for the first time in our long period together, we were finally going to be honest and unguarded with each other.

The fight resolved in affirmation and kindness. Later, at home, I told him a little more about George, sharing pieces of his life because it was interesting. My boyfriend joked about working out extra hard because I had "a lover who's an ex-con in 'great shape.'" That he could tease me about the other man I fucked struck me as a promising development.

~

Bad events converged in the larger world. There were constant busts and rumors of stings involving well-known clients who'd been established as safe and large chain hotels that were assumed to be good for working in-call. Several highly visible escorts fell offline. One, allegedly, because she'd been involved with a pimp who'd been busted. The other, allegedly, because someone threatened to out her.

A longtime friend of Emma's stole her cash savings, a six-figure amount. The Supreme Court kept releasing rulings that made it feel even scarier to be a woman in the United States. Redbook was busted, and I laid awake next to another favorite client texting and tweeting feverishly, wide-eyed with panic. Not because I was involved with Redbook. Because of the illogical urgency mounting inside of me that even my home wasn't safe so I needed to move, to hide money in random places where no one else would find it. Because of the feeing of being hunted.

"A sense of closing in, of extermination," I wrote to myself on the night the news about Redbook broke. I'd been sex working for a decade without ever being crippled by fear of arrest or outing or assault. That was changing. Even reminding myself of my privilege, trying to extend my concern to more vulnerable people, wasn't working. I'm in a position to protect myself some but I still have a lot to lose.

Usually I can get ahold of my mind and my emotions will follow, but this time, it was like dipping a cup in a river. I'd hold the cup still but the river kept rushing. I was unable to focus, vaguely unhappy and nervous all the time. I became even more strict about my diet. I scheduled my breast surgery. I opened safety pins and picked at my pimples.

This year will forever be the year I got paranoid. I stepped away from work and that move turned my life into a mown field, wide open and prepped for possibility. That explains almost everything about what happened with George.

≈

We were in a car on our way to dinner when I passed yet another one of his company's signs, and I smiled in spite of myself. My boyfriend saw it. "Why are you smiling?" he asked.

"No reason," I said, then felt bad about lying. So I asked him if he'd heard of the group where George works.

"Yeah," he said, and described what they do, which I already knew. Then he added that he had hired them before, and had them doing a project for him now.

"Oh," I said. Then I paused. "George works there."

There was quiet.

"You said his real name is _____?"

". . . Yes."

"Is his last name spelled _____?"

"Yes." I had never told my boyfriend George's last name.

"AH!" He shouted like he'd smashed his hand with a hammer. He shouted the appetite right out of me. He kept asking dazed questions to reconfirm the obvious, which is that George was the same man he knew.

"Another escape route sealed off," I wrote to myself, selfishly. I felt bad about everything; that my boyfriend would know about George's prison history, that George might see me with my boyfriend and know my boyfriend's girl is a slut. I felt like I couldn't be trusted with anything, not keeping myself safe, and not protecting people I cared about.

A long time ago, during the molly night, George asked about my sex life at home. I'd told him we had sex but not a lot. He asked me what not a lot was.

"For you, less than once a day," I'd said. "I don't want to talk about this. It doesn't feel right."

"That means it's bad," he said.

I didn't like seeing my boyfriend's reaction to our discovery and I didn't like feeling as if I'd endangered the privacy of other people's personal lives, so it was easy to offer not to see George for a while. I had a lot of travel coming up, anyway. I pulled away from him in our remote communications, mostly because the dynamic felt altered. Not because of a sense of duty. I wasn't sure I'd ever be able to see him again, knowing what I knew.

It was three weeks since we last saw each other when he sent the email saying he loved me. I read it with my boyfriend next to me and an IV in my arm, on the hospital bed waiting to have surgery on my breasts.

ALL MEN
August 12, 2014

George didn't really love me, I knew that. Or maybe he loved me similar to the way I cared for him, but without my cynicism, which stops me from naming it something so large. At best, we were using each other to imagine love. My boyfriend drove me home from the surgery and brought me pain pills while I sprawled on the couch. He slept in bed next to me as I took up too much space.

The day before the procedure I was struck with urgent horniness, and gave myself permission to post an ad online. I reasoned I could use the better responses after I was healed and coherent; the winning cock wouldn't go bad in the meantime. I never included a picture because the post would be flagged as spam immediately if I did, but I generally wrote the same thing and gave the same stats. Which meant I was recognizable to someone paying attention. George answered with the following: "I know new dick is always exciting. Hopefully I still rank high on your list of contenders. Forgive the same old lame pics!"

The sad truth about Casual Encounters is it's mostly the same group of people posting and responding again and again. This includes George, whose ads I passed over regularly for months while browsing for the rare new guy or out-of-towner. And it includes me. There was never any hiding our promiscuity from the other and I assumed this was in part what fostered the impression of a connection. Even though there was still a sense of propriety when it came to discussing details about recent or current partners, there could be no delusions of ownership or commitment.

But the impulse toward alliance, allegiance—that's normal, maybe even inevitable, when two people keep choosing to fuck each other. Placing fences around sex to separate it from the rest of your normal life makes it more intense, not safer. I've gotten to feel that rush so many times through work. Not always or even often. But for years, I've practiced parsing out what is real and enduring from what's artificially heightened.

Fucking outside a relationship has no plausible conclusion other than an end. Conventional romantic relationships end too but they usually flourish inside the hope that they won't, that something permanent is being built. So our sexual lawlessness itself became the common thread, our bond amid the sea of other people we were "intimate" with. (Who, presumably, were not as dedicated to the cause.) That and our criminality. "Bonnie and Clyde," as he was fond of saying, though we kept our enterprises separate and he insisted he'd sworn off anything that could land him back in prison.

～

I slept poorly after the surgery because I hated being propped up on my back, the prescribed position to keep swelling down. I wasn't supposed to wear anything other than the large surgical bra, which had to be on all the time; it looked awful underneath any clothing. I barely left the house except to run the occasional errand two blocks away. I was tired, perpetually exhausted and yet understimulated—probably the worst possible combination for my personality.

But George saying he loved me was a secret I could fall back to for a small thrill. It also gave me a sense of triumph and confirmation. I make men feel like they're in love with me for a living. Though seeking out George was in part to leave behind the efforts of work, I hoped and expected that some habits were too ingrained to be so easily jettisoned. His confession of love meant another scalp on my belt.

The bad news was such gloating only carried me so far. Because it wasn't only my wiles that were validated, it was my suspicion that I would lose respect for George if he truly started acting like he were in love with me, as I'm almost always put off by an ardent man. He wasn't really, not yet, except for some slips here and there. But I thought this was probably the beginning of our end. Already I felt benevolent toward him, indulgent. The one with power.

~

I took the prescription meds for two days. The pain wasn't bad but I stayed in a deep fog from the anesthesia and blend of other unfamiliar chemicals circulating in my blood. I've had true surgery twice before and I couldn't remember feeling so fuzzy headed after either of the previous ones. I kept telling people that physically I was fine but my mind wasn't working right, as if my brain existed apart from my body. One of the tasks I was best suited for was sorting through Craigslist ads and replies, which requires barely any mental activity at all.

I'd sent George a picture of my new boobs, which I didn't look at until 24 hours after, afraid the bruising and swelling would be too grotesque to handle. (When I was 16 and uncovered the scar left from my first surgery, I cried so hard to see the raw mess of purple surrounding the staples, the meaty seam. I was doped up then, too.) Surprisingly, they were pale and pink and healthy looking, with most of the bruising confined to my sides instead of my front. He was perfect in his enthusiasm, per usual.

"Holy shit, I'm so excited for you. They were absolutely amazing before, I can't imagine what they'll be like now," he said when I texted him from the hospital bed. "You picked a good doctor, they look fucking great," he said after I sent him the picture. He tried to convince me to invite him over the next afternoon.

Later that night, I found his newest ad. It was his picture, his succinct and casual style. No spelling errors or glaring punctuation problems. The typical fudging of his neighborhood and his age. (Did he lie about his location because he was trying to hide the ad from me? From other women he'd met this way?) I smiled, though, at the one change: "Big breasts and small frame desired."

Some men on Craigslist always state a preference: MILFs, Latinas, etc. Normally you can tell they're saying whatever they think will get them laid—"I bet some horny mom is just dying for a young guy like me …" —but George had never done that before in any of his many ads I'd seen.

So big breasts and small frame—what else could I think? He was looking for someone who'd remind him of me. He described himself and that was it. I probably reread it to bask in the glow of feeling wanted. It was during this second look that I saw the word "generous."

~

For months I've thought about writing an essay on the idea that all men are clients. All men are johns. Meaning there is no identifying characteristic that fingers purchasers of sex from the ones who finagle it for free. The entitlement, the capacity to commit abuse, the cruelty, the kindness, the sincerity; it's always all there. But spending time with George swept a lot of sex work concerns out of my head. He made me feel I had something so worthwhile and joyful that any achievement through work or income was trivial and irrelevant. That was a big deal because at one time, for a long time, making money and feeling like a successful whore were all that mattered to me.

When I saw him looking to pay for sex, I experienced an emotion that has no word. Regret, betrayal, shame—they all sound too clichéd and there was only a spoonful of each involved. I didn't know if I felt struck by a bolt of pain because I wanted his money, because I felt incensed that he should be having me for free while paying for someone else, or if it was because I was repulsed by the idea of him being anyone's client. Did I want him to be my customer, or nobody's? Since when did I want him to be anything at all?

I sent him an email from a different account with a faceless picture of someone else's body in response to his ad. And then I wrote him as me to his direct email, asking if he was still up and if I could come over. He replied to real me within 15 minutes.

"I'm awake. Come over. I just made a fruit salad," he said. He included a picture of it.

Fuck his innocent-seeming bullshit, I thought. I went to bed without writing back, to another tits-up night of barely sleeping.

In the morning, he'd replied to my other account. I decided I was going to dedicate my entire life to sleeping with as many men as possible who weren't him. But not before I rubbed the salt a little deeper.

SOME GUY
August 15, 2014

Tacking "will have sex for money" onto "small frame with big breasts" should have affirmed my belief George was looking for another me, not interfered with it. But finding out that he would pay for the sex we'd had for free—or, more likely, sex not as good as what we'd been having for free—upset me in the logically irrational, emotionally rational way I most associate with being in a body thrown out of a chemical balance. It was the trauma and drugs lingering in my tissues, I hoped. Why aren't I yet beyond my heart?

I cried to my boyfriend about it, not on purpose. Only one short sob with my hands covering my face, but it was enough. I'd been trying to explain how frustrated and mad I was, pent up with nothing more than the internet and my discomfort. I wanted to force myself to talk about what was easier not to say, but my cloudy brain and rambling mouth couldn't put it together right. Then everything was wormy on that end, too.

I wanted a number. George had said many times Craigslist was low-end. So what would he quote a girl he'd promised that he was "generous"? I emailed him under the new account to find out. And I emailed him as he knew me, "Hey sorry I didn't reply last night, I went to bed early. What's today like for you?"

"I've been wanting to fuck you really bad for a few days now," he responded, immediately. "When can we meet?"

When I responded to his "generous" ad, he waited 90 minutes to write back. When I'd written as me right afterward, the reply came back in minutes. So he'd waited to see if I'd come to him. Because I was free (for him) or because he wanted me? He hedged in his emails to the other account. He wouldn't name a price without seeing my face.

I went for my mini walk with my stitched tits bound in the bright white bra. The sun was on and I had the world to myself. His scalp, my belt—why would I think that way about love? I wanted it to happen, then when it did I felt powerful but disappointed, like I knew I would. Like I wanted to have an excuse for detangling from him. First things first. Why would it be easier for me to reject a man who said he loved me, than it would be for me to cut off one who hadn't?

If a man says he loves you, it's because he wants to control you. That's what I decided. No man says, "I love you so go be free. I expect nothing." Not in my experience, anyway. Every man since my father has loomed his love over me like a sentence.

My fear wasn't that George was lying. My fear was that George was lying to manipulate me. I didn't think he was, and my intuition is the most important asset I have. I've spent so much time learning men and I have financial proof of some mastery. But I try to stay humble. I make an effort to be paranoid. I don't want to be a fool.

Who he slept with and under what circumstances was only a distraction. He could be otherwise celibate and I'd still feel the same; I worried he was taking something from me, or trying to. But there was nothing he could take from me unless I was willing to give it.

I resolved not to talk to him for a week. The urge to spite him was not diminished. I emailed with a guy who lived near me about getting together to fuck.

Nearby Guy had seemed convenient at first but his emails quickly got strange quickly, with him proposing we travel somewhere farther away from both of us to fuck on a rooftop because he thought exhibitionism would be sexy. He seemed both overeager and flaky. He'd say something stupid and I'd ignore his barrage of emails for the rest of the day, then he'd send a semi-sane note the next morning and I'd reply. My boredom knew no bounds. Even the cats couldn't keep me entertained by day four of self-imposed house arrest.

I'd already decided I would never meet him when he asked how I'd like to be with "two fit guys" at the same time. But I responded out of curiosity, to see what ridiculous scenario he had in mind.

"I'd love it, if they both knew what they were doing," I said.

He told me he knew just the man—his best friend—and flew into a flurry of logistical questions.

"I'd have to see pictures of this other guy first," I said.

He sent me a picture of George.

No one could believe this development. I called one friend immediately and made her listen to me detail the build up for a half hour. With others I merely stuttered to them on text, then gave up trying to explain the layers of fucked-up coincidences that had accumulated over the past month. According to Emma, someone was messing with me. Either my boyfriend or George himself. The latter made sense but not the former, because where would my boyfriend get a naked picture of George?

Flaky Guy knew where George lived—he replied with the neighborhood almost immediately—and when I asked if we needed to do it there, he said his place was also an option. I wanted to follow through with it to see what would happen next. Show up and act surprised or better yet, totally blasé. But surely this guy had sent George my pictures. George would know it was me, he would know who to expect. It took an hour for him to text me with, "Sweetie, some guy is sending me pictures of you. I can forward if you want to see."

Some guy. Some guy who knows where you live and has a picture of your dick.

I pretended to be confused. ("Who? What guy?") I ignored his attempts to chat around the issue. ("How are you?" "How are you healing?" etc.) I wanted this weirdness over with. I needed to see his face so I could decide what was true, for my own sake. And then maybe I could climb out.

To my boyfriend I explained there was a hole in my life left by the transition of formerly caring about work to not caring about work at all. I needed something new to propel me but I hadn't figured out what that was. George wasn't the replacement. He was a piece of grit trapped in the absence, something lodged through the virtue of me having too much space. I imagined it like emotional diverticulitis.

"I don't love him," I said more than once.

I dressed to go to George with my anger growling. I wanted to punch him and felt putting my fist into him would be the best possible outcome of the night, until I remembered that not long ago I'd fantasized about us fucking while we were mad at each other. It rebooted me. I told myself that no matter what had happened or could happen, this person was not my enemy. I'd been cold to him all week and he'd processed it with a dog's abiding patience. I didn't think he was fortifying himself for a fight. Or for anything.

In his home I held myself with a swan's mild disdain. I acted mostly normal but I wanted some falsity to come through. I was playing the part of a bad actor, which I'd never done to him before. I wanted him to be uncomfortable. I wanted to seem a little cunty in the pedestrian way, to take away anything about me that he (or I) could pretend was special.

"Are you sore?" he asked. He meant my breasts. I said not really, and he asked how I'd been otherwise.

"Some weird stuff's been going on lately," I said. But whenever he asked for elaboration I'd give him a cryptic smile until he finally said, "You're not going to tell me, are you?"

I thought about it, though. Being with him again tempted me to tell him about finding the "generous" ad, and even replying to it. He is a spell. I was wet before I even left my own home, wet in spite of my irritation. I realized it while I was getting ready, and felt held in the hand of something inevitable. Not scary or big or unmanageable, but a fact nonetheless.

The texts he exchanged with Flaky Guy didn't convince me of anything. The details are boring, but the gist was that they'd been texting for a few months, sporadically, whenever FG said he knew a girl who wanted to be with two guys. It didn't make much sense to me, and I figured some messages might have been deleted before I came over. But George maintained they'd never been together in person before, and they internet-met because the guy replied to George's Craigslist ad, saying he was trying to find a third party.

"He called you his best friend," I said.

"You know I don't have any friends," George said, like this had been explicitly established more than once. Later, he suggested FG didn't actually have a location though he pretended he could host, which explained all his abrupt and bizarre propositions.

"Let's send him a picture of us together right now and be like, 'We're on the roof, where are you?'" I said.

George died laughing at that. Naked next to him, I wasn't quite the cunty swan anymore. But I knew I couldn't trust him.

Nothing felt solved in me. I was back where I started: did I have this man right or didn't I? The next morning I texted him and said that I was bored, and he should entertain me. He sent me a screenshot of some other girl telling him she wasn't wearing underwear, and him responding that he loved her.

IMAGINARY
August 18, 2014

I met Emma the way I meet lots of people in my life: remotely, through words, then pictures, then in person. Years and years ago, we worked on something together while living on opposite ends of the country. I knew she once identified as gay and I thought she still did, though her boyfriend confused that point for me. When we became friends on Facebook and I saw her there, I felt shyly attracted. I showed her pictures to my boyfriend, confessing. I hoped maybe she would find me pretty but she didn't seem interested.

I don't remember when we first met, but soon we were sending each other clients and sleeping together in the same bed when we intersected for a night. Being with her always felt like an adventure, a little electric though familiar and safe at the same time. We snorted meth in her city before the writer/editor/whatever the hell he calls himself these days, the one I thought was my friend, masturbated on me. (This is what I wrote about it in my blog at the time: "I am still capable of feeling used. I am still capable of having a sexual experience that makes me feel like my entire life has been a mean joke.")

She'd left us alone together but came back over while he slept in my hotel bed, and we listened to Mazzy Star and Fleetwood Mac, and then I made him go away early in the morning because I hated him and I had a client to meet. Two clients, actually. Who became regulars, because I'm sexier when I'm high.

It happened that way for us often, the pattern of male sex and sororal aftermath, and not just because we sometimes worked together. The last time we saw each other, I was working in her city and had arranged some unpaid sex after. The first man I picked was a limp-dick disaster who repeatedly tried to stuff himself in me without a condom until I stopped telling him not to and let my own body become as floppy as his cock but only everywhere it didn't matter, clenching my pussy shut as he mashed against me in vain. In my experience, it's better to bank on a man becoming bored or embarrassed enough to stop before he'll listen to "no." He came without ever getting hard, and I threw him out when Emma was on her way from an hour's distance, and went back online to find someone better, a ropey swimmer who was fine with the rush.

"You want to come down and have a drink with us?" I asked the guy after I noisily orgasmed on him less than 10 minutes after we met. I didn't even take off my dress. He said yes, but by the time we got downstairs Emma said the bar was closing. He and I kissed each other goodbye, why not, and she and I went upstairs without him. I met Nick the next day.

I was fucking everyone except Emma. She'd complimented other female friends to me and in front of me, and I heard the stories about how she'd make out with them while high but she never said anything nice about my appearance, not even around clients when you're supposed to coo about how sexy the other woman is. I thought she found me ugly. I laughed about it to my boyfriend more than once, how convinced I was she found me unappealing to the point of incredulity that I could work as much as I did.

"I think she thinks it's a miracle that anyone pays to have sex with me," I told him once.

Her impending visit was hugely exciting. She'd never come to my home before, or even my city. And almost as soon as she planned to spend the weekend with me, I imagined the two of us fucked up with George. It was a thought that wouldn't leave my head, probably because he and she were the only two people I'd ever been around while on molly. But they had other things in common. Their bodybuilding, for one, though both were lean and taut instead of bulky and thick. And George's home was a perfect setting. Just dark enough, warm enough. Cozy without being sloppy. Masculine without being cold or corny. He always had fresh towels.

As things between he and I became more complicated—for me, anyway—I realized I needed another woman's opinion of him. I also wanted to see how he would treat her and how he would treat me while the three of us were together. Though I wasn't dwelling on particulars, the notion of this night was so appealing, so necessary, that as much as I told myself I needed to be done with George, I didn't want to give up the opportunity. She was going to arrive the next day, and I'd laid all the groundwork: gotten extra pills from the client who gives them to me, mentioned her to George many times before. I don't like it when plans change.

When George sent me the screenshot of his conversation with the other woman, it was after he'd asked me to meet him out in public that afternoon. Meeting in public was something we'd never done before, especially not in the middle of his workday. It felt slightly urgent on his end, like there was something he wanted to tell me.

"You love a lot of people for someone who doesn't have any friends," I said back to him, buried under a few lines about other things. Trying to play it off. He ignored me.

"Are we really getting together for tea?" he replied.

"I can't right now."

"Yeah not now but what about later?"

"Prob not, sorry," I said, unnecessarily abbreviating like a bitch.

"I've got an appointment at 5:30, then heading home," he said. "I'll reach out to you then."

That night, I went to get my nails done. I didn't want to, but I needed to for work and there wouldn't be many other opportunities between now and next stretch of dates. I wanted to find out what he had to say and I wanted to make the night with Emma happen, but I also never wanted to see him again. I was performing for myself. ("I'll go out to get my nails done but not because I'm hoping to already be near George when he's finished. I always put on makeup to get a pedicure.")

He messaged me around 7:30, when I was just sitting down, and I told him it would be a while until I was free and he probably didn't want to wait that long. He said he would sit with me while I was having it done, but I felt edgy about him knowing my regular nail place. I was still trying to hide my real life from him then, though I knew the boundaries were fraying.

An hour after he first texted me, I acquiesced and told him where to find me, and he sat next to me while I asked the technician not to cut my cuticles and the gel on my fingers dried.

We went across the street to eat, and he paid for my dinner, which I wanted him to do and expected him to do but still felt strangely about. The gesture was somehow too tender or too gallant for what we'd been through. What was he after?

We ate and then we walked and we talked for hours. He told me about his first endeavor after he got out of prison. It collapsed when one of the guys he met there, and later hired, committed credit card fraud with the company's machines and wiped the business out. He told me again about the woman he lived with briefly, and how he first cheated on her when one of his friends talked about hiring an escort from Backpage—how cheap it was to find a girl who did anything you wanted. He said he and his girlfriend vacationed in Mexico and when they got into a fight, he went to see prostitutes there too. Gradually he started meeting people for free, and he moved out.

And then he said he thinks of his life as having two chapters, Before and After Prison, and he always feels like he's making up for lost time. We talked about his current work a little. I didn't ask him what it was like for him to be the client of a prostitute after his wife had worked as one, if that changed anything for him. I didn't ask how often he still paid for it. Maybe he wouldn't have answered those questions. We'd never spent so much time together clothed.

I told him that when we'd met on Craigslist, I'd been looking for another Ethan, someone to have a torrid emotional affair with, even more than I was looking for the sex, which had been the best of my life. I told him about how Ethan wanted to marry me but I wouldn't leave my boyfriend; how he threw himself into a relationship with another woman and still wrote me fraught emails while engaged to her; how he disappeared and I missed him but had no way to find him. "I'm not looking for that anymore," I added. "Because things are so good with me and my boyfriend now."

"For a while I didn't really believe you had a boyfriend," George said.

I thought this was hilarious. "What? Why would I make that up?"

"I thought it was just a convenient excuse for why you couldn't get together or stay longer or have me over." It was testament to how little he knew me that he thought I'd feel compelled to invent any excuse.

"And what do you think now?"

"Now . . . I don't know."

The imaginary boyfriend was not happy about George and I staying dressed. When I told him via text that we were just talking and having dinner together, not having sex—a message I thought would be reassuring—he didn't respond well. And so I had to leave to do damage control, though we did fuck a little. I told him I was too sad and distracted by my boyfriend drama to come, but I didn't mind being with him until he did. He said seeing me sad made him too sad to get off. I don't know how all that fit into my boyfriend not being real.

He sent me a text a few hours after I left saying he was still awake and thinking about me and wondering how it was going. I didn't reply. Over dinner he told me he had two secrets, his time in prison and his incredibly varied, nonstop stream of Craigslist-supplied sex partners, and that I was the only person who knew about both. I couldn't believe that, and I told him as much. He said it was true.

I did not, and would not, call him out directly for telling me he loved me. I would never bring that up directly to him. But in bed, the time before, I said there was a lot we didn't talk about and he was holding me when he said, "But I would be open to talking about that with you." The tone of his voice was so . . . adult. I assume that exchange was why he took me out as he did. By the end of the night, I didn't know what I wanted from him anymore or what was possible.

There wasn't time to think about it anyway. My boyfriend and I stayed up late talking. A few hours later, Emma arrived.

ORBIT AND SHINE

August 25, 2014

On Emma's first day in town, she met Drunk Client. Naked, she and I kept the respectful distance from each other that we always have at work. When he said he wanted to see us together, we exchanged a quick look and finessed the thought from his mind. At night we hung out on the couch with my boyfriend and the cats.

Pretty soon after her arrival, I outlined my plan—that we take molly on Saturday night and go out, and she could meet George at his place or have him come out to us—and she said it sounded good. George, meanwhile, was determined to prove himself worthy of a visit. He sent me regular messages from Friday morning on about preserving his energy, i.e. not fucking anyone.

Saturday night arrived slowly. We went to a movie first, then she to the gym and I to a lingerie store to which a client had given his billing info. I left an hour later, braless and near tears, having been told I'm now a 30G, which might as well be a size in Wingdings for how easy it is to find in fancy shops. Emma and I went to dinner where I sad-ate too much in spite of knowing I'd want to give the drug quick access. We didn't take our pills until 9:30 p.m. We were still deciding what to wear, putting on clothes and then pulling them off, yelling about implants and beauty standards from respective bathrooms while we did our makeup.

The clubs nearby were dead so we went for a walk. I didn't feel anything but Emma said she did, which made me a little jealous and frustrated.

"Do you want to take another?" I said.

It wasn't until I was shouting in the cab about how happy it made me to think about dying young and giving away all my money and clothes and books to my friends that I realized I may have been a little high.

"Well, don't die," Emma said sincerely.

"Ok, I won't," I said. "Let's take a picture together."

I gave Emma strict instructions not to mention my real name around George, or my boyfriend's name, and not to tell him we'd taken two pills when I was only bringing him one. We pulled up outside his condo and I realized I hadn't even told him we were on our way. Who knows what I said to the front desk attendant. When George opened his door for us I hopped into his arms.

"We're here!" I said. I wish I could remember what he was wearing. I know he looked tall and lean and louche as always. Behind him, his home was dark and glowing.

When I went to introduce him to Emma, I realized I wasn't sure what name he wanted to go by; he has two that are legitimate.

"What should she call you?" I asked him.

"Call me Carlos Danger," he said to her.

"Don't call him that," I said. "Isn't his place great?"

I presented his pill with a flourish from my back pocket. "Take it right now."

"I'm scared!" he said, and I squeezed his waist.

"You're going to be fine, you'll love it. We've already had two."

"You're talking about everything you said you didn't want to talk about," Emma said to me.

George offered her water, fruit. They talked while I drifted deeper in.

"Oh no, the laundry," I said in dismay when I noticed a big pile on one of his two couches. It's a fixture of his place but I'd imagined straddling his lap there, before things progressed. "I thought you stayed home all day. You couldn't clean this off for us?"

"I know, I'm always behind. I feel like my whole life is doing laundry."

"At least you do it. Some guys don't even do it. It's because you fuck so much. I'll help you fold it."

"Will you? I hate folding."

"I love it."

Emma asked George if he had any weed or coke.

"Emma's a fiend," I said slyly. "Once she gets started she doesn't want to stop."

"Um, sure, I have something," George said, his typical accommodating self.

"You have something to smoke it in too? I don't want to use, like, a can." Prescient Emma. They ended up repurposing a ballpoint.

"Oh my god, this is so high school," I said, refusing it. "Is it ok if I take off my jeans? I'm not trying to be sexy or anything I just really don't want to be wearing pants right now."

George and I went back and forth from the living room to his bedroom with the folded clothes and sheets.

"I think I'm starting to feel it," he said to me.

"Really? I think it's too early. Have you not eaten today? I try not to notice when it starts. I just assume I'm going to keep being normal. I've never forgotten that thing from high school where you give a girl a nonalcoholic drink and then watch her act really fucked up even though she didn't drink anything. I never want to be that girl. So I don't pay attention at all."

The couch was mostly cleaned off in a few minutes, but Emma was already on George's bed, smoking, unhappily staring at his TV.

"Why are we watching sports?" she said in that way she has, laughing a little but seeming stressed at the same time. It was baseball or hockey or something. I don't know.

"Oh she gets so picky about what's going on when she's doing drugs," I said. "I brought my laptop so I know we'll have music she likes."

George turned the TV off and approached me, leaning back into his own body. Pelvis slightly forward. His "I'm going to start touching you" stance.

"Can you get me a washcloth or something?" I asked, his arms around my shoulders. "I'm really wet. I'm not even feeling that turned on, I'm just super wet." Then, to Emma, "I get really wet."

"She gets so wet," George confirmed.

"Yeah, it's embarrassing actually. I'm glad you like it."

"I love it," he said.

"I have to wipe it off sometimes surreptitiously with the back of my hand, I feel so embarrassed by how much there is."

George brought back a hand towel, which made me laugh. "Oh ok, you went for a big one, that's smart. Thanks. Good call."

I pulled off my underwear and before I could put the towel there he reached a finger in.

"Do you want to feel?" I asked Emma. George went to get us water.

"Is it ok if . . . maybe in just a little bit?" Her forehead creased.

Nothing felt sexual to me, at least not sexual in the usual way. Everything felt friendly, so I'd been offering in case she was curious, in the same spirit we talked about our implants. You can be curious about another body without it being sexual. But through my haze I remembered all the evidence that Emma wasn't into me, and found me unattractive, and I felt bad, like I'd pressured her.

"Yeah of course," I said, frowning back, but sadly. I reached for her but didn't touch her. I was trying to be reassuring, push the sincerity through however goofily I might otherwise have been acting. "You don't have to do anything you don't want to do. And whenever you want we can go back home."

George got on the bed with her, so I got on the bed too. She'd taken her jeans off. And her shirt. She was stretching with her leg up by her ear.

"Can I use this?" she said, standing up and gesturing to the pull-up bar over the door. "It won't fall or anything?"

"Do you weigh more than him?" I asked.

"Yeah, go for it," he said.

She did two pull-ups and jumped off. In her underwear, her long hair loose. "I can never get to more than two! I can take a break and do two again, but I can't do more than two in a row."

"It's great that you can do any," I said. "I want to try it. But maybe not right now."

"Yeah, not today," George said definitively, in a way that threw me into laughter. My implants weren't even two weeks old.

"Not today!" I said. Hugging him, him hugging me. He was in his underwear too. Ok.

"I want to fuck you," he whispered in my ear. His strong, prickly thighs against me. His familiar, knotty abs.

"You will," I said, beaming. The happiest human on earth.

"Take a picture of us together," Emma told George, meaning she and I. "I want to send it to Chris." Chris was the guy Emma hooked up with most often. She'd wanted me to sleep with him when I was in her city and she wasn't, so I could report back on whether or not he knew she had implants.

"But won't he wonder who took the picture?" I asked.

George showed us.

"Wow, that turned out perfect," Emma said. "You're really good at that." It was blurry but only slightly so. Our breasts, my smile, her great ass.

George got back onto the bed and put his arms around Emma. They each closed their eyes, which made me nervous. They were too mellow from the pot, and I didn't want them mellow. I launched into some story—I can't remember what—and in the course of it I recounted someone speaking to me. That's when it flew out of my mouth, my real name, the whole name before I could even stop halfway through, though I realized my mistake immediately and started yelling, "Fuck fuck fuck fuck."

"_____!" George repeated it the instant I got it out. He fell back on the bed laughing and then popped up, grabbed me and kissed me.

"Fuck," I said, a puddle. He kissed me again.

"Do you really not like kissing?" Emma asked me. She'd been incredulous about that for years. "Even when you're not with a client?"

"We're working on it," George said.

"My boyfriend's a good kisser and George is a good kisser but . . . I don't know. It's hard for me."

"I love making out," Emma said.

"Can I feel your boobs?" I asked.

"Yeah," she said. George had pushed her bra up.

Emma's implants were over a year old and they felt amazing. Better than I ever would have believed implants could feel. They were impossible to detect, I thought, even though she said there were some angles where they looked funny under the skin. Mine were still stiff and pokey. Too round. But seeing Emma's gave me faith they'd improve.

I said to her, "I was so shocked when you said you had them. I'd thought you might be like, 'Why would you do that …?' when I told you I was thinking about getting them."

"Really? I thought you would too, to me. That's why I didn't tell you when I did it." We laughed a little at how wrong we'd gotten each other.

"I don't understand how Chris could tell," I said. "It all feels totally real."

Then she said, "I told Chris to have sex with you because you're my hottest friend and I wanted to live vicariously through him and know what it was like to fuck you."

"Wow, you've really gotten used to saying things for Adam, huh?" I said. Adam is Emma's only remaining client, her de facto sugar daddy, who somehow believes that she and I are in a serious sexual relationship.

She paused. "No."

"What? Are you serious? Wait. Hottest? You've never even complimented me. I always thought you found me really unattractive!" I thought about how just earlier that night, on our way to a club, I said I wasn't affectionate and she said she was, and that she always wanted to be petted. How many nights we'd spent bare in bed together without even our extremities touching. *More evidence*, I'd thought then.

"I'm sorry," she said, sincere but confused.

"You don't have to apologize, it's just . . . I mean, even when we were working together."

"Yeah but we're friends. I think it's always that way if you're really friends. I didn't want to make you uncomfortable."

I addressed George, trying to convey how shocked this situation made me. "For years I thought she found me totally gross!"

"That's crazy," he said obligingly, his hands on us both.

I wanted to put my music on, and we tried to get my laptop to play through his Bluetooth speaker but I was too high and I just gave up and let the music come through my computer. I kneeled to plug it into power, and when I came back up on the bed George had his hand in Emma's underwear and his mouth on her breasts.

"I love being fingered," she said.

"Me too," I said. "But most guys are so bad at it. Or they don't even try."

I was on my knees next to her and she reached her hand between my legs and rested it on my inner thigh. "Is it ok if I . . . ?"

"Yeah of course." I said. And she slipped her slim, cool finger into me.

"She's tight," George said to me, moving aside for me.

I felt, gently. "Wow yeah she is."

Then I noticed he had his fingers in her mouth, and she and I talked the day before about how much we didn't like that. So I took his hand out and moved it away. Then, so he wouldn't feel corrected, I leaned over and kissed her. Her mouth felt smaller than mine, which surprised me. There was the densest, softest fuzz above her top lip. I tried soft, then aggressive. Then I stopped.

"You can take your fingers out if you want," I said to her. "I don't want them to get prune-y."

"They already are a little but I don't mind," she said. But then she did stop, because George moved his body over hers and reached for a condom.

I got distracted by the music, and Beatrice, who I have to talk to when I'm high because I love her so much. I laid on the floor sending Snapchats and back-dancing, playing Beyoncé and Missy Elliot remixes. When I thought maybe I was being too antisocial, I came back up on the bed and Emma put her hand out for mine. I'd told her and George about working a long date with another escort once, how she'd held my hand while the client was on top of her and how special it made me feel. I'm sure Emma was thinking of that. I mostly stayed out of the way until Emma came. George peeled off his condom.

"I want to fuck you," he growled again when Emma went to pee.

"You will," I said. "We have all night."

Emma and I talked about how we masturbated, and Emma asked many questions about George's sex life, most of which I think he earnestly "umm . . . I'm not sure"-ed his way out of. I wondered how much of the questioning came from genuine curiosity and how much was her attempt to keep from asking about prison.

"Is he on probation?" she asked me before we went over.

"I don't think so," I said. "I'm pretty sure he at least doesn't get tested. But you can ask him if you want, I don't think he'd mind."

And she said, "Oh, no." If he were, that would have been something else they had in common, in addition to the serious working out. But then we were all normal-looking criminals; I was just the luckiest.

George fucked me until I came, which took much longer than it usually would have because of the drugs. As soon as I finished, I said, "Your turn!" Which made him laugh. I don't think he remembered saying it to me in the hotel weeks ago, the day we'd heard the World Cup audience cheering outside and I thought I would burst into petals of light from the joy of being with him.

When Emma was gone, again in the bathroom, he said while inside of me, "I really do love you a little bit."

"You say that to everyone," I said. "You need a new line."

"But it's true with you!"

"Well, you need to get a new line. Maybe if you say it a different way I'll believe it."

He didn't come. Emma and I took turns sucking his cock—mostly Emma though. "I really like doing it while I'm high," she said. "I'm worried I'm not very good at it." I only went down when he insisted upon it by pushing my head. I didn't want it to be a competition or for Emma to feel pressured to do it the way I did it.

"You guys should charge people to watch you fuck," she told us, which was probably the last thing George needed to hear.

"I told her I wish I could keep her in a cage in my room so she'd be here whenever I wanted," George told Emma, about me. I'd actually forgotten about that, but he would say it again in the following days, in a text. ("I wish I could reach into that box under my bed and pull you out.")

Emma asked me if I really didn't like it when someone went down on me, and she said it in wistful way that made me think she wanted to do it to me. I couldn't figure out how to answer.

Mostly I didn't care what was happening. I just wanted to dance and sing. I played Miguel and BANKS and told George he owed many of our meetings to these artists, because I would walk around the city with them in my ears and fantasize about fucking him. I played "Hanging on to My

Youth" and told Emma Ellie Goulding always made me think of her.

"Aw, thanks," she said. She loves Ellie's voice.

I played "So High." I played "Do It Again." I played "Retrograde." I played the remix of "Do a Trick" and said to George, "This is our song."

"Oh really? Why's that?" he said from the edge of the bed. I just kept dancing and singing along in front of him, smiling while I looked into his eyes.

After a few hours, Emma dozed off, or pretended to because she wanted to be left alone. I pulled him to the floor when he wanted to go again, so we wouldn't bother her.

"What are you guys doing?" she asked when she roused for a moment.

And George said from his position kneeling on the floor, "It's still my turn!" Scrubbing rug burn into my elbows. He came on my chest profusely as proof of how he'd abstained the day of and before. I left it there because I wanted to come again and I liked the idea of doing it with him still on me like that, but he wouldn't move his hand the way I was trying to show him so I gave up and left the mess. My boyfriend would touch it hours later, flake some of it off with his finger.

I started getting nervous about sunrise. I hate coming down in the morning—as if there's any other way. I could already tell light was seeping through the windows. "I'm starting to feel anxious," I said.

"Smoke some," Emma murmured.

"Yeah, here," George reached for it but I refused. I got the last piece of laundry from the couch, a fresh white sheet, and dragged it into the bedroom so I wouldn't have to try to pull any covers off of Emma. George laid between us and I curled up against him with his arm around me, willing myself to sleep before I could panic. My brain was moving but not loud or scary. It was a little like hallucinating but I knew nothing was real because my eyes were closed. Various images, half-images and half-thoughts, would rise and dissolve without logic.

We only slept for an hour or two. Emma woke up and George fucked her until she came again, and this time I stayed on the bed next to them and watched, and was struck by how boring it was because the sensations were inaccessible to me. There were Emma's noises encouraging him, but I couldn't tell how much of it was for his benefit rather than out of her own pleasure, or just involuntary from the impact, or if, like me, she went into autopilot sometimes.

After she came, she was ready to leave. We'd talked about going shopping together, and we were meeting Adam later that night.

I dressed quickly and swiped at my chest with a wet cloth. Emma was showering when I kissed George's soft penis as he sprawled on the bed, then laid my clothed body over his and kissed his face.

"You know," he said as he held me, "this is how my ex-wife and I got started. Addicted to pleasure. I had a job, but then she would come over and we'd just lay around like this all day and I wouldn't go. That's why I started selling drugs, and she started the escort service."

"So you could spend more time together?" I said.

"Yeah. Like, if you wanted to come back tomorrow, I wouldn't go into work all day."

But I wouldn't come back tomorrow.

"Don't you think it's sad that George was in prison?" Emma would ask me later, while we were out at lunch. Of course it was sad. Distractingly, oppressively sad. For a while after I learned that, it was all I could see about him. That loss. It was too hard to think about him there, for a lot of reasons. So I had to give up my irrelevant sadness which felt too close to pity. He was, and he deserved, more than that.

In the days that followed, instead of pining for George I felt heartsick for Emma. Her first day gone left me inclined to do no more than lie on the couch and cry. I didn't, but I wanted to. Where George was concerned I felt not closure, but completion. Like we achieved something that made me feel freer. I didn't need to see him immediately after, or even a week after, or even two.

"I miss you," he messaged me. And then weeks later, when we still hadn't seen each other: "I've been fucking other girls and thinking about you."

But when I thought about that night, I didn't think about him as much as I thought about Emma's fingers inside of me.

The completeness was characterized by peace and gratitude. He'd made my world so much better: my relationship with my boyfriend, with Emma, my work. My own mind. In spite of all the drama, or because of it, everything in my life felt stronger and more flexible.

"We must be soul mates," he wrote me in response to something innocuous I said about managing my time. I know he sees his ex-wife in me. Because she and I have sold sex for money. And because he wants to.

Some distance felt like the right thing. I wasn't sure what positive influence I could have on him, if any. So I thought maybe for a while I should stay out of his way.

RELEASING

September 2—December 23

BLUSHING IN LONDON

September 2, 2014

Much of what I haven't said about my boyfriend will remain unsaid. He is the most private part in all this. But he went to my home the morning of the threesome, bearing breakfast for Emma and me. He saw that we weren't there, and, from what I gather, took the breakfasts somewhere outside to be destroyed in a dramatically violent way. I felt badly about this but not guilty, which was new. Never guilty, because I had kept him apprised of everything. I would have come home that night if he'd replied to my texts.

When we finally arrived, he acted normal and nice for Emma. I could see there was an awed wildness underneath, like he couldn't believe what was happening. Not the circumstances, really, but what was happening inside of him, a response. He pushed me down on our bed and put his tongue in my asshole, fucked me, and rubbed George's dried come off my chest. I smiled and held him and asked him to stay a little while longer, but he had to go.

Two opposite things were occurring, and they could not be unknotted. We were being drawn closer together by what should have pushed us apart. I had spikes strapped to my chest but he was hugging me even more tightly, blood leaking down his legs.

Our love felt to me like it never had before, like a giant sleeping bag that cocooned me all the time. It created possibilities. It supplied energy and courage.

"How is there so much love between us?" he asked, a month or so after the threesome.

"I know," I said. "It's sick."

In the hours after we left his place, Emma couldn't stop talking about George.

"He's so hot," she said. "And he's such a good fuck. He has a great ass." And so on. New things to appreciate would occur to her, she'd voice them, and then we'd lapse back into silence. She asked if I wasn't bothered by his spit, by which she meant how much he'd apply between her or my legs, and I said that if it were almost anyone else, I would be. But somehow with him I didn't care at all.

I told her that when my boyfriend found out he knew George, he said several snide things about his appearance. Something stupid about how he didn't think that would be the type of guy I'd go for, that his body clearly wasn't as impressive as I'd made it out to be. And there was some minor race-based friction that I'm not sure I should or can write about, related to how George reads as black but my boyfriend doesn't, even though their skin tones are about as dark/light.

"He was saying that because he was upset," Emma said. "George is basically the man every guy would be afraid of his girlfriend getting with. Because he's so handsome. I mean, [your boyfriend]'s handsome too. But George is so tall and sexy . . . and masculine and . . . confident."

My boyfriend admitted feeling some pressure to work out harder. He said he was secure in himself and didn't feel threatened, which I think was true. But our egos work on us still, in subtle ways. And he started losing weight. I told him he had a better cock, because he got so hard and didn't take an hour to come, and he accepted this with a quality I know well from inside myself, hopefulness and gratitude mixed with suspicion.

I didn't want to explicitly compare them or make it into a competition, but some things were true; I thought about them, and I wanted to share those things with him. I pointed out this fact once while we were locked together: "I've come more with you than I have with any other man." Years and years of it.

My boyfriend has said before that he wants to redeem men for me. There is some larger responsibility, in his big brother mind, to convince me they are not all like my father, or my father-replacement, the much older man I lived with for a while, or my clients. It's like he's offering his body as a platform, so I can reach something above my head.

We went to London and it was there that he leaned toward me across the restaurant table, earnest and focused and not exactly serious but telegraphing intensity.

"Ok, what do I need to do to make this happen?" he asked, collecting both my hands in his.

"What happen?" I said.

"Tell me. Give me a list of requirements. Whatever I have to do to make you my wife."

A fan of hot blood filled my face from the bottom up. I felt it when it started, and that made it worse. It seemed like the first time in my life I'd ever blushed.

"Are you blushing? You're blushing!" he said. He knows a miracle when he sees it.

It was after we came back to the hotel from the restaurant that we saw the rainbow. What a cliché. It was the biggest I've ever seen; it spanned the available sky with its colors in bright, clear bands. People stood in the street and took pictures. I did too, though it made me feel vulnerable and stupid to acknowledge such pedestrian beauty, if there can be such a thing.

On our way home we ate breakfast in a pointlessly stylish airport restaurant with tons of natural light and an extensive view of the metal procession outside. Birdy's cover of "1901" played on the speakers overhead and we were the only ones there aside from the staff. Two people sitting across from each other while the day woke up around them.

My boyfriend first told me he loved me when I was sitting on the toilet. It was eight years ago. We'd been at it for a long time, the only way we fucked back then, and I left the door open when I peed, which I think no other woman had done around him before. He came in and positioned his body between my legs and we were probably talking about something. He laughed with his hands holding my face and pulled back a little, shining, to say, "I love you."

"I love you too!" I said. I'd realized it once before and brushed it aside, because a lot of our relationship didn't make sense to me. But when he said it, it gave me permission. I could believe it was real and not a flyaway piece of emotion caught for a moment on one of my wires.

It happened a little like that when I discovered I loved George. That's how I recognized it as true, because of what I'd learned with him.

WHY LOVE
Sept 10, 2014

"So what's your boyfriend like?" George asked. "Is he white, black, Latino . . . ?"

I took his dick out of my mouth. "Not white," I said finally, witheringly.

He laughed. "Well I sort of figured, with a name like _____."

I don't know how he found out my boyfriend's first name. I texted Emma to ask later—did I accidentally let it out the same night I'd let my own name slip?—and she said she didn't know. It's ambiguous enough to mask his race. But it's original, unique. I worried if George said it too many times, it might click in his head that they'd been introduced before. So when he started in on how my boyfriend was imaginary, I played off of it in what I hoped was the most distracting, unworried way.

"Oh you don't think I could have a boyfriend?" I said, pretending to be hurt. "You don't think anyone would want me?"

Minutes ago, still naked and on each other, he'd asked, "What does your mom call you?" She'd visited recently, and I mentioned her because she saw my rug-burned elbow from the night of the threesome and said, "You must have hit the ceiling when that happened." She meant only the pain, but it was hard not to laugh given the context. George thought it was hysterical.

"The only name she knows," I answered him. "The one she gave me."

"Your name is _____, and your boyfriend's name is _____, right?" he said, laughing at himself a little as soon as he got it out. "Why does that feel so weird?"

"Because you just named my imaginary boyfriend," I said with what I hoped was a masking disaffection. I was unnerved to hear him speak our names aloud. It was weird. George's home was supposed to be a world apart, a world where I wasn't quite myself and the unspoken rule was usually not to talk about my boyfriend at all. Which didn't mean he was far from my mind. When George was heavy on me, I started to wonder if he could feel the implants as separate from my natural breast tissue when they were pressed against his own chest. But I felt too self-conscious to find out from him, and resolved to ask my boyfriend instead.

Maybe it was the sporadic boyfriend talk that put George in a reflective mood about his ex, the slightly older woman with whom he used to live, who wanted to get pregnant. He'd been this way a few times before, preoccupied enough to ask my opinion as to what he should say or shouldn't say, should do or shouldn't do. Currently, he was both wistful and anxious because she bought a home near his, and there was a business event coming up for her, one that they'd always gone to together. He told me who she was, and I knew her. Not *knew her* knew her, not like she would recognize me, but:

"With the little dog?" I said.

"Yeah."

Our world is just too small. We met online, for Christ's sake.

"I feel like we're Spartans when we're fucking," George said as we cleaned up.

"Well, you have the body for it."

"So do you. And the dark hair."

"I should make you wear the leather kilt next time," I said. I didn't mention he probably wasn't quite ruthless enough to be a Spartan. He stopped thrusting from behind at one point and asked if I was ok with a concern so genuine it almost frightened me—I thought something must be so wrong.

"Yeah, why?" I answered.

"Because, um, you're bleeding."

"Is it bright red?"

"It's just sort of pink . . ."

"I'm sure it's fine, I don't feel any pain," I said, and we kept going. Later he said, "We're so messy," and I glanced down at the puddle on his sheets, which truly was a series of small, muddy puddles and not just smears or individual translucent drops of lube and spit, and I said, "It looks like someone spilled a cappuccino."

"I sort of feel like, the intellectual connection isn't there," he said, of his former girlfriend. It felt like he was trying to imply it was for us, though that's about the level of our usual discourse. Observing the sexuccino.

I think it was because I read his appeal that I asked about the tattoos. I don't know why else it would have been on my mind. I'd googled his full name hoping to find the details of his original case, but the denied appeal was all that was online. I tried to read it but had trouble focusing. It felt too much like a violation to read these things about him not being read his Miranda rights, etc.

"You got this tattoo after?" I said, touching his chest.

"Yeah, all of other ones were before."

"And none during?"

"No. I wanted to, but then I saw how they were doing them and I was like, 'HELL NO.' They're really good on the West Coast, though. They do this one to represent every year you've served . . ."

I started laughing as he described them, and I couldn't stop. His enthusiasm was so quintessentially him, so pure. Talking about tattoos in prison like a cool pair of shoes. I hugged him, and that's when it almost slipped out—*I love you.* I could have gotten away with it. My laughter would have made it seem nonthreatening, figurative. as in, I enjoy you. But when I felt the words in my mind before they could leave my mouth, I realized they were true.

"You're so great," I said again. I hugged him hard, then harder still. "I'm so glad we're friends."

"Me too," he said, hugging back, his voice a little strangled because he was short on air.

I can never tell him, I thought to myself as I walked down his building's hall. *I can't even contact him until he says something.* I knew we would be together again; it wasn't about that. My fear of giving myself away was too great, if I were left to speak first.

"Do you feel like the more we have sex, the better it gets?" he emailed me the next morning. "I hope I didn't confide too much, I never want you to feel uncomfortable." *He feels the same way too*, I thought. Then I told myself that was ridiculous.

~

Once I realized I loved George, I was consumed with urgency to tell him in spite of my suspicion that would be a bad idea. Recognizing my love for him somehow felt like I was granted permission to release my full curiosity. There was so much I could learn about him now! So many things I could ask.

Thankfully, I wasn't in a position to do that right away; I went sailing with a client for five days. Holding thoughts of George in my head was probably a great boon while being stuck on a small boat with this elderly man, since it kept me from going too stir crazy. I played Jimmy Cliff and Solomon Burke on the cabin's sound system, pretending George was there and that he would have liked those choices. I took pictures of the sunset for him. He'd told me once, several months or so ago, that he had a ritual when he received emails from me while I was traveling. He would pause, close his eyes, and imagine being wherever I was. He hadn't seen much of the world, for the obvious reasons, and he dreamed of international trips he couldn't afford.

But my chain-dreaming was interrupted by an email from him saying, "You'll never believe it—well, actually, you probably will." He'd struck up a conversation with a woman while he was having lunch that day, and quickly deduced she was an escort. He said he was still with her and would keep me posted.

My response to this news was not exactly rational. I fell into such a self-absorbed funk that I could barely even pretend to be interested in my client. Hours later, still troubled, I climbed out of bed and told him I was going to go write notes while I read, which had to be done upright. I don't like it when I have emotional reactions too strong to be easily parsed out. Yoga helped me establish a practice of looking at my responses to the world instead of avoiding or ignoring them. So I sat down and created a map.

For some time, as far as George was concerned, I worried I was going through the emotional process of a smitten client. Was I being manipulated? Should it have been obvious? Was I making a fool of myself? I know at least one of my friends thought I was being played, and badly. But I thought he was a special person; I couldn't help it.

Sometimes I felt so greedy to talk to him, to tell him things about myself, but maybe that was because who else could I tell? My work is usually being present while someone else talks, and the response is better if I don't add anything of my own—which wouldn't be particularly intimate even if I did. Men think they want to hear it, but they don't, because it is Their Time. Those hours are supposed to be about my interest in them. Sometimes when I offer up a thought or anecdote, it's as if I farted. They pause, then change the subject entirely. Was what I called love just relief at finding someone who would indulge my self-disclosures?

I wanted to be special to him. I wanted him to feel for me as I felt for him. And so it was threatening when one facet of my specialness, my sex worker-ness, might be shared by another woman in his life. I immediately imagined her as a peer and therefore a rival, someone who charged very high rates and targeted businessmen. I knew how ridiculous it was to take the secondhand notes of a brief conversation as evidence of a future regular sex partner, but I couldn't immediately quash the resulting panic. It seemed inconceivable to me that any woman wouldn't seize the opportunity to be in his life.

If I had been in a saner headspace, I'd have assumed the woman was trying to hustle him. I might have even been wryly amused by his gullibility. Whatever dynamic was actually established between them, I couldn't be sitting on his dick 24 hours a day, so why or how would it matter to me if he was with other women? It didn't, and I knew it didn't. I wasn't bothered by him having sex with other people. This was about a deeper insecurity, which was that I might not be as significant for him as he was for me. Though ultimately I was willing and ready to accept that, too. It wouldn't deter me from being with him when I could.

I thought of my love for George as a love that wasn't wanted, and hadn't been asked for, but I wasn't sure that was true. I'd been looking for a redo of my affair with Ethan when I met him, even if I didn't think George was the one it would happen with. I'd cared for Ethan in a protective and connected way, but this was different. Sex with Ethan had been more powerful than sex with George. Sometimes I wondered if I weren't having sex with George mostly just to be around him, a thought that never arose with Ethan.

I didn't want only a friendship with George—the thought of never fucking him again was a sad, painful one—but if he wanted to be friends without sex, I would accept that. Though it would be hard to sacrifice that closeness with his body, which was one of the most beautiful I've ever been held against, and which I love, covetously, with awe.

It feels good to be loved, but if you aren't in love, you're getting the lesser joy. The thrill is in loving, not in being loved. Ethan was in love with me. He got there first, and he stayed there longer, at a higher pitch. I indulged and withstood his love while it vented in my face like a well-fed flame.

My feelings for George were something else. To experience them was to be the flame. I wanted so many good things for him. I was so happy to be around him. My love was spontaneously arising, either out of need or desire or the pure imperative of my meeting George's self; that didn't make it uninvited. Whatever the reason, it was here, it was a gift to me. I had to treat it with gratitude. It gave me numinous pleasure. It was its own reward.

I stopped picturing myself telling him I loved him in a cute or romantic or sexy moment and started imagining it as a clear-eyed conversation, face-to-face instead of side by side. The only way to stop the confession from being wholly selfish would be to make it clear it created no obligations and that I expected nothing.

How could I explain it to him as honestly as possible? I didn't need him to be a certain way for my feelings to be real or stay real. The weird anxieties I have about being duped or self-deluded are my own garbage, and not his responsibility to dispatch. I would make no demands of him.

The next morning, I sat in the sun at the stern and watched the water gathering and glistening like a reptilian skin. I was being paid so much money to meditate here on the water, paid so much to be near another person. Who else has this life, with its relentless abundance? I hope I die believing what I realized on that boat, that loving someone is a good thing no matter who that person is or what they may have done. Love exists for the subject, not the object. Your love is for you.

"You know I treat our relationship like gold," George said after I asked him not to mention my name to the other escort, just in case she was of my circle.

Of course I didn't know that. How could I know? But I wanted it to be true.

GO INTO IT
September 16, 2014

After several long nights wrestling the alligator of love, I resigned myself to not seeing George for at least a day or two after my return. My boyfriend found out before I left, for one thing. He saw my texts to a friend: "Bleh, I love George." Though he brought it up with impressive mildness—"I trust you"—it seemed impossible that, after five days away from home, I could run to this newly loved other man without hurting him deeply.

"Yeah, I love him, but I'm not *in* love with him," I said when he confronted me.

My boyfriend gave me a look like I usually give him.

"Ok," he said after a beat.

But before my flight back, while we texted, my boyfriend was oddly permissive to the point of being outright encouraging almost pushy. I gave myself an excuse to give in to his prodding. *I'll go to George now, and tell him, and then be free*, I reasoned, as if the telling would alleviate my interest in being with him. Like once I delivered the message, I would be released from my desire. Curse lifted.

George and I texted throughout the trip. "Are you back yet? I miss your face," he said. He tried to get me to come to him straight from the airport, but I wouldn't. I had to at least see my boyfriend first, and fuck him first. That was only fair.

My boyfriend mentioned he saw George not far from our condo building.

"He was probably stalking you," he joked.

"What building do you live in?" George would ask later that night. "I keep thinking I'm going to run into you. I keep an eye out for you. I want to walk by while you're looking out your window, or leaving, or going in with someone."

"And then what would happen?" I asked.

"I don't know," he said. In the time since the threesome, he'd often brought up wanting to live closer to me or visit my home.

"Us not being neighbors is cruel and unusual punishment," he wrote in an email on the night my love for him broke out of my heart like a fresh, greedy stalk.

"I wish you lived next door," he would say when I left.

I didn't have a plan about how to tell him. I figured I would know when the moment was right. When I got there he was in the shower, as always. We shouted back and forth about the escort he said he'd met, who apparently he didn't see again after their first random encounter, though they emailed.

"I think she thought I was trying to pimp her," he said as he stepped out of the bathroom naked, scrubbing his neck with a towel. "You know, because I knew a lot about the business? And I guessed pretty early on what she did. I think that freaked her out."

"That makes sense," I said. He'd sent me her website the day after he told me the story about meeting her. She was nothing like I'd imagined in my head. Not someone I would have crossed paths with, or will. "So you didn't have sex?"

"Nuh-uh."

"Was she trying to get you to hire her?"

"Yeah, maybe." He hustled me into bed. Normally there's no hurry on his part but this time it seemed more urgent.

"I missed you," he said. "How long has it been? Four, five days?"

I didn't tell him. I couldn't bring myself to. Early on while we were lying together, he started telling me about a girl he was screwing who visited him that afternoon to complain she worried he was "only using her for sex." The girl has a boyfriend. She and George had sex only once before—news that surprised me, because he'd talked about her several times. And apparently she came over that afternoon not for sex, but to talk and cuddle, which turned George into a whiny teenager, rolling his eyes, impatient—or at least he was now, with me, while remembering it.

"I started thinking, what if Charlotte came over here and started sucking my dick," he said.

"What do you mean? Like, I just walked in and started going down on you while she was trying to talk to you?"

"Yeah," he laughed. So that was why he'd tried to get me to come over straight from the airport. To show this other woman how she was supposed to act. I laughed then too, out of disbelief at my own stupidity and out of ruefulness. Yes, that was what I was to him. Exemplary, convenient cocksucker. Why would I think otherwise.

"She says she wants someone to be vulnerable with," he went on.

"Of course. Of course she wants that with you, because—" I cut myself off and shook my head. Because that's his whole shtick. To make you feel cared for, special, interesting.

"What? What is it?" he asked then, and would keep asking as we fucked, and I smiled the private smile of the corrected fool.

"I'm just incredulous," I said eventually.

"Incredulous," he repeated. "I'm going to have to look that word up."

"It means . . . you can't believe it. You can't even believe what's happening."

"I really did miss you," he said while he was inside me, over me. To this, I arced my arm out and around from under our bodies to settle my raised middle finger directly in front of his face.

"What are you thinking?" he said, pulling away to lower his face between my legs. "What? Tell me."

"No. Fuck you."

"If you were really my friend, you'd tell me," he said.

"I am your friend," I said, abruptly earnest and a little indignant, hurt.

"I know you are." His mouth on my thigh.

The friend line hooked me. The next time he asked why I was laughing, I said, "Because you're manipulative."

"You think I'm manipulative? And I don't know it?" He feigned some outrage over this but was too amused to do it well. He laughed. He tried to be curious instead.

"That's one option," I said.

" . . . Or that I do?"

"That's the second option." These were both possibilities I'd considered extensively since we'd met. I thought they didn't matter, and I'd told myself they didn't, but now I realized they were all that mattered.

The sex was forgettable. I looked up at my bouncing foot and the ceiling behind it while George rocked away and I thought about how many fake flash points I'd tried to set up for myself in this regard, even though I should know better. The first time I faked an orgasm with him, I thought, *I'll never have sex with him again. That's the end.* Whenever our sex lasted longer than I wanted or I found myself wondering when it might be over, I thought, *It's boring me now, I won't come back.* But I would. Those weren't the significant pieces of him that stayed with me.

I kept looking for an end. I didn't find it.

After he came, he snuggled me close to his chest.

"Cuddling, your least favorite part," I said, giggling, still feeling shocked and sour and alone in love. I'd thought so much about how and where and when to tell him. I hadn't been ready to consider not telling him at all.

"Your favorite part," he said.

"Oh yeah, the only part I like." We both laughed, because the truth is I normally bolt as soon as the sex is over. I disentangled myself from him then as I looked at the clock.

"My boyfriend jokes about how 90 seconds afterward, I reach for my bra," I said as I dressed. "It's because of work."

"So you really do have a boyfriend," George said. And I finally had my answer about how sincere George had been all those times he said he didn't believe I was partnered.

I thought about how I'd never spent the night with him except for when I brought Emma, how I'd never seen him and not had sex with him. I thought about how I rush to leave once it's over. Of course he only saw me as a dick sucker. How badly I'd misunderstood my own life.

He was reluctant to let me leave. He wanted to show me something on his computer, then wrapped his arms around me and drew me to him as I stood while he sat.

"We should take a vacation together, to Barcelona or something," he said.

"But then you'd get annoyed when I didn't brush my teeth enough and you'd go see other prostitutes." I was referring to when he snuck away from his ex to hire sex workers while they were traveling in Mexico.

He considered that for a moment, then said, "We can post Craigslist ads there." I laughed. Go overseas just to fuck more people. It was ridiculous, and yet very true to who we were.

"I don't think you lie," I said as he held me. What I really meant was, *I think you're too slick to have to tell outright lies.* That's what I count on for myself, anyway.

"I don't. Well, not to you. Why would I when we're so straightforward?"

I went home and got into bed with my boyfriend. My heart was gulping like a hungry flame. I still hadn't found the ending. I kept trying to trick myself into letting it go but I couldn't. There's no point fighting for something circumstances aren't ready to give you.

So I was afraid. So what? I've been afraid before. I'll be afraid again. I knew what to do with this type of fear.

I roused myself in the dark to write one phrase on the paper by my nightstand: *Go into it.* The next morning, I told George I loved him.

SECRET LIFE
September 22, 2014

I dressed that morning with an intention I'd never had before: to tell a certain man I loved him. I put on gray jeans and a sleeveless cotton top the color of linen, a half camisole underneath to make its slit-down neck more modest. Flats. I kissed my boyfriend goodbye.

"What are you doing?" George asked me that morning after I told him I woke up wanting to be with him again.

"You don't want to know :)" I replied, my boyfriend's body against mine at that very moment.

He knew what that meant: "Are you getting fucked? Tell me . . . Since when do we keep secrets?"

That was the deciding factor, his asking that.

"Ok, no secrets," I said.

He was in the shower when I arrived, his door unlocked. Our routine so well established. On his couch piled the ever-present laundry and I set about to folding it. Sunlight everywhere but soft and kind. It wasn't even noon yet.

"I'm such a whore," he yelled out, still in the bathroom. "That's why the guy at the desk was giving you a hard time. Because once he let someone up and there was another girl here already."

"Right, I remember you telling me about that," I said. "He's looking out for you."

"And one of them was a woman from this building's management! I've hooked up with three women who work for that company, and then there's a fourth I'm talking with . . . One of them forgot her top and she keeps bugging me about coming over to pick it up. I left it out so I can take it to her and get her to leave me alone."

There was indeed a bright pink bra lying on his desk with a shirt wadded around it. "Sounds stressful to be you," I said.

He came out with a towel tied around his waist and saw me sitting beside the folded clothes. "I can't believe you folded the laundry. You're so sweet." He sprawled down over me. "I didn't even shower after you left last night. I wanted to sleep in your smell. Don't you want to go lie down?"

I touched the droplets of water still hanging in his hair. "Yes, but it's nice to be here too. This is a good couch."

"Yeah, it is. My sister gave it to me after I got out. And this, and that," he gestured about the room to other pieces of furniture. "And a four-poster bed that I gave to my mom."

"It got in the way, huh?" I pictured the amount of space our limbs took up when we were there together. "I still want to see pictures of you right after you came home." He'd told me he was bigger then, even more muscular. And he got work as a bouncer, which was how he picked up so many women. At first.

"I know, right? Maybe I can find them now . . ." He did a cursory search in the other room and came up empty. He put his body back on mine.

We talked about the woman he'd mentioned the day before, the one who kept pressing him for some type of emotional confirmation or commitment even though they'd only had sex once and she has a boyfriend. He showed me things on his phone, business things, explaining what he had going on recently. I knew more about his finances than I ever thought I would know; somewhere along the way we started talking about that.

He brought up having sex in his office again and I said, "Isn't it all glass? How many other people have keys? Couldn't anyone walk in, even on the weekend?"

"Well, yeah, that's kind of what makes it fun," he said, utterly sincere, and I couldn't stop laughing at that. I was so maternal because I worried about him jeopardizing his job. I just wanted so badly for his life to be good.

I wanted it more than I wanted anything for myself.

My love for him pressed against my insides, straining to get away from me the way a dog flings itself into a leash. But I couldn't release it yet.

"Let's get in bed," I said.

He said he'd need to get more condoms because of how much we were fucking, and I said, "Oh no, don't worry. There's a huge box under your bed—"

"Shut up!" He wheeled up on his knees, laughing, mouth open. "Shut up. You saw that?"

I'd noticed it during the threesome, when he was fucking me on the floor. I loved that I could call him out and that I didn't give a shit how many condoms he had or went through because I didn't give a shit about anything except him being happy. Sometime back, he complained to me about a woman who spent the night and in the morning took his brown bananas to make bread. After that, I joked to him that I was making banana bread, and he took it seriously and asked how it tasted.

"Yeah right, I would never do that," I said. "Then you would have two chicks named 'Banana Bread' in your phone and you'd be totally lost."

He fell apart laughing: "Oh my god, how did you know? How do you know me so well?"

He said he'd read about a service that wipes all your data and gets rid of incriminating things when you die. I said I had someone to do that for me. He said I would have to be that person for him.

We went for a bit and then we took a break, and then started up again. He'd asked me if I had already had sex that morning and I said yes, and then he asked me how many more times I would before the end of the day and I said, "at least one."

"So, three," he said. "Is this going to count as the third?" Meaning our second round, but he hadn't gotten off yet, so I said no.

Then he slid inside me and I looked up at his face and I said "Ok … This feels good enough. This can count as number three. Next time I spend the night we're going to fall asleep this way."

"When you spend the night . . ." he said, to himself, like he were cradling it.

I can't remember anything about the sex except for a moment when he said, "That's one thing I love about you," and I said "What?" and he said, "Your flexibility." A few weeks ago, maybe the second or the third time he'd come inside of me instead of pulling out, I told him how much I love it, how it makes me feel like I might orgasm instantaneously even if I've already come or I wasn't close before.

"You should have told me sooner," he said. "I'll only do it that way from now on."

And he did this time. I remember that too. Because he stayed in me afterward and we talked while we were still joined.

I used some word he didn't recognize and he said, "That's another thing I love about you. Your writing. That you're so well read, so smart."

I wrote these words down then, That's why they still remain.

"Remember the first time you came over?" he said. He loved reminiscing about our first time. "You blew me away, literally, and then I didn't see you for like a year?"

"I remember," I said. Aching from love, his head against my breastbone. Why was it so easy to feel but so hard to say?

Sarah," he said, teasing me. The fake name I'd first used. Then, "_____."

"You think _____ is my real name?" I said, with a mean chuckle. Ashamed of myself the moment it came out, but it felt like a necessary response. I still wasn't used to hearing it in his mouth. He wasn't supposed to know; that had been the deal. But then suddenly I couldn't take it anymore, the idea of having to try to play these games or assume he was playing them with me.

"I love you," I said, not even looking at him. "You know that, right?"

"I know," he said, quietly, like maybe he didn't. "I love you, too."

We squeezed each other tighter, then he lifted his head and we kissed. But I wanted to make sure I said what I really needed to say.

"And . . . it doesn't require anything from you."

"What doesn't?"

"The way I feel about you. I used to worry you were fucking around with me, lying to me about stupid shit I don't care about. And then I realized it doesn't matter. I feel the way I feel.

"I had a friend I used to love a lot, I've told you about her before. I mean, I still love her. I'll probably always love her even though she's doing awful things to her ex-husband, who is still in my life. But after a few years I found out she'd lied to me about all sorts of dumb things, probably even how close she felt to me. And I wish I could have communicated to her that I would love her no matter what, because maybe if she knew she didn't need to lie to me to impress me, she didn't even need to care about me as much as I cared about her . . . "

He was thinking. "We have so much in common, and for us to have had such different lives but to end up together like this—it feels really special."

"Yeah, it's crazy."

"It's like, we both have to keep a lot of things from other people about our pasts and our present. But we can tell each other. I don't like lying and hiding stuff but sometimes you tell someone and then you regret it. So it's better to keep it to yourself.

"My ex got so mad at me one time. She said, 'Just stay there in your apartment with your secret life!' Your secret life," he repeated the last part in an imitation of her tone. It had hurt him.

"She doesn't want to be left out," I said, my hand on his chest. Sad for her.

"I know," he said. "But I don't think she could handle the truth. That's why it's so great to have someone like you in my life. Sometimes I wonder if things could be stronger between us but trying for something different always has the risk of making it worse. So it's better not to fuck it up."

"If you wanted something different we could talk about that . . . But I'm happy right now."

We got dressed to take a walk. I wanted to find an ATM and he wanted to show me some of his neighborhood. He kept trying to feed me watermelon, asking me what I liked, what I did and didn't eat. We were exhilarated, giddy. He mentioned the laundry again before we headed out.

"I like doing laundry," I said.

"Yeah, you said that, but I didn't think you meant it."

"You thought I was being sarcastic, like, 'Yeah I looooove folding laundry, you fucking jackass.' But I really do."

We left through the building's back stairwell. Something occurred to me while we were walking out.

"Was Krista the woman who caught you in your apartment with someone else?" I asked, naming his ex with the little dog.

"Yes," he said.

Outside, we talked about his time in prison and about my work, how I pay taxes, how I got started. We talked again about his work, too, the possibility of me trying to charm some of his clients. And we talked about the next weekend. My boyfriend would be out of town so he and I could have the whole night together for whatever we wanted. There were too many things to plan. We suggested ideas and then replaced them with others. Get stoned and watch a movie about the man he'd done time with. Go out and get drunk. Go to a strip club. He wore long shorts and a white shirt and he noticed several men in a car staring at us, and wondered aloud who they were watching.

"The other day when I was walking, a car full of guys pulled up near me and yelled, 'Do you want your dick sucked?'"

"What did you do?"

He shrugged. "I didn't look at them, I just kept walking. I try not to make eye contact with other guys in that neighborhood." It was memorable for me, that even a muscled ex-con can be cowed by street harassment.

I was sweating by the time I hailed a cab. The sun had become too much. George pulled me into a tornado of a hug while the driver waited impatiently.

When I got in, the man laughed and said, "He's gonna miss you! Wow, he's gonna miss you so much."

"Right," I said, laughing some too.

"Are you going to miss him?"

I hesitated. Maybe it was just the newness of someone seeing our relationship and commenting on it, or my standard prickliness to strangers. But even before we left George's place I already felt a vague sense of trepidation.

"Yeah," I said. The window was right there, but I didn't look back.

THE GAME
September 25, 2014

The summer when I was 11 or 12 years old, I began having long daily phone calls with a boy named Casey. We went to a small private school and had been in the same class since first grade.

Casey was distinctly a weirdo, someone who would loudly live inside his own fantasies with no hint of shame or defiance. If he wanted to speak in a creepy voice, he'd unleash a creepy voice. If he wanted to contort his face into something hideous, he would. His behavior was abrupt, often nonsensical and always unselfconscious. But all that strangeness didn't really make him an outcast. Being in that cramped school for so long meant most of us endured each other with the weary, mean familiarity of siblings. No one could shun anyone else very effectively; the class was too small. So the social order was more a suggestion than a mandate. We all ended up going to each other's end of year parties.

Taking Casey's calls wasn't any issue for me popularity-wise. Some years there were as few as three girls in the class, including me, and we existed in our own gender-defined clique of mostly equitable (though fluid) friendships. And beyond that, it was the summer. Our phone calls were a secret between the two of us and another schoolmate who spent lots of time at Casey's house. Or they were, until Andre was introduced into the mix.

At some point after our aimless, mostly flirtation-free phone calls had become routine, Casey told me a new friend of his was visiting, and he put Andre on the line. He didn't go to our school and I'd never met him before, so I had no idea what he looked like.

Andre, if I remember correctly, was a little older than us. His voice was definitely deeper. And he would whisper to me, which Casey never did. He would ask if I were alone and tell me to get someplace private and I don't think it took more than a week before he said, "Charlotte . . . I love you."

I was already in my mom's closet and she wasn't home, but I covered the mouthpiece with my hand anyway. "I love you too," I whispered back.

I knew I didn't love Andre. At least I was pretty sure I didn't. But it seemed inconceivable that a person would say this to someone else and not have it given back. Was that even allowed? Nothing I said to him had any tangible effect on my life. I hadn't even met him in person. I could brag to friends about my secret boyfriend without ever bothering to verify if he were handsome or popular. His existence would surely scandalize my parents if they ever became aware of him—that was part of the fun—but this status as my secret boyfriend was safe since he would never come to my house nor I to his.

It was exhilarating to say those words to a nonfamily member, and to hear them in the mouth of an unrelated boy. It felt illicit and passionate and risky and exciting. Our conversations were boring but the fact of having them was not. I loved the sneaky circumstances and all the possibilities they suggested, though I couldn't love the kid. I didn't even know him.

∼

I had this ancient memory in mind when I tried to reassure my boyfriend that the situation with George was not serious. I insisted that he and I were not suddenly in a "poly" relationship and that everything was under my control. I told him I knew the circumstances made the emotional dynamic more heightened. As with most things in life, the boundaries were intensifiers. I see this all the time at work: there is a large obstacle in place that makes a more conventional relationship impossible and so emotions can run wild without requiring commitment. It's easy to believe you're in love with someone when you're exempt from doing the real work of loving them.

I couldn't think of how else to explain some of the starkly earnest emails from George. After we said goodbye that day in the sun, the day we declared our feelings for each other, he sent a message a half hour later: "I feel euphoric right now—I miss you already and I'm wondering what you're doing."

I emailed him a link to the article that first got me into sex work, and his response stunned me: "I can see how it inspired you. You picked all the good things and added your own flair. You are a genius and an amazing person. I love you." A few hours later came the message that he was fantasizing about us "traveling the world together, exploring fresh water caves in Greece, riding camels in Africa, partying in Santorini & Ibiza ..."

I worried his feelings outweighed mine considerably and had to remind myself that he was probably just playing, not in a manipulative way but in a lighthearted and happy way, enjoying the same headiness I was. Drinking the sand of a mirage like it were clean water.

Knowing intellectually that much of what I felt was probably circumstance-specific had little effect on my most intense spasms of George-love. I drifted through dreamy states of thinking about him idly and happily, to more urgent cravings, to anxiety that he felt more for me than I for him, to a sense of complete distance. I went to bed convinced I couldn't go another day without seeing him but then I'd wake to my boyfriend and my cats surrounding me and I knew I needed nothing more than this family, and that George was an expendable and frivolous accessory to my real life. Whatever state I was in felt like the truest, but none was as powerful as yearning to be with him. Those were the times when my love for him beat inside me like a second heart and I couldn't concentrate on anything else.

When I was on the sailing trip, the thought first entered my head of him telling me he loved me while he was inside of me and that was a wish I couldn't release. I returned to that idea again and again. I'd never wanted any man to do that to me before, not even the ones who had.

I went out of town. I worked.

"It's going to be awesome to do other things together soon like watch movies or spend the night together," George wrote me while I was away.

I remembered the feeling of permission I had once I realized I loved him, like it wouldn't have to only be about sex anymore, and to know he felt the same was so cheering.

I sent him pictures of the bruises his fingers had left on my leg.

"How many times did you get fucked today?" he wrote.

He invited me to an upcoming business meeting of his, still daydreaming of me charming his clients for him. We ricocheted back and forth like that: sex, not sex, sex, not sex.

"All I want to do is sit on your dick and talk to you," I said to him. It was the purest distillation of my sentiments.

"I want to grab you by your throat, not to choke you but to kiss you so deeply you forget whose air you're breathing," he said.

The next time we saw each other he was fresh from the gym.

"What'd you work?" I asked.

"Guess," he said.

I looked at the lifted veins on his bicep and said, "Arms."

He started talking about wanting to gain weight for the winter so he'd be warm in fewer layers, and he plotted where the muscle would go, gesturing at his own naked skin: how much on his legs, how much in his torso. And I marveled at his body again. It never stops.

He told me before I arrived that it wouldn't be a quickie, and I knew what that meant. The other girl with the boyfriend had been over earlier.

"Do you think girls leave things in the trash on purpose?" he asked. "Like, for other girls to see it?"

"I think they probably just need to throw things away," I said. There was a condom wrapper in his bedroom trashcan that wasn't ours. I liked that he hadn't felt the need to hide any evidence.

It was a short visit, and as I was getting ready to go, I said something offhand that made him laugh. He walked to where I stood in his bedroom doorway and put his arms around my shoulders.

"I love you," he said, still smiling.

"I love you, too," I said, surprised.

"I don't know what we're doing or where this will go but I'm happy.

I'm liking it." He'd email me the next morning: "You're one of my closest friends . . . I'm excited and curious about forging ahead with you. I often wonder what 'our story' will look like when we reflect back 20 or 30 years from now."

Why this romanticism crested in him when it did, how true it was, what it meant for him or for me, I had no idea. I told myself I knew how to ride it all out—manipulation, infatuation, sincere devotion, whatever it was—because it was my job to handle the emotions that pass like shadows over men's souls. But my intuition was failing me. That's why I was in love with him. He disabled all my normal powers of perception, which made me curious. The curiosity was what was toxic, and addictive.

~

When Casey told me there had been some bet between him and Andre to see who could be the first to trick me into thinking they were my boyfriend, I was confused more than hurt. I had the sense to feel shamed in a minor way, just from the sheer fact of people conspiring to make me vulnerable or appear stupid. But I never had a great capacity for embarrassment, at any age. And their prank made no sense to me. Hadn't we both been playing? I didn't realize it was supposed to cruel, that it was intended to hurt.

I think I remember Andre apologizing to me, but maybe I made that up. I might not have been willing to talk to him again. I know I didn't miss him, but I did miss the idea of him and what he briefly symbolized: romantic success, the ability to appeal to the opposite sex. A secret.

~

"Can you imagine if you didn't have a significant other?" George asked me when we'd been lying together.

"Yeah, you'd get burned out on me so quick."

"No, I'd be like . . . go to work and bring me back money while I stay here!" He laughed. It wasn't quite what I expected to hear. But I still had a lot left to learn about George.

HEAD SHOP
September 29, 2014

Friday stood at the end of the week like a church at the end of a road. It would be our first night together in love, my boyfriend gone so I could sleep over; the perfect time to finally tackle our agenda. Going out drinking or to a strip club or both. Or maybe not going out but staying in, getting high. Watching the movie about the guy he served time with. Laughing, fucking, talking, fucking some more. I wanted to feel him still inside me while we lay together before sleep. We would wake up against each other. Just us this time, all night.

"Do you have Amazon Prime?" George texted me.

"You want to order something to smoke with that will get here in time?" I asked.

"You're always reading my mind, honey bunny," he said, partially in emoji.

"Let's just get something here," I said. "There's a place not far from your office." I was excited but busy. It was Wednesday. I had to work all day Thursday into Friday.

"Are you free at 2?" he asked. I wasn't. I told him to go pick something out and I would buy it.

He said he had a meeting at 5:30 but then it was pushed back to 6, a few doors down from the shop. I was free at 5. He told me to call him. We'd never spoken on the phone before.

"I'm at the office," he told me. "My business partner's here, so I thought it might be a good time for you to meet him."

George brought up his business partner to me ages ago, before he knew my real name but after he knew about my work.

"He wants to meet you," George told me then. "Not for sex; he's gay. But he thinks we might have some business opportunities together."

I assume he'd shown the man my website. It didn't bother me too much then, when George was only some guy I'd slept with a few times. What consequences could it have? How could it matter what he told anyone? I wasn't entirely convinced George had a serious job then. I thought he was probably doing something smalltime and a little shady, not working with a company that had offices all over the city, where my boyfriend had been a client.

"Well, I'm wearing my workout clothes," I said. I was not in the mood to be introduced to a man who hoped to exploit my whore-ness for his own economic gain. Even if I were, I couldn't. My boyfriend had probably met this other guy. He might deal with him in the future. It was too risky. If this guy knew about my work, or even about me having sex with George, I couldn't give him my face.

"It's ok, that doesn't matter," he said. As much as George was starting to learn about me, he still didn't realize he'd met my boyfriend. Or that my boyfriend used his firm. Or—how could he know—how often my boyfriend and I were out together in the neighborhood where we lived, which blurred into the neighborhood where he worked.

"No . . . " I said. I went for diplomacy to end the conversation quickly. "I'd rather meet him when I'm dressed and ready for it. Let's not do it today, it will be rushed anyway. Just meet me there. I'm getting into a cab now."

"Ok, I'll leave the office in five minutes," he said.

"Oooh, it's underground and scary," I texted him when I was out front. "I'm not going in there alone."

"Not that one," he replied. "Across the street. Walk over and I'll be right there."

I crossed, still unsure of where exactly he meant. I felt giddy, maybe because we met in public so rarely. This was only the second time. I was supposed to tell my boyfriend in advance whenever I met George but I hadn't told him about this. All he and I talked about anymore was the other man.

I looked at all the people passing. I waited edgily—it felt strange to think of him seeing me from afar. And then I saw him coming. He was not alone.

I turned away at first. I laughed in my shock. I started to text him, "You are a jackass." But then I stopped and put the phone away. I pulled my sunglasses down. I would maintain control. I would mitigate the damage.

"Hey," he said when they were steps away.

"Hi," I said. George leaned in and I thought he meant to hug me but then he kissed me and cupped his hand around my ass.

"How are you?" he asked, his hand lingering, his gaze intent. In his intimate voice. My boyfriend and I don't even use our intimate voice in public with each other. Not like that, not right out in front of everyone. Why didn't he just take out his dick and piss on me?

"Fine." I was not using my bed voice.

"This is the guy I've been wanting you to meet: my partner, Dave," he said.

"Hi," I said. I shook his hand with my firm, not-afraid-of-you handshake. Dave was wearing sunglasses, too, and his face was impassive. He did not seem desirous of the introduction, though it was allegedly his idea.

"Where's the place?" I asked George.

"Just up this way," he said. We all started walking together. To Dave, he said, "She just wants to get something for a friend, I'm going to help her pick it out." Every second of silence made the gaps between us stiffer and, impossibly, more hostile.

My escort training kicked in, as it always does in unpleasant situations with men. The old backup generator whirring to life.

"So, you guys have a meeting at [a restaurant]? Have you eaten there before?" I sounded very invested in knowing the answer to this question. Small talk is always the shield.

"Um, yeah, well the owners wanted to talk about selling," George said. Then, tenderly to me, as if we were alone, "How's your day been?"

"Busy." My god, I was angry. He couldn't even play along for a minute. "You guys have been busy, too?"

They both ignored my question.

"So, Dave, this is the *strategic partner* I've been telling you about," George said finally. In the heaviest air quotes I'd ever heard. "She, um, works with a lot of Jewish clients too. So I thought we could all help each other out."

The innuendo was rank and artless: heavy cologne, a sucker punch, a sexist joke. If there had been any doubt he'd told Dave what I did, it was gone.

"What'd you say your name was?" Dave asked me, still not smiling. Like a police officer, so secure in his unearned authority.

I opened my mouth; it felt full of disbelief rather than air, shock sitting against my tongue like a stone. For all I knew, George had already told him my real name. But I wouldn't be cornered into giving it up myself. "Sarah," I said eventually, flatly. Making it sound like the bullshit answer that it was. Let him know I'm lying. Fuck him, fuck George. Once I got out of this trap, I was never coming back.

Almost as soon as we stepped inside the store, Dave went back out without much explanation. I could be projecting, but he had a disinterest and irritation about him that suggested George pulled stunts like this all the time. I imagined George describing me to Dave, suggesting some connection to be exploited, and Dave's impassive nonresponse translating to George as, "Yes. Brilliant."

After he was gone, George stepped toward me and looked down into my eyes. Innocent. "I think I'm going to go, because things seem a little uncomfortable."

"Yeah, no shit! I told you not to bring him."

"Oh no, I'm sorry. I guess I didn't get that," he looked mildly concerned. A confused puppy. "I must not have understood that. But we're ok, right? I mean, we're ok? We're still on for Friday?"

"Yeah, yeah." I lied, eager to get rid of him, brittle with impatience. "Just go to your meeting. Go get ready for your meeting."

He kept looking at me. "Are you sure?" He was standing too close to me. I wanted to be alone, immediately. So I did what almost every woman knows how to do when a man has violated her in some way: placate, affirm, reassure.

"Yeah. Yeah it's . . . fine," I finally forced a smile onto my face. The way ice cracks in water. "Go make some money."

"Ok," he said, but pausing until I smiled again, or more, or something. Who knows how I finally got him to go.

Then he left, and I held still and breathed. My body was a sleeve. One of the men who worked the shop started coming at me and I worried he might get mad I was loitering but he didn't so much as glance at me, just moved around me like I were part of the display case. I stared down at the pipes and pretended to evaluate them. My mind was empty. No decisions. No reactions.

I didn't feel myself closing. I only had the sense of being already closed. I knew it then. In that moment, it was the only thing I knew: I can never see him again.

LONG LOST

October 6, 2014

I met Ethan in the time after my boyfriend and I survived an event many other people did not—a large-scale terrorist attack. We failed each other in the days that followed but I don't think that failure was evenly distributed. He was cold and cruel to me even though I cried, asked him for comfort, and told him how he was hurting me. A few weeks later, back home, I received a voicemail while working at the massage in-call; the FBI was at my home. They came into my apartment, three of them. They met my cat.

I was hopeless in the subsequent months. I felt terribly alone, and I went about addressing this in the familiar ways. That's why I found Ethan, the single, skinny ex-military man who picked me up from my apartment in his car, then fucked me in the backseat. His cock was like a truncheon, a battering ram. I was confused by the blood but he was used to it.

A long time passed before I saw him again. Half a year? Less? More? Then on a whim, one of us contacted the other—I can't remember who— and I went to see him where he worked. This is how I wrote about it at the time:

"What are those?" I asked. I knew, but I wanted to hear it. I was wearing suspender pantyhose, the kind that leave your thighs and crotch bare. I felt the air under my skirt as we walked.

"Bulletproof. Shields, in case some crazy person comes out shooting. All of the windows are blast proof."

"Blast proof," I repeated, scanning the face, imagining slow-motion footage of those imploded buildings with that leisurely, thudding impact, smoke billowing out.

When he closed the door behind us, I said "I can't believe you're willing to lose your job for this. Would you lose your job?" He shook his head, but he wasn't listening. He was taking off his suit jacket. When he met me at the entrance I noticed the gray in his hair for the first time.

I gripped the sink with both hands, bent over. I didn't look at our faces in the mirror. I looked at the black stockings and my skin. I tried not to make noise but I couldn't help it. He made noise. He whispered to me the entire time.

On his lap I leaned back and watched my patch of pubic hair move up and down. There was a faint pink stain on his white shirttail. I couldn't think of what it was from until I saw the bright ring of blood at the base of his cock.

"Oh baby," he groaned. I held the handicap bar behind his head. "You're going to make me come. You're so beautiful. Oh . . ."

Afterward, I wet a paper towel and tried to wipe it from him. It was stuck on the underside; it stayed flecked there and I didn't want to rub too roughly.

"It won't come off." I was still trembling. Sex with him involves so much adrenaline, and it starts before he's even inside. It's like he's caught me wild, escaping from a fire. Like I'm trying to run from him before he fucks me.

"It doesn't matter, sweetie. I'm going right home." I passed him dry paper towels and he wiped his hands.

"Does that always happen?" I'd asked him this before.

"Not always. Normally. We go really deep. And you're so skinny. I think you're skinnier than me."

"I'm not," I said. He wrapped me in his arms and I ran my hands over his back, then up to his head. His hair was soft and short in my fingers. I kept trying to slow my breath. I wanted to lie down with him. He kissed my cheek and my neck, held me patiently. I didn't want to be that girl, using sex for affection. But I wanted so much affection from him. Where had that come from?

He asked me my real name. I'd promised I would tell him and I did.

"Oh baby, that's a beautiful name," he said, as though I didn't think so.

On the escalator he let his hand drift down my arm and pause over my fingers. He looked at me with that faint smile.

"There are a lot of hot women here," he said, and I thought he was joking, but then a petite brunette in a pink shirt walked by.

"She was hot," I murmured.

"She was. I liked her sweater. It looked so soft."

I stared out the windows as we passed. The trees in the courtyard were covered with snow. Nothing was coming from the sky.

"But not like you," he said, low. Men and women in wool coats moved around us. So much black and gray. "Nobody here is like you. I fantasize about you all the time."

"And how many of your years in the army were spent in Telling Women What They Want To Hear boot camp?"

He laughed. "They don't teach that. That sounds like something you'd learn in law school."

I have to believe he's playing a game. I tell myself: This is not a real connection. You are a foolish girl. You are easily taken in by men who know what they're doing. But I don't know if he knows what he's doing. I do know that I don't.

～

It only became more intense after that, a continuous acceleration.

"What do you want out of this?" he'd asked me so many times. I could never answer. "Besides sex?"

Tonight I finally replied, "It doesn't matter what I want. It's already here. We can't change it. We can't do just sex. It's either this or it's nothing."

The city night was around us, black punctuated by neon. Wild wind and girls in dresses. I was late.

"Thank you for saying that," he said.

I took his face in my hands. "This is horrible," I said, and kissed him.

He'd fucked me hours earlier on the high counter in a public, family bathroom. Took my jeans down to my ankles and then lifted my feet to slide my thighs down over his body. I held the backs of my knees to get the best angle. It felt so good. Sometimes that's all I can think to say about sex with him. It felt so good. Someone pounded on the door. He flipped his tie over his shoulder. It was red.

~

The tenderness and gentleness between us stood as a stark contrast to the sex, which was ferocious and brutal and unequivocal. "It's the difference between taking a large bite of food and having your jaws held open with a dental gag," I described it once. It felt good to be held open. Yet giving each other something we both badly needed ultimately fostered more desperation.

He asked, "Are you like this with every guy you sleep with?"

I didn't answer because I knew he wouldn't like the truth. Which is yes. Sometimes. Often. I touch their faces. I push my mouth against their necks. I fall asleep on their chests. I stroke their hair, always.

The silence made him restless. He came on my face, then lifted my leg and fucked me for a few strokes, pulled out and came more. It was heavy on my eyelids, streaked through my hair. I wiped my face with the top sheet.

He was kneeling over me, his cock still hard. "It has to be just sex between us. Just business."

"Ok."

"That means no more touching my hair."

"Oh. Ok."

When he lifted his chin in a kiss request, I said, "If there's no hair touching, there's none of that either."

"Right. Just business."

"It can't be business if neither of us is making any money."

"We'll film it."

When I tried to sleep away from him, he pulled the length of my body against his.

When we first laid down together he cupped my pubic bone, splaying his long fingers down over my lips.

"You don't know what you do to me." He said, sliding one finger inside. I arched against it. "I crave you." He slid in another. "I crave you."

∾

Ethan was a good, thoughtful, lonely man. He told me often that he loved me and wanted to marry me. When I told him some of the bigger truths about myself, when I hesitated before doing so, he said as encouragement, "You know I love you." Not necessarily committed to me, but committed to loving me, to answering every aspect of me with love. He told me things like, "I want to know you. I want to be your best friend. I've never liked looking at anyone as much as I like looking at you." He washed me in the shower as if the lather were abrasive, as if I might break from a wrong touch.

I didn't make him happy because I wouldn't love him as much as he loved me. Meaning I wouldn't leave my boyfriend. Eventually he told me not to contact him, though it took many tries to make that stick. The problem was that he'd email me first. He'd say he was in a better place but it would quickly devolve into the old patterns: him provoking me, trying to make me jealous and failing. He threw himself into a relationship with a woman he met after me.

They got engaged quickly. I knew how threatening she found me or the idea of me; it was obvious from the way he wrote about her interest in meeting under the guise of a threesome. And also because he was so bad at disguising what he still wanted: me. He and I together. He said he was accepting a job out of state. He deleted all his old email addresses. He changed his phone number.

I had no right to think there was something unfinished between us. How much more warranted could the separation have been? I know everything ends. But in my mind, somehow, everything ends yet nothing is over. I pined for him periodically over the years. When I was loneliest, I missed him. I missed our sex. I wrote and deleted incredibly earnest, detailed Craigslist ads about what unfolded between us and how I wanted to find that again. I emailed addresses when I knew it would only bounce back. I googled him, every now and then.

Years. Years and years from when we'd last spoken and even longer from when we'd seen each other. I'd told George about him because I wouldn't have met George if it weren't for Ethan. If I weren't looking for an Ethan #2.

~

My boyfriend was still going out of town on Friday night, so I posted an ad. I wanted someone to distract me from George. I wanted a sexy story to tell my boyfriend that wouldn't be fraught with emotional risk. I planned to find someone I could meet with briefly, then leave to read and write and enjoy my home alone.

His was one of the earliest responses. I knew it even though he was wearing sunglasses in his picture. I didn't want to say his name yet, or frighten him with anything too pointed coming from someone anonymous on the other end. I thought I should make sure.

"Are you in the military?" I asked.

"Former military," he wrote back.

I took a minute. I wanted to say it right, without him feeling panic for even a second. "I would love to meet you," I replied, "but I'm not sure you want to see me. We were together a long time ago and you asked me not to contact you. I want to respect that. You only ever deserved happiness and peace."

"Charlotte?" he said.

It was Ethan.

INTERLUDE
October 13, 2014

He was shorter than I remembered by at least a head, but still taller than me.

"I thought you'd be wearing a suit," I said.

"Not anymore," he said with a laugh, as he let us into his office building. I'd said we should do it there, "like old times," even though we'd only done it in his old workplace once, and this new building was very different. We passed through the back corridor to avoid the security guard he thinks has a crush on him.

"How long have you been in the city?" I asked in the elevator.

"Two years," he said.

"You moved from New Jersey?" I was referring to the job he said he was going to take before he deleted all his email addresses.

"No."

"But I thought—"

"I didn't end up taking that job. I just stayed in where I was."

So he stayed for years in his old apartment. I believed him gone in a more literal way, not a few miles outside my own neighborhood, where he had been before. Not passing through the same rooms where he'd screwed me, washed me, told me he loved me. Not sleeping with his new wife there after she became his wife.

His office was trendy, wide open, full of light. The only person there was a janitor whom he spoke to briefly and then locked out with an all-glass door. He led me to the darkest room, the only one with three opaque walls. Even there he retreated to the darkest spot to unfasten his jeans.

"How do you like being married?" I asked with a small, teasing smile.

"I hate it," he said with the exhale of an almost-laugh, looking down at his belt. Then, "It's not that bad."

I set down my bag and slipped off my shoes, keeping my eyes on him. I took everything in. Took him in. The body and face that were both new and old to me.

"Come here," he said as he sat in a chair wedged into the corner. "Sit down."

I peeled my pants off and swiveled my hips over his, reaching down to draw him out. Through his legs and through my own, his massive penis draped against my inner thigh. I held it with both hands. I didn't set my weight entirely down but stayed light on his lap.

"Is your boyfriend's dick this big?" he asked, vaguely combative.

"No one's dick is this big," I deadpanned, and he laughed.

"You're so tiny," he said, which I always found funny coming from him. "Remember how you bled the first time?"

"I bled all the times," I said. One of the first things I liked about him was how nonchalant he was about my blood. That was manly to me, the way he kept fucking right through it, that he didn't pause or bother to wipe it away.

I bled again this time. It's why I didn't stop him right away when he lifted me up and knelt before me. I stayed bemused for a moment or two, still touched by his willingness to put his mouth on it all, the blood and the lingering latex taste, compelled only by his own exuberance.

"Oh my god," he murmured again and again as he placed his hands anywhere on my body and then withdrew them. The potency of his memories became accessible to me through the way he touched me as he said those words. Like I were a foal and he were imprinting me with his marvel. Oh my god: this skin, again. My hands and this skin. The ribs, the waist. The elbow. The hip. This human. Like he were welcoming me home in the dark.

It made me happy to be privy to his rediscovery even though it also felt so personal as to exclude me. It was a conversation between his past and his present, my body a tool for measuring memories against the truth or rather what was now the truth. "You got implants," he said immediately when I took off my bra. Clients who've seen me regularly for the past several years still haven't commented on it but this man who hadn't seen me once in the better part of a decade did. "They were perfect before," he said. And then a moment later, "They're still pretty good."

I wondered so often what sex with him would be like now, whatever "now" I was in when I wondered it. Would it be as powerful, as good as it was back then? Or had my idea of good sex, my body's tastes, been too altered? Had his style of fucking turned into something different?

I'm not sure I got an answer. It wasn't that I felt nothing—there were moments of pleasure and more moments of pain—but mostly I waited for it to end. Waited for a conclusion so I could come to my own conclusion about it. I was too stunned from George. I missed my boyfriend. I would have probably preferred to be by myself if I couldn't be with either of them, but how could I have declined being there with him? The timing was too eerie. It was felt like I was being given a key already fitted in a lock; I only had to turn my wrist.

I held him when he came, his body over mine and my back on the floor. I put my fingers against his hair. There it was still. The place above his collar I'd touched when I realized we were about to go over the cliff. Soft and short.

"I've been looking for you for a long time," he said as he dressed, ducking his head as he smiled. "I stalked you a little bit."

"Oh, really?" I had no fear of him so this only made me curious. "Like how?"

"Yeah. I was pretty infatuated. You probably remember."

"I looked for you too," I said. Neither of us said, "And now I found you."

While we walked down the hall together, he said, "I've changed."

"In what ways?"

"Not too many. But physically."

And it was true. He was less muscular, even skinnier than before. He'd always had bad skin and now his face was drawn, lined. It wasn't noticeable, much, but he had lost hair. I'd been overwhelmed by this man once. Now that intensity was only an echo albeit one full of warmth and familiarity. The difference between a fetus hearing its mother's heartbeat from the inside and then born, a child listening to it against her chest.

We walked outside together.

"It was good to see you again," he said. It's his eyes, I think, that give him his appeal. "I know women like me," he'd told me years ago, not bragging. Matter of fact. He has the eyes of a faultless father. Benevolent. Approving.

"Yeah, it was . . . so unexpected," I said. There was a time when I couldn't meet his gaze and now I was as bold as I've ever been, though it didn't feel like boldness. It felt like research. Peering at him as if what used to be there would surface legibly on his face.

It wasn't bad to see him again but it was a mistake to think there was something left undone or unsaid between us. We hugged and I kissed the corner of his mouth.

I kept wanting to say, "I was only a baby when we met," but that's not true. I wasn't a baby at all. I was simply younger than I am now.

I'd been making a playlist for what was supposed to be my big night with George. I debated putting serious romantic songs on it. I wasn't sure he would like that, and it might be too heavy for us and make me feel self-conscious, but I wanted to listen to London Grammar's "Interlude" while with him. In the time after the ambush with his partner, I realized I could listen to it with my boyfriend. He doesn't like having music on as much as George does, but he wouldn't object.

When I came home after meeting Ethan, my boyfriend wasn't there. George wasn't there. No one else was there. I put on "Interlude" anyway and got into bed alone.

POST GAME
October 27, 2014

Severing myself from George was hardly a clean process, nor was it truly a severing. He texted me almost immediately after we separated in the shop.

"I feel like a jackass," he said. "I need to learn to be content with our situation the way it is and not push things . . . I'm really sorry about what happened. It won't happen again."

I didn't read it until hours later. I didn't want to think of him.

I had a facial at a hotel spa, so I went there and cried in the empty anteroom for only an instant, because "Lay Me Down" was playing and I became overwhelmed by what my boyfriend had endured on my behalf, only to have it come to this. What he might endure still. How could I tell him what happened? Wait until that night and spring it on him right away, as soon as we saw each other? Wait until later in the night and be accused of dishonesty by delay? There was never a right time or way for me to initiate a conversation about George.

I decided to text him then: "Something happened. I'm fine, but I think it's finally over, I will tell you everything in person." I padded it to sound lighthearted and amusing so he wouldn't be worried.

That night, George emailed me: "Is this our first misunderstanding? I think there was some miscommunication earlier . . . I needed my business partner to attend that meeting and I wanted to see you. I don't know if, in my excitement, I didn't hear you clearly or what happened but I really hope you're not upset with me."

I recognized this as bullshit. I might have been in love with him, but I wasn't an idiot. What he said next made it clear he knew exactly why I was upset, and why I had the right to be: "I don't want you to think I'm reckless when it comes to you, I would NEVER do anything or bring anyone around you if I thought they were suspect or that it would hurt you in any way. I've confided things from my past with my partner that no one else knows about, things that could damage my livelihood, but I have extreme confidence in him when it comes to our privacy. I hope in your heart you know that I'm genuine and sincere."

But there was no "our privacy" or "our" anything. I learned how to handle situations like this from work. When a man wants something he doesn't deserve—like immediate, unearned forgiveness—when he feels entitled, when he is willing to gaslight or beg or pressure or manipulate, you have to disengage and give him nothing to work with when you do.

"I know you're not a malicious person," I wrote back the next morning. "I just need to take some time to think about my decisions recently." Done.

I was still in that post-impact moment when you've hit your head hard and your nerves haven't decided what alarm to sound. That moment when all the adults wait to see if the fallen child will stay down, wailing, or get up and keep running. It was easy to hold George at a distance because I felt nothing except incredulity. I knew there was still love underneath, but on the surface, shock spread like oil. I kept thinking of something I'd written about journalists and sex workers a long time ago: "I won't let my anonymity be yours to give." To not see him again was necessary, automatic. It had none of the resonance of an emotional decision. It was self-preservation. An instinct, not a choice.

When my boyfriend and I went out to dinner the night just after, while we were marveling at the stupidity of it all, I started laughing.

"Hey, Dave, here's that whore I've been wanting you to meet," I coughed out, stripping George's act to its barest terms. "I think she can fuck her way into a few deals for us. Now can you hang out for a minute while we buy a pipe?"

After all, Dave was not truly George's partner but his mentor, his superior. That George could have thought anything about the situation would have made him look good or savvy or put him in a position to earn more money was ludicrous. It was so ill conceived I almost felt pity more than anger, and a low, sad thrum from having to articulate all of George's flaws to the friends I explained it to. He really wasn't malicious. But he was selfish in a lazy way, immature, shortsighted, too used to getting what he wanted from women to bother thinking about their lives or needs. I knew all of that when I started to love him.

Now one more offense to add to the list was that he put me in a position to articulate these shortcomings. I didn't want to think of someone I loved as dumb.

I woke up the morning after to more emails: "Thanks for responding … I can't get out of bed this morning. I care about you more than I realized. I don't want to lose what just started blossoming between you and I."

"I'm in love with you," he said a few hours later.

And an hour after that: "I share all of my sex stories with you, like the one that happened last night which I wanna talk to you and laugh about so bad . . . The thought that we might not speak makes me so fucking sad … And you know more about me than any single person. This is so unfair."

I got these all at once on my phone while I was with a client. I wasn't surprised that he would have sex with someone else right after hurting me so much, but I was a little surprised he would think it was worth mentioning now.

George and I don't sex the way most people sex, and that's ok. The fact that he'd fuck someone while claiming to be in pain didn't, for me, negate his claims to care about me. But because I have sex to comfort myself, not to damage someone else, I wouldn't use the fact of that sex cruelly. I had no idea how else to interpret him bringing it up, though I wanted to. Was he petty enough to hope to hurt me that way, or stupid enough to believe that was a good way to hurt me? Me, who'd never once objected to his many partners or shamed him or done anything other than encourage him?

What bothered me most was the whininess, his own sense of aggrievement. I'd been ready to give this man my leash, to bring it to him like an eager dog, to let him take it from my mouth. But he could not give me so basic a thing as a truly repentant apology. Maybe he thought that's what being loved means: he says he's sad and I fix it. Maybe he believed I was wronging him in that way, to let him suffer when he said it was all a mistake. But he said he'd loved me too.

When I went to look at the last email a second time, I noticed he attached eight pictures: his semen on someone's asshole, his finger inside, his dick inside, both at the same time. Eight of them.

Against my silence, George texted me a picture of his backyard full of people. There must have been some concert or outdoor event. It arrived on Friday evening when I was on my way to see Ethan.

"It's too hot for that," I said.

"I'm in the shade," he said. "Did you already make other plans?"

For a moment, I thought of saying yes. I could have replied honestly, *I'm going to fuck a man with a much bigger dick than yours, the man I was looking to replace when I met you, the one I told you about because I thought it was over.* But I didn't say anything.

I would have forgiven him if he could have said something sweet and kind. That was the truth of my sad, soft heart. One message that felt sincere and I would have gone over to his place after I saw Ethan or instead of seeing Ethan at all. But George didn't send anything like that. His next text was a Dropbox link to a recording of him having sex.

GAVE FREELY
November 3, 2014

I used to have a regular who spent most of our time together talking about his devotion to a stripper less than half his age. I'll call him Bill. He was a recently divorced father of two who used tanning beds and hit the gym in the hope of lifting away his 50-plus years being upright against gravity. He plaintively, repeatedly told me that women his age seemed so old, so un-fun, he had no choice but to go after women in their early 20s, whose vibrancy and energy were so much more on par with his own. He had many pictures on his phone of the various dancers he'd convinced to fuck him—I hoped desperately they'd received some sort of compensation, though I worried it was not what they deserved—but none of them captured his heart the way Melody had.

Melody, he told me more than once, was not a stripper but rather a girl who stripped. She'd gone on a few trips with him to Vegas, often with a friend of hers in tow, and it seemed she rarely had sex with him anymore, if she ever had. As far as I could tell she milked him (financially) far more efficiently than any of her colleagues, and I'm sure it was her success they chased when they posed on Bill's sad, frameless mattress.

I don't know how much of this was calculated on her part. All of it was clearly intentional but Bill was deeply, deeply in love with Melody. So it didn't require much on her part to get him to give her cash. He covered her bail when she was arrested in another state. He covered her lease when she quit stripping. He bought her new furniture, though she wouldn't allow him to pick it out with her or see the home it would go into.

I swung back and forth between feeling tenderly toward Bill and finding him utterly pathetic.

"I would do it all over again with her," he said. "Kids, marriage, everything." He was so sincere. He knew how foolish he looked but he didn't care.

Meanwhile, Melody despised him and resented his presence in her life but felt it too lucrative a situation to terminate. (I'm extrapolating some from my own experiences.) To her, his devotion seemed misplaced, indicative of weakness. Something nasty comes out when you're being idolized by any man you don't care for, but especially a much older man in midlife crisis, a man who you met as a client. His "love" seemed selfish, maybe, because it was. And the ardency was suffocating.

When she told him he was in love with a fantasy, he insisted she could not be more wrong. He believed if he were patient, his love for her would engender in her a love for him. He forgave her any mistreatment. He knew she was using him but it didn't matter. I saw pictures of her and thought her aesthetically unremarkable. Who knows why she triggered something so profound in him.

"I gave freely," he said to me. He could only ever look at their relationship in retrospect, since it existed in a constant state of being over except for her dips back into his bank account. "That's what I want her to understand. I've always given freely."

～

George didn't stop with the pictures or video. Those clumsy cuts would have been hard enough to endure, but he went further. After the Dropbox link—"What does this have to do with me?" I asked him wearily—he texted that he felt lost, and then much later, that he was starting to find himself with me. The next morning, he sent a picture of a pile of clean laundry.

"Wow, full court press," I replied.

"You are irreplaceable, for more reasons than just the laundry," he wrote back. But then, "Check out the job this girl did last night—so sloppy, and didn't even fold the blankets, ugh." He attached another picture. It was laundry he folded himself, obviously, but I was impressed by how thoroughly he wanted to make me feel common and expendable. Why did he want to be mean, and why was his sex with other women his go-to way of hurting me?

I shouldn't have said anything, but I couldn't help it. "What is wrong with you"—no punctuation.

"There's an old Chinese proverb my friend taught me," he said. "*Mei you yao neng zhi ni*—no medicine can cure you." So self-satisfied. Suffering from the great delusion of men everywhere, that their disregard for other people makes them interesting.

"Ok," I said. "I can't talk to you for a while."

∼

He still wasn't done, of course. Late that night he wrote again: "If you genuinely wanna know what's wrong maybe I can tell you one day in person."

"I have always been genuine with you," I texted back. Sad. Raw. Already preparing for whatever selfish, narcissistic reveal he was baiting me with. This felt like dealing with a preternaturally unpleasant child, someone you're supposed to protect and care for because you're older, you're wiser, it's your responsibility by sheer circumstance.

George was revealing himself to be so emotionally immature that no matter how much he hurt me, I had to take the high road. Not out of principle but out of maintaining order in the universe. Maybe he didn't know how to treat someone, but I did. I had to negotiate my love for him, which was not gone, with my need to uphold my own dignity and self-respect. I kept hoping he would take some of that burden away by not actively working to insult me, but he didn't.

What he said next was unintelligible, something about the income that could have resulted from the deal he wanted me involved in. It frightened me, truthfully, to think he was telling himself I'd cost him money. He'd told me about his finances; I knew he needed a sale, badly.

"What's there to be mad about though? That's more for you," I said. I hoped his ego wouldn't let him accuse me of ruining the deal, that he would want to be seen as capable of closing on his own.

"No, I already have my split," he said. "More for you."

I realized he was probably fucked up, and then he confirmed it: "Forget it—I'm smoked out. But you got mad and there's no other reason, I can't explain it."

"I didn't get mad. I just said I needed some time, and you know why."

"No," he said. "Tell me."

"It's irrelevant." I shouldn't have replied but I wanted him to say something right. I kept giving him the chance to be a good guy, silently screaming for him to take it.

"Irrelevant, why? Not for me, maybe for you." And then he did it: "I'm the one feeling pain. You're seemingly fine."

While I struggled to contain my rage, he added, "And you're lucky I deleted our texts." Lucky. Because I should be grateful, I suppose, that he wasn't amassing our correspondence to somehow use it against me.

The following week, my boyfriend saw that George recently viewed his LinkedIn page.

~

You can imagine what it felt like to get those messages and then to think of him in the days afterward, to recall this person I had such tenderness for who'd proven so eager to diminish me. It felt like pain. It takes a lot for me to stop loving someone but I've always found it easy to honor myself in the process.

When Brandon, my first real love, wouldn't admit he didn't love me the way I loved him, when he flatly lied to me about it, I slept on his couch until the morning, hauled my roller bag through the frigid cold to the train, and didn't see him again for years. It was right before the holidays and I've still never felt so bereft. My love for him was like a piece of oversized shrapnel lodged under my lungs for months. I could barely speak to my family during Christmas dinner. I loved him so fiercely for so long, but I had my pride. And I would not stay in the home of a man who withheld the merciful honesty for which I begged.

Now, in terms of my feelings for George, I found myself thinking, bemused, "I can take a lot of abuse." I thought about how ridiculous it might seem to still care about someone who'd illustrated again and again that he didn't care about me. It was a battle not to give into the suggestion that he was a villain who'd taken something from me, which was a nagging suspicion I'd had since I first started to care about him. (Taken what? My virtue, my self-respect, my dignity. That he'd conned out of me something finite and rare. The same propaganda all women are exposed to, the vague threat that hangs over our heads when we have sex for sex's sake.)

But I remembered an Alice Walker quote: "The animals of the world exist for their own reasons," and thought of how many men need to learn that about women, and about sexual women in particular. All the important and enduring things about me are permanently mine. They don't go away or tarnish because a man treats me poorly after we have sex. I had always done as I wanted to do with George. Everything—the sex, the love—had been given freely.

It's hard to understand intellectually; how can you give freely if someone is manipulating you? How can you be in charge if they're using you? But it's what Bill tried to explain to me. You can't pick a lock that's already open. You can't steal food left to be taken. This is the twist inherent in love affairs that look lopsided. People on the outside pity you, even the person you're ardent for may pity you, but on the inside you feel strong because your love is strength.

I felt so strong, still loving, not giving up just because it hurt. And my pain was not for nothing. The greatest human mission is to love someone else and there I was, doing that, while also learning about myself, which is the second.

A few days after the situation became so ugly, I went to Las Vegas with a client who shares Bill's name. I was not good company—too busy pulling thorns out of my heart—but he didn't seem to mind. He was in a reflective mood, and asked me about losing my virginity, falling in love, being happy. He said the only two women he'd ever been in love with didn't love him back. He chose his wife because she loved him; no other woman had before or since. He said he'd never known happiness and he didn't want to keep waiting for it. But he wouldn't divorce her until he had someone else waiting for him. He was too scared to leave the bubble of being loved no matter how little pleasure he derived from it.

This is a recipe for misery, and I know it because I've made it myself. You can never properly respect the one who deeply loves you without you loving them back. It's better, and far less toxic, to do the loving in spite of its risk. Be the subject, not the object.

"How many people have you been in love with?" he asked.

"Hmm," I said. "Fi . . . ve? Six? Maybe seven?"

He marveled. "You're so lucky."

"Very lucky," I said instantly. "Very privileged." Which I meant, and not because all of them loved me back. (Obviously, they didn't.) But because of what heady joy it was to care about some of them, and how instructive and slow growing the experience was with others. Nate, Brandon, Michael, Julian, my boyfriend, Ethan, George. All the men who are most romantically significant in my life.

I've never been sure how to define "in love." It's like a measuring rope that keeps changing length. When Brandon's lie broke my heart that night in his bed, I thought, "I'll never love anyone like this again," and I haven't. I've never intensely cared for any man in a way that feels identical to how I cared for another. I found George because I was yearning to replace Ethan, and look what happened. I just added another love to the list. The mistake is in thinking there is only one spot. You divot the sand and the tide fills it in and then you create another pocket while the tide drains itself out. Same properties. Different shapes. It's never the same.

～

One night we went to the Stratosphere for the rides—or really, only one. The Big Shot. I was nervous since it had been so long since I'd been on anything like it. More than a decade, at least. I trusted myself not to puke or scream or do something embarrassing, but I worried I would hate it underneath my composure.

Yet it was beautiful. Deeply calming in a way I could not have expected. First there was the extreme acceleration to the top, to which I shut my eyes on instinct. Then we started the plummet back down, but the nest was caught and raised again with a sort of bounce. It repeated. Loft and drop. Loft and drop.

I opened my eyes. I breathed, my lower legs dangling. There was only lit landscape before me, homes and the spaces in between sprawling into the dark horizon. And it was quiet in spite of the happy screams. I felt singular and cradled. I don't feel it often but that doesn't mean I don't know what it is: the true sensation of grace. Gently tossed into the air. Gently let fall. Gently caught. Gently lifted up again.

WORK SEX

November 14, 2014

I woke up today to one of my best regulars, a man I hate having sex with more than anyone else I can remember. I took solace in the fact that in the mornings sex is usually shorter. It had been almost unbearable the night before. I clenched my jaw as hard as I could at one point. If I could have jammed my hand down on a tack, I'd have done it. While he was coming I thought, "Thank god it's over, it's over, it's over, it's over, it's over, thank god." My relief more powerful than his orgasm.

I'm nearly immune to bad sex at work but being with him reminds me how corrosive it can be to give intimate access to your body to someone you wouldn't choose to be intimate with. With him, I sometimes put my own hand over my mouth in an attempt to hide the expressions I can't keep off my face. I pinch my fingers over my lips like I'm pinning in a scream. I sense my own mind becoming tighter and smaller but the process is already out of control because the way to make the sex stop is to see it through, and I want more than anything to not be having sex with him. A constrictive panic mounts. The sensations are not painful in the usual, physical way, but they function like pain in that they obliterate any desire other than that for cessation. I have no life outside of wishing it done. I have no interests, no personality, no future. I have only a prayer for termination.

This is labor beyond most labors. This is not forcing yourself to go to an office in the morning when you want to sleep in. It is not sweating in polyester in front of a fryer. It is not washing the ass of a bed-shitting patient. What this feels like is a psychological test devised by military sociopaths. How much effort it takes to part my thighs even slightly for his vile claw of a hand to rasp between them.

I know it's profane to admit, but I almost think it would be better if it were truly forced, if I were in some circumstance where I might feel emboldened to fight back. Being complicit may be the worst part. I'm compelled to accept the indignity of faking an orgasm while I mentally gag against our contact. I do it out of desperation and a hope that it will speed the process along though I'm never sure it does.

I don't know why it's so awful. It may be because his body genuinely disgusts me. He is stooped and short, old but even older-looking, with sun-ruined skin that puckers where it hangs off his skeletal arms, his drooping ass.

We've known each other for years. I've tried to cut him off several times, but I relent. I tell myself it cannot be as bad as I've made it out to be. My learned talent is in the forgetting. I recognize the horror the moment it starts but otherwise I can keep it out of my mind.

He's not fun to be with but he is fine to be with, more or less. He loves me. That doesn't make his company any more appealing, but it seems worth mentioning. He watches me while I sleep. He tries to look into my eyes while thrusting his wretched penis inside me. Of course that makes it more repugnant.

He's not a bad person—that's the refrain I find myself returning to when I struggle through sex at work. Sometimes I even feel guilty for hating it as much as I do. The hatred is not reasonable, it is so intense. The act is offensive to my soul in a way that defies articulation.

∾

For months I've wanted to write about why enduring detestable sex is a special challenge of will. Much more than I have just now, I mean: a proper essay. I think about how much there is to say, how I imagine I could say something useful for other people, mostly other women. Something accurate. Then I lapse back into not writing about it.

Sex is a bad topic for a woman to write about it. It's cheap and easy, it's self-centered, it's boring. Nobody wants to read about what makes me wet. Even I understand—you should believe I of all people understand—how tiresome it can be. Sex again? More sex? Like being served the same meal every night for dinner.

I'm sometimes irritated by women who frequently write about sex because I live in the same world we all do, so my instinct is to see them as pandering for attention and affirmation. *She must write about sex because she wants to seem sexy. Why else does she keep putting the idea of herself having sex in people's heads? Ok, we get it, you've had sex. Is anything more pathetic than a slut begging to be acknowledged as a slut?*

But I write to understand, to describe something that escapes my more casual mental attention, and the best egress I have into any idea or inquiry is the pinhole of my own life, and my life is full of sex. This state of affairs does not seem remarkable or odd to me now, if it ever did. It's my setting. It's my environment. And the most exciting change in my life this year has been my own sex drive's return from years of exile. I lived without it for so long because I thought that was the best thing to do. I didn't believe I could have the type of sex I wanted but nor could I have no sex at all, so my response was to shut down sexual interest or desire.

Now I believe the antidote to work sex isn't no sex. The antidote is at least as much sex as I have at work but on my terms, with people I choose. I think I realized this, strangely enough, because of something that happened at work.

~

The last entry in my gone blog was about Hot Client. I don't think anyone but other sex workers could understand it. My boyfriend read it while it was still online and then confronted me even though it didn't make sense to him. He went looking for evidence of me doing something wrong because I'd tried to tell him a little about what happened, what I felt. I told him I had a daydream about us, the client and I, being married, a very specific one that involved me joke-bragging about sex with him to some of his colleagues at the massive tech company where he worked.

I go to the client's Facebook page sometimes; there are no new public updates. But I can see the pictures that don't do him justice. I can see him sharing innocuous links. I've let men pay to get at my body for a decade and no one's ever affected me the way he did. We haven't seen each other in over a year. We haven't spoken, either.

We saw each other once after the night described below. He booked me for 24 hours. He had spent at least $4,000 on three pairs of heels, which were waiting in our suite for me. There was champagne, too; he had no idea what I liked. I sat on the couch and he put his head in my lap with hesitancy, and I stroked his face and hair. He looked like the most tired man in the world. I could swear we were both afraid of each other in the best possible way. I didn't want to go to dinner; I only wanted to be in bed with him. But we went to dinner. He was trying to do things the right way. I can't believe I didn't write about this then, that I only have my memories.

If he liked me even half as much as I liked him, I don't understand how he could leave me out of his life. That's why I go to his Facebook page: What happened? His wife found out. Or she didn't, but he renewed his commitment to her. What was it?

I try to have faith he'll come back, just like Ethan did. Everything ends, but nothing is ever over. Even now I tell myself that; among a crowd of men I've chosen to have sex with for free, I think of him. *Let me have left a stain on you like you left a stain on me.* My motto. My hope.

GLAMOUR

November 17, 2014

I'd gotten Don off sporadically over the phone for a year before we met on the eighth floor of Saks, in the Louboutin section, at his suggestion. He's a tall, round man. Bald. Bashful. It was my first time seeing him in person. I made him pay me the full amount for our date in advance because he wouldn't give me any screening information. He's into financial domination, a touch of public humiliation, and, in the right mood, forced bi scenarios. Like many men deep into a fetish, he would tell me what he wanted.

"Should we go to the ATM?" he asked after he paid for my six pairs of heels.

"Should I take out more?" he said after he passed me the first $500 from the machine.

At the cafe, he wanted to know how much it would cost to set up an exclusive arrangement and I said at least $750,000 a year. The shopping bags full of shoes as cumbersome as children. It was winter, and the wind made doors heavy.

Don is an ideal client because I've never been physical with him beyond a kiss and a caress of his pants-clad crotch. Spending time with a paying man without fucking him always feels like getting away with something.

Other clients like to go shopping, too, but not to the extent he does, and not to the exclusion of any other activities. I think there's some tension around this point in the "high-class" stratum. Lots of women make it out like their clients are eternally splurging on gifts. Maybe that's true for the blondes, but for me it's usually a decent dinner followed by sex. I think we all sometimes feel that we're not as elite as everyone else. Even other escorts can be misled by escort marketing.

I'm not trying to downplay my extraordinary life, which is a charmed one full of generosity and conspicuous consumption. But people with money can have strange tastes, and lots of them are frugal in unexpected ways. My best regular loves Marriotts and uses a Velcro wallet. One man used to dress me in elaborate outfits, five or six over our hours together, but they were ill-fitting, off-brand, and sometimes smelled bad; he got them from thrift stores and eBay, and I'm sure he didn't wash them. Several guys I see don't like using any valet service and will circle over and over to look for their own parking. The first and only time a client chartered a jet for me—after I missed my commercial flight—I texted Bea immediately, in total shock.

"This is like a Lifetime movie," she said.

Don likes stories about me being spoiled and powerful, so I accommodate.

"Have you known any other guys like me?" he asks.

"Oh yeah," I say. Which is true to some extent, but not really.

"How much money did you take from a man the last time you made him go to the bank with you?" he asked me.

"$20,000," I tossed off. Sometimes it all feels like make-believe, including the seedy parts, which makes it even easier to pretend for them.

∿

The last time I worked with Emma we saw Adam, her only client and de facto sugar daddy, in a hotel suite with a spectacular view. Another of Emma's friends was there, and they looked beautiful together: fit, made-up, dressed in black lingerie and heels. Fireworks went off outside while we put

Adam in women's clothing, spanked him, took pictures. I tried to tell my boyfriend about it later; while Adam, in a maid's outfit, crawled to pick up items from the floor, I thought about how quintessentially salacious and sex work-y this tableau would be for outsiders, how provoked they would be by every detail—three women! cross-dressing! Adam's wealth!—but how mundane it seemed. It just wasn't a big deal. It's easy. Pleasant. Almost boring.

"It's really not that weird, you know?" I said to my boyfriend.

"Well, yeah. But . . . it kinda is," he countered. Such a civilian.

$\sim$

I don't hear escorts describing their work as "glamorous" when talking shop with one another, but I think we're continually attracted to our own work by the perceived success of others doing it. Even when you're in it and you know better, when it's come to be routine and unremarkable like most any other job. That's what the word "glamour" means, that's how it operates. It's the casting of a spell, and spells don't wear out. It's reaching one oasis to discover it's a mirage and, as you sit in the hot sand of reality, becoming all the more entranced by another shimmery faux oasis in the distance.

Emma's told me that she wants to work regularly again when she listens to me talk about my appointments because it seems "so glamorous." And I never brag to Emma, ever. I rarely mention details. I just sketch out travel plans sometimes as they relate to her and me getting together. What's comical is that her situation with Adam is the true *Pretty Woman* dream. He's obscenely rich, says he's in love with her, travels with her all over the world, and they never have penetrative sex.

Sex work can seem glamorous because it can be made up of elements of glamour: a relatively high hourly wage. A young, attractive woman. A rich man. Sex. The power differential. The heightened femininity performed for the client's benefit. The heightened masculinity bestowed by the act of hiring a sex worker. The secretive nature of it all. And so on. An aura of celebrity comes over me when I'm working because it's a performance, and it loops back on itself. As I project specialness the client believes I'm special, as he treats me like I'm special so do I feel more special, as I feel more special so is my attitude of celebrity increased. That's when it truly starts to feel like a movie, for me anyway. It's not about circumstances, like being catered to in a Dolce and Gabbana boutique or fed room service snacks while I soak in an oversized bathtub. It's about believing my own hype. Getting high off my own hooker fumes.

The second time I saw Don it was for a spur of the moment shopping spree. I'd just finished my overnight with the client I most hate to fuck— yes, the contrast is dizzying—and Don emailed to ask if I wanted to meet at Saks. I had two hours before I needed to meet another client, so I agreed. Only three pairs of heels this time, since we didn't have as long to spend together, and we skipped the café but not the ATM. Then we headed downstairs because there was a handbag I wanted. While the saleswoman fetched it from the back, Don asked, "Do you want me to get out my wallet and give you all the money in it?"

"Yes, hand it to me," I said.

"Right here? What if someone sees?"

"Well, if it's a man, I'm sure he'll recognize how lucky you are. Don't you feel lucky I'm letting you buy me all this?"

"Yes, but . . . convince me a little," he whispered in a pained voice.

I just looked at him, grinning my dumb grin.

"Take it out," he said. "It's in my back pocket."

There was only $400, but I confiscated it. He bought the bag. I let him ride with me in a car to the hotel where I was to meet my next client.

"How does it feel to know you have so much power over me?" he said in the backseat. "I'll do anything you tell me to. I love you."

I already had five figures in cash on me when I stepped into the lobby, purchases in one hand and overnight bag towed behind. I practically kicked over the doorman who tried to take my things from me; I was there to collect even more. Attitude, not circumstances. I felt like a colossus of capital, of men, of the city. I set myself in the corner to unpack and repack, discarding the superfluous as I went. I moved efficiently and swiftly like a machine programmed for consolidation.

"Sorry to give you this, but it's trash," I said to the concierge as I handed over the massive Louboutin shopping bag full of empty boxes. My next client wouldn't want to see me with a gaudy pile of expensive new heels, so I made sure he didn't. All I do is manage other people's impressions of me. What does it mean for a young woman with a messy blowout to cram a small roller bag full of just-purchased designer goods? Why would she do that in a hotel lobby? It speaks to some wealth, but not class. And not to truly shocking wealth, but a lower, tacky level.

At the right times, I like to let my bourgeois roots show a little; I revel in being new money. It makes me feel more beautiful. I want strangers to know I earned what I have through fucking, but I want them to think it was greedy and easy sluttishness on my part, not calculated, not clawed out. Let them think it was fortuitous, that I was born with some face and body that paved my way with invitations, and that I'm too stupid to want anything except luxury in exchange for sex. They should see only an edge of the truth so they think they've seen it all.

I want to make my work invisible because then I can feel more powerful than those who overlook it. Cannier. Slippery. A rich witch. A ghost.

EVERYTHING I WANTED
November 24, 2014

He wore gray sweatpants—the same pair I saw laid long on the chair in his bedroom months ago, the ones I fantasized about finding him in—and a white ribbed tank left scrunched like a scarf around his neck. He looked better than I'd ever seen him look. He looked the best. I wonder how it feels to him when I touch him.

He was high. That was part of why I decided to come. I thought maybe I could catch him honest if he were stoned, and it was another Friday night with my boyfriend out of town. Since our bizarre, confrontational text session, he had changed his approach. Now he acted as though everything were normal and there had been no fight or betrayal. This felt safer to me. Better to have him deluded than angry. I said little in response to his casual texts and emails, but I didn't say nothing. I was angry yet I still wanted amends, contrition, repair.

He smelled more like beer than weed. Every TV in his place was on, and music overtop it.

"I wanted to show you the scratches I got from this nurse!" he said, bringing his body into the light and reaching around his ribs. "I think she was mad because I spanked her too hard. But she was telling me to."

I turned off the first TV and herded him into his bedroom. He kept laughing. He fell on top of me heavily from behind, with our hips stacked and hinging over the edge of his bed.

"What happened?" he asked.

"Yeah, what did happen? Why did you send those pictures?"

"Well, I guess it was a little bit about my ego. I try not to do that but . . . it's so important."

"It's so important?" I said. He dissolved into laughter. Too high to make sense. I thought I heard him call me by my work name, Laura, but I didn't want to dwell on it and I didn't think he'd be able to answer me even if I asked. Later I wondered if he'd been studying my online presence at the same time as he looked up my boyfriend on LinkedIn and that's why it was fresh in his mind.

"It was so cute when you said you were in love with me," he said, his head in my shoulder blade, still laughing. But I never told him I was in love with him. I said I loved him, and I know everyone else thought the distinction was meaningless, but it mattered to me.

"You're a piece of shit," I said, but now I was laughing, too. Angry, incredulous laughter. It'd been a while since I smoked but none of the drugs I'd tried ever made me into a different person, only a more transparent version of me in whatever mood I was in. So when he said it was cute, and he laughed, it felt like a confession that he'd been toying with me all along.

On the bed a moment later he made a move with his hand toward my face that made me think for a minute he was angry, too, like he wanted to touch me with violence, and I felt so much aggression well up inside me; it was one of those moments when the animal part rose with full readiness and verve to say, "Yes. Finally. Finally."

I wanted to hurt him with sex, with my body. I didn't know what other tools to use.

"Oh baby, I missed you. I missed you so much," he said, kneeling above my face. I moved my mouth off of him and said, "My god, can't you ever take a break?"

And he laughed and said, "What, we just started!"

"No, I mean give this a rest," I reached up for his lips with my hand. "Just shut up."

But he couldn't. "How's your mom?" he asked while inside me from behind.

"Thinking about you, probably. How are the 8,000 other girls you're fucking?"

"Not one. Not a one," he muttered. "No one. No one compares."

When I talked to Bea before I went over, I said I didn't understand what he had to gain from continuing to try to pull me to him. But then he straddled my face and plunged into my throat and I thought, *Oh.* He grabbed my hips and flipped me over, and my knees and hands swam underneath me but he dragged me toward him and then yanked me up, positioning me like I were a doll: *Oh.* Free sex from a hooker. It didn't hurt, it was funny. Not funny enough to smile about. But neither was it scary.

To be maneuvered and manhandled like an oversized Fleshlight—the truth was, I liked it, because he wasn't putting me in any position I rejected. I was fascinated by the feeling of not being able to control my own body outside the confines of what he wanted from it. It was the best sex we'd ever had, my orgasm strong and easy.

"Your hair is the perfect length," he said, wrapping it around his fist. "Everything is perfect." And then it began building from a breath into a murmur into a low speech:

"I love it. Love all of it. Sarah . . . Laura . . . _____. Whatever your real name is. I love you."

I dreamed of that moment once, him calling me my real name, telling me he loved me while plugged deep inside. It meant nothing to me now.

≈

As far as my body was concerned, I woke up the next morning wanting more. But then I want more even when he's in me. That's me, always; that's my whole life. I have so much, I love having so much, and yet I still want more.

He took our fucking as a sign that things were restored to normal. He texted and emailed frequently. I was distant but not unresponsive. He told me he loved me with some regularity. I still loved him too—it doesn't turn off—but I wouldn't say it back.

Integrity, I'd kept thinking during that first time seeing him again. My brain processing while my body got lost. I wanted to tell him, "You don't have to work so hard to get what you want. You could get what you want with integrity." I don't think he knew. It's like he was climbing barbed wire to get into a locked back door, when he could have knocked and been let in the front.

Or maybe he did know. After all, it wasn't that his actions didn't have clear consequences but rather that the consequences didn't matter to him. He said he'd stopped going to his usual gym because of how often he ran into his ex, Krista. They would make eye contact but not speak. Hearing him talk about her reminded me that he's avoidant and cowardly, but not a threat.

"She got fed up," he said of their not talking. And he let her go.

∽

Because our sex the first time back together had been so good, I went over again. But this time his high had him struggling to stay hard and it wasn't sexy. I left disappointed but even more prepared for a real end. Either we'd fuck and not try for a friendship, or I'd fade out of his life entirely.

I gave him one more chance so I could find out which it was. He was baked then, too. Maybe it was just that he found someone good to buy from, or maybe work wasn't going the way he wanted it to, but he was smoking a lot, too much. I could tell from our communication and he admitted it in person as well. He'd get stoned instead of jerking off, which to me seemed a serious sign. He'd get stoned before he went to the gym.

The third time, the last time, when he started losing his erection I said, "I'm leaving," and began moving out from under his body.

"What?!" He thought I was joking, so he laughed.

"I'm leaving, man, I came here to get fucked!"

"Just give me a minute. You're not going anywhere." He pressed me back down. "You'd seriously leave?"

"Hell yeah," I laughed.

"You fucking bitch. You slut." He gathered me up against him. He put his hand on my throat. He pressed inside me. "You try to leave while I'm fucking you? Don't you ever fucking leave. I'll find you. I'll come up behind you in an alley. I'll grab you when you're coming out of your building, when you're done with work, and I'll fuck you right there. Don't you ever fucking leave, you hear me?"

I was still laughing. I wasn't afraid of him. He'd hurt me as much as he was going to, no matter what power he thought he had left.

His energy was short-lived. After a few minutes of thrusting, he pulled out and dropped to the bed on his back.

"Krista wants me to come over," he said, catching his breath.

"What, tonight?"

"Yeah, she says we should talk."

"Don't do that. Don't go over. You're too high."

"Yeah but I don't know what to tell her about why I can't."

"You can't tell her you're blazed and want to have the conversation sober?"

"Should I say that?"

"No, send her some pictures of you fucking another girl. She'll like that."

"What, really?" He propped himself to look at my face, then laid back down. "Oh, you're joking."

"No, I think that would be fantastic. Just, like, send her a video of you fucking some chick. Women love that."

"You're trying to mess with me," he said. "That's not nice." He turned plaintive in a way I'd never seen before: "Will you tell me what to say? Will you write it for me?"

I was on my side, looking at him. You can't turn off love. But you can decide how you act. "He's not a good person," my boyfriend had yelled at me more than once. "It's not good for you to be around him."

"I have so many thoughts about you," I said to him now.

"What, tell me," he said, and I just shook my head.

"I think you're going to have to figure it out for yourself," I said, "through trial and error." I was thinking of how many errors he'd made with me, and how he hadn't figured anything out. But maybe he would now, once I was gone.

I started my drift. He sent me little messages trying to pull me back in. At first just through casual conversation and small talk-type questions, which I ignored. Then he forwarded me an email chain of ours he titled "Love Letters."

"We were so cute," he said. It was just us arranging a time to meet, a year ago, through Craigslist: where, when, complimenting each other's pictures. Once he asked what I was up to and responded with the right pointing and the ok emoji, "The usual."

"Lmfao, you're my idol . . . I love you so much," he replied. And days later, "I wanna fuck you so bad."

"You just wanna fuck so bad," I said.

"No," he wrote back, "actually I want you to stay the night. But I know that's rarely a possibility. You know there are certain people you really connect with—you've consistently been one of those for me. Our sex is always amazing . . . I don't mean to sound cheesy but lately I've been getting tired of having sex just to have it. I wanna have sex with people that I care about, people that stimulate me mentally and physically and make me feel good and have good energy . . . People who are special to me. I try not to bother you because I know you have a whole other life—but the truth is that I think of you nearly every day at some point (little things like your smile, or your demeanor). It may sound juvenile but I don't care because it's the truth and it's how I feel."

I never responded.

∾

On that first night back together, before I left, he asked, "Do you remember the first time you came over?" He'd done this so many times, and almost always when I was trying to go home.

"Yes."

"You were wearing a raincoat?"

"A trench."

"Yeah, it was beige?"

"And an orange dress," I said.

"And you started going down on me and I thought, 'Who is this girl? Where did she come from?'"

I'd heard all that from him before. He loved to tell the story of our first time. But suddenly I had a vision of a woman doing this to him, reminiscing about the first time they met or the first time she saw him, teaching him possibly without him even realizing it: this is how you show someone you care about them.

Then all I could see was his mimicry. I googled the "kiss you so hard" line I'd been struck by him texting me weeks ago and found it as a common Instagram meme. I searched for another quote he'd seemed proud of, that he recounted telling to another woman once—"I'll rip off your logic and make terrible sense to you"—and it was the same.

I didn't even have to go looking to make discoveries. A month or more later when I was on the other coast, I saw a local Craigslist ad featuring a cock shot George had used in his original ad. I'd always chalked up the discrepancy between his dick and the one in the picture to funny lighting and a clever angle, but no—it had simply been stolen. I thought of the "kale yeah" shirt he'd given me, the one he claimed to have bought for me, which was an XL when I wear an XS.

"I figured you probably wanted some extra room," he said, and I became certain he won it at a festival or that someone else he fucked gave it to him as a gift. This was how I knew it was over. It wasn't that he'd lied to me. It was that I pitied him for his lies.

And when he reminisced about our first meeting, a wistful feeling came over me. Not for him, but for sex with a total stranger, which is probably my favorite thing in the world. I realized how much I missed walking into an unfamiliar home, seeing an unfamiliar man. How much I missed the anticipation and curiosity and the defined unknown in the moments before. I hadn't met anyone new that way in a long time because he had been all I wanted. Now I was free.

∽

I couldn't fault him entirely for copying behavior to learn it or understand it. I don't think it's necessarily synonymous with insincerity. But it is at least synonymous with immaturity.

The week after we fucked for the last time, I cut my hair. I met Ari. I met Tom. I met James. I met Bryan. And my boyfriend bought a new home so we could move in together.

THE URGE SYSTEM

December 1, 2014

Too many men have the same name. In the pie chart of whom I've had sex with, a considerable slice would be Johns—one of whom is a large, dear man I've seen regularly for several years. The first time we met was for an entire day and night, and I texted my boyfriend that I might finally quit, because I couldn't keep enduring the sex with this man, or with anyone paying me ever again. I just wanted to be done.

I felt like I was falling apart, and I almost never panic. I couldn't make sense of his lumbering body over mine, all the sweat, the saliva, the panting. The sheets wet in a ring like a chalk outline around us. The fundamental strangeness of our forms together: the age difference, the size, the histories. Like two dolls mashed together by a graceless child. He insisted on eating me out for so long, so many times over. I think he'd been regularly seeing one of those "mature" escorts who takes it upon herself to teach a man "how to please a woman," as if paid sex should be like sex with an unpaid partner. That infuriates me.

But I didn't quit, to state the obvious. And I love him now, now I know all his sweetness. He's been incredibly kind and generous to me. Sometimes he makes me angry or annoyed, just like anybody else, but mostly I'm all warmth for him. And if it weren't for him I wouldn't have met Nick.

They don't live near each other anymore because Nick moved for work, but when I was last out in his city, Nick happened to be there, too, for a weekend trip with his guy friends. I was supposed to have an hour and half between landing and working but my plane was late and I ended up with only 30 minutes. Nick and I had been texting for at least an hour, trying to figure out a place to fuck, and we finally settled on a bathroom in the hotel where I had to be. Not that Nick knew I had to be there, or knows anything about what I do.

I staked us out a capacious single stall on the highest floor, near the rooftop, and waited on the bench near the elevators. We did an awkward dance around the employee who tried to hold open a door for us to go to another part of the building.

"You look damn good," he said, smiling, once we were shut inside. He gripped my hips.

"You too," I said, pressing against him. "You look … the same."

He didn't need anything more to make him hard but I wanted to do it, so I bent over at the waist to use my mouth and he watched it in the mirror above the sink. He'd already pulled my jeans and underwear down to mid-thigh before I backed up and bowed. He couldn't see anything from his angle but I arched as if he were watching my pussy from behind.

I held on to the handicapped bar around the toilet while he fucked me. It didn't last long.

"I'm sorry, you're too hot," he said. "Is there anything I can do for you?"

There wasn't.

In the wake of George, I met a respectable number of men from the internet for strictly sexual purposes. Most of the encounters were not noteworthy. I didn't find anyone I responded to the way I did George or Nick or Ethan. Some of them I forgot about entirely a day or two later. But I felt unusually placid about all of it.

Charlie was a contractor from out of town with a heavily muscled body and a boyish face. He was easy to be with and could stay hard for a while, but had a dick too skinny to be any fun. Quinn talked a great game about being dominant and we sexted furiously for a week before we finally got together. He trembled walking next to me in the wind; I could feel his entire body shaking when he grabbed me to kiss me.

Ari was thoroughly handsome and winsome. I kept forgetting he had a halfway beard even as I felt it against me. I touched his neck, his throat, liberally, like I owned him. "I bet you know how to make a man feel like a god," he said to me. Constant compliments like that, superlative and sincere. But his beautiful cock and fingers were a total waste; even after I put my hand on his to show him how I wanted him to move it between my legs, he couldn't understand. He came immediately, over and over again. By the sixth time he pushed inside me it was only pain but the good kind of pain, better than nothing, and I made the same noises I'd been making before. Painful sex can still satisfy something.

He spent the night, and I ached to get off for every hour of it. He was maybe the best find since we still regularly send each other selfies and praise. I'm happy to be in contact with his beauty and his sweet heart.

I met Tom after months of correspondence because his "girlfriend" was finally out of town. (After seeing his home, I felt certain he was married.) He asked often if I was nervous, once while he had me backed up against the low wall above the staircase at the highest level of his row home. "No," I said. "I doubt you want a dead body in your house."

While he was trying to coax me to come, I admitted I could be bratty and hold out for a long time because I liked the build-up more than the climax.

"Don't be bratty," he said in an unconvincing warning tone, the nervous way men sometimes talk to children. He was out of breath from all the thrusting.

I just giggled at him and bore down and spread wider and at the moment when it felt best to me, too, he came. He gave me a ride back home afterward, reaching over now and then to grab my thigh, my crotch, my tit. "Sorry," he would say, and drop his hand. When I saw him a second time he laid me down on the dining room table and it was over right away. He got hard and we did it again, but it wasn't as fun as before and he knew it.

I worked on figuring it out. Everybody needs to have something that matters to them. This lets me be private-but not alone. Powerful and not challenged. Full and away, drawn inside myself and then released, with the sensation and then gone.

When I was younger and newer to sex work, brand new to in-person sex work, my impulses were so strong they ruled me. I would fuck some massage clients just because I was too turned on not to, almost always without protection and never having negotiated an extra fee in advance. Usually they would leave me an extra $100 and thus a norm was established. But sometimes they didn't give any tip. One of the first times it happened I emerged from the bedroom to tell Tina, the booker: "I had sex with Mike." I was exhilarated, ashamed, confused, or none of it—I can't remember. I just remember the need to tell someone. I don't know what I thought she would say.

At least half of the others were fucking clients but they had the sense to ask for something extra, or use condoms, I hope. I had no idea about anything back then, no anchor. Then I found the ground under me and wised up. Then I lost my libido entirely and could not fathom being that girl who got so wet the man behind her could slide into her ass without any extra lube. It seemed like a detail about me someone else had made up or something I must have been faking. Who could ever, *would* ever choose to be that way?

Tina was a chubby, fast-talking girl who always had a bag of something crunchy nearby. Once a client convinced her to come into the room and watch me giving him a hand job, and he gave her a $20 tip afterward, which was exactly what he gave me. I'll never forget that.

There's a lewdness I embrace on my own now that I would never show a client. I think that's new. The personal nature of it, and the fact of it. I learned lewdness at work, for work. Practiced and honed it there, not without occasional joy and arousal. Then I gave it up because I hated sex. Now I like sex again, and I have a voracious appetite for performing it in the raunchiest ways possible. It keeps confusing me; why am I so happy to do this?

Sometimes it feels like a curse or a mental illness to want it as badly as I do now but I try to remind myself it's better than the alternative. Better than deadness. It seems the urge system has kicked in now to drive me toward correction. Overcorrection. My body, my subtle self, any layer more intelligent than my conscious mind, all collaborating to make me into this, which perhaps should be embarrassing, but isn't, because it simply feels true.

Maybe this is aging: running through a cycle, running through it in reverse, resting, diving back in. Maybe that's why, these days, I take pleasure in almost being chaste when I'm paid but wild and insatiable when I'm not, even though the refrain used to be that we'd die before giving away that which we could charge for. "We" meaning me and my sex working friends.

I don't know how they fuck unpaid these days, I only know how I do. And I'm so tired of having to understand my sex life through the lens of my job. I don't want the unpaid sex I have to be a comment on my occupation, or vice versa.

Once freedom felt like earning money for sexual labor that would otherwise go unacknowledged and unappreciated, but now doing it for free feels like freedom. Now the freedom is in not experiencing sex as work.

IN THE PAST
December 10, 2014

I cried after I met him. It was winter and I felt skinned all year, like I was stripped and raw. The cold made that vulnerability so much worse. I had a lot of money, and a lot of yearning slowly calcifying into resignation; I believed my loneliness was permanent. I tried to live like I was inside a shell but it felt more like being inside an iron maiden. "All I can think to say about 2011," I wrote, "is that I made more money than I probably ever thought I would make, double what I made the year before. I'm not sure I feel richer but I do feel older."

He dressed as though he were going to help a friend paint. He wore huge, ridiculous black gloves, like something he'd found in someone else's house, and one front tooth was slightly chipped, a different color than the rest. He asked if I had change for the parking meter. It shouldn't have been a big deal but it was. After we sat down inside a largely empty casual restaurant, I asked him what his sheaf of papers was and as I asked I saw, under the torn corner of one paper, the image of my foot. He'd printed out my pictures.

"You don't look happy," he said.

"I don't think . . . I think I . . . "

To his credit he understood. We shook hands and he got in his car and drove away and I stood on the street corner trying not to cry, waiting for a cab to approach. You have to realize, it never starts like that. The men I see are gentlemen. They at least have the air of having lived and functioned in the world for a long time. He'd cashed in a bunch of stocks, he told me that much. I won't even say what type of car he drove. I'm never this much of a snob. I never have to be.

"I am experiencing regret," he texted me. And he called, but I didn't answer. He sent me an email. ("What was it? I went home and I had everything ready and I really wanted to be with you.")

I agreed to meet him again, because I needed money for my pain. That was the only thing I knew to do with it: profit from it. Suffering was a waste only if not sufficiently compensated. Even when that man tore my asshole and I was wiping away blood in the bathroom, I thought, *I hope he leaves me a tip*. But I knew he wouldn't. And he didn't.

It was horrible. The restaurant was crowded, which was a surprise.

"Do you have the envelope?" I asked him, when I started to sense the rapid slide downhill. I never have to ask that.

"It's a bank envelope," he said.

"Ok, well, you can still slide it over to me." Not giving a fuck. Angry. I have an anger in me. It's rare that I let it come out around clients.

"It's _____ dollars," he said. I just kept looking at him. "Do you want it?"

I flashed my eyes. Who cared. Let him see my greed. "Yes."

"Then are you going to come back with me?" he whisper-hissed, leaning toward me.

"No," I said. "Not today."

"But maybe later?"

"I'll think about it . . . " Meaning no.

We'd been together for 10 minutes and he said he was going to leave. I said he should do whatever makes him comfortable, which I knew was ambivalent enough to keep him seated. He said I wasn't being open to him. We fought about what had gone wrong, misunderstanding each other.

Finally I couldn't help it; I started thinking about the table of tourists next to us, and how obvious our conversation was, how obvious our arrangement. I started smiling and he thought it was for something he'd said.

"That's the first smile you've ever given me," he said.

"That's not true," I said. "I was really trying yesterday."

"You're a hard woman," he said. "A hard fucking woman. I won't lie. It's kind of hot." We started smiling at each other, laughing a little at ourselves.

"I'll give you all the money to come back to my place right now for one hour," he said.

And his house was just like it should be—wood paneling, an old family home. His family's old home. Great, cold spaces because no one but him had been inside for some time. Full of emptiness. It felt almost abandoned, like a mausoleum holding the bedroom of a friend from my adolescence.

I took off my underwear and tights in the bathroom and stood before him on the rust colored carpet. We kissed. I got wet. I usually got wet with a first time back then. But this was very wet. He felt me with his fingers and laid me down on his bed. I cleaved to him.

"I don't want to come," he said.

"Don't," I said, clinging like a barnacle, like a monkey to its mother. I didn't want either of us to come. I wanted it to last and last. He repositioned me with pillows underneath. He pressed my face flat to the side with his palm full on my cheek. He wrapped his arms completely around me while I lay on my stomach, He said things I didn't hear into my hair. It was so good. Luminous. Inexplicable. One thick gold smear.

At one point he tried to distract himself, to stall by talking to me while inside me. "When was the last time you cried?" was one of his questions.

I didn't want to admit it had been the day before, so I said, "Recently."

It never ran smoothly with us but the jaggedness felt right. I saw him again and it was combative from the start as we sat on the couch in a hotel room. This was when I still occasionally offered in-call.

"It never gets easier with me," I told him.

"Really? Why would you say that? Why? Why are you like that?"

"I don't know why, that's just how it is."

"People have told you that?"

"Yeah, people have told me. I'm telling you what people have told me."

"It's cause you're a hard woman. I think you're a bit of a seductress, though." He said it as though he were talking to himself. "But you're a seductress."

Shuffling his sentences, repeating words as he refined his thoughts. He teased out every one of his reactions at once. Somehow that made it harder to be evasive. Maybe it confused me.

I was dressed in a black strappy tank top and my hair was in my face. I hadn't shaved because he'd asked me not to.

I said, "What's up with the aversion to showers, like you're a little kid?"

I didn't treat him like he was my client and he didn't act like he was. He almost acted like he'd been sent to deal with me, not against his will, but there was an inevitability when we were together that let me show him my edge. I knew what I could get away with; I knew my hostility was provocative, maybe necessary. I thought he was a man who needed to be challenged. Our chemistry was already there, it wasn't some fakery I had to create through polite omissions and accommodations, so my coldness couldn't threaten it.

I can't remember how we ended up in bed. I remember him pulling back the covers and me asking, "In our jeans?" And he said yes, but then we both took ours off. Partially undressed, ungracefully on opposite sides of the bed, like adversaries or spouses.

Up close, with my nose at his neck, he smelled good. I thought to tell him that but I didn't. He lips were so soft and he kissed conservatively. It made me wonder if he didn't like the way I kissed him and I almost didn't mind if that were the case. It was such a relief to not have my mouth violated by an unwelcome tongue.

"So you said you're seeing someone," I asked him, only curious. But he pulled away.

"Alright, let's set the table here," he said. I laughed at him for that and repeated it later: *Let's set the table.*

"Do you really think we have amazing sex or is that something you tell everyone?"

"I don't think I've ever told anyone that before," I said. I meant that I'd never said it to a client but I may have never said it to anyone. He was quoting an email I had written him, when I joked about needing to find someone else to do it with.

"Ok, so am I just like any other client to you? Because if I am, it's fine, I'll keep seeing you and paying you."

"And if you're not?" I asked.

"I'll . . . probably keep paying you," he said, and I laughed.

The exact words with which he asked me to tell him he was special—they escape me.

"We have an uncommon . . . " I answered with hesitancy, trying to find the right words. I can't remember what I said or if I said anything more at all.

"I want you naked and on top of me," he whispered.

"That can happen," I said.

He rolled us over. "But I want to be patient."

It's redundant to mention the wetness. He breathed something to me that I couldn't completely hear: "Last time, when you were on top of me, I came because you . . . "

We didn't get together again.

I offered him a discounted rate once, since I knew he couldn't afford me otherwise. But we still didn't meet. "I draft emails to you all the time," he wrote after multiple cancellations. "I can explain." He'd pissed me off too much by then. I didn't care what our sex had been or would be like. We didn't speak for all of 2013. He reached out again a few months ago and I could tell it was going to fall apart like before if I didn't remove an obstacle.

I have enough money. Money isn't what I need more of right now. I emailed him, "I actually want to see you."

"I would like to meet you for coffee and then make the win-win arrangement," he wrote back. "I know you are a businesswoman and I respect that."

"I have a counter proposal," I replied. "You get the hotel room, I will show up. That's it. Don't be suspicious."

"I don't mistrust you. (Double negative.) The opposite. See you in a few days at most. Or . . . what's good for you?"

"The sooner the better. I am eager. Have you changed much? In the looks department? I don't care about anything else since I only want you for your bod."

"Bod is better than ever."

I couldn't actually remember what he looked like, only what I'd written about it. *His stomach was firm with give, full but lean. I noticed his body when he got up to adjust the floor heater. Unintentional. Just right.*

We had some trouble communicating in a timely manner. He said he realized he had a filter on my email address: "I am laughing aloud, sheepishly. Wow, did I do that back then? I remember being in love with you but . . . the only times I've used such a filter is when I wanted to train myself to stop checking whether someone wrote me or not."

I would say our biggest problem is that we're both writers, the type of writers given to poignancy.

I hadn't seen him in over two years. And then we met again.

PURSUITS

December 23, 2014

He said he would be free at 11 but I wasn't sure that was definite, so when he told me he was 10 minutes away and I said I was 30, he texted back, "L!" This was from a game he invented the second time we met, where I had to tell him if he guessed the first letter of my real name. I said ok because I thought he would never get it, and then he guessed it on the first try, and I said no to that but yes to the second one, L. Earlier that morning when I tried to goad him into checking into the hotel sooner, he said, "Hold on, I'm suffering, too."

"No suffering is like my suffering," I replied. Tongue in cheek, because we were only talking about wanting sex. But don't most of us think that when we feel denied or delayed? Uniquely frustrated? The theme for this year would be my burning for it, constantly, in solitude, not knowing what "it" is but believing sex is the closest I'll get.

His exclamation at my tardiness flustered me. The hotel was swarming with conference attendees and I got the room number wrong, which made me even later. I reminded myself I wasn't working now, and how dare he make me feel like I was. I worried meeting him was a mistake. Would I know how to be with a client who wasn't a client? Is running 30 minutes behind something a nonclient would get mad about, or have a right to?

I hadn't been in this hotel in over a year. It was where George had provided protection for the outcall date that went wrong, and hotel security came—but that was years before I even lived in this city. It was the same hotel where a dominant client elaborately tied my arms behind my back, with rigging between my legs, then covered my nudeness with my buttoned coat and told me he was going to take me downstairs and walk me through the common spaces. But I was too unbothered by the idea; he decided not to.

He'd thrown the lock so the door would stay ajar, and sat in a chair at the corner of the room facing the entrance.

"Have you been waiting like this the whole time?" I asked. I'd forgotten entirely what he looked like. Seeing his face again wasn't quite recognition. It felt too fresh for that, though he wasn't a stranger. I was still reminding myself I wasn't getting paid, so I didn't have to act like I was. I didn't know if I could pull it off, whatever I thought should or could happen.

He stood without urgency to approach me. As I shut the door, I told him: "I couldn't remember what you looked like."

He blinked to show surprise, his eyes widening a bit. "Did you know it would be me?"

"I knew it would be you. I just wasn't sure what you would look like."

"I didn't forget what you look like," he said, staring at me. His face is moonish, with heavy cheeks. He'll have jowls when he's older. And his mouth is heavy, too. Soft. The chipped tooth behind the lips. A beard, still. Youth.

I thought there was no way the sex would be good, certainly not the way it was good before. It would be something to get over with, I'd already decided. A mess I made and now had to wade through. But I was wrong. It's unusual, self-erasing, amnesiac sex. No details can be sifted out. It all settles like the finest sand. The same way I forgot his face. I can't find purchase in it.

"You don't have any of it memorized?" I asked him when he said he forgot to bring a copy of his book to read from to me.

"No," he said. "I've only memorized you."

Afterward, he started addressing me and then stopped himself. "L—what's your name, by the way? Does your first name really start with L? Or did you lie to me?"

I paused only briefly. "I lied to you."

"What does your name really start with? Or are you not going to tell me? That's fine. You're not going to tell me." When we first meet, he speaks words like he's inventing them. Slow, everything considered. So it's a compliment when he starts speeding up. I take it as a sign he's relaxed.

"I like L," I said. "Why don't you give me a name?"

"Linda."

"Oh, come on. Don't punish me."

"You don't like Linda? I had a crush on a girl named Linda once. How about Lexi?"

"Lexi's ok," I said, although it doesn't suit me at all.

I'd been tempted earlier to tell him I'm the better writer. I arrived at the hotel ready to tell him that. I'm sure it's true, and I like to lean into the brattiness he tempts out of me. But I think writing is his softest spot, so that possibility started to feel cruel and irrelevant. He talked to me some about a writing group he joined, how there were people in it better established than he but they didn't seem to understand his work. It sounded predictable and immature, and sexist, too. Then he told me one of the female writers whose work he didn't think much of red-penned the submission she requested from him in conjunction with rejecting it flat out.

"For instance," he said, "she told me I'd used the same word twice in one sentence."

"Oh god, that's sad." I was embarrassed for her. "That's so . . . basic."

We walked out together. Miraculously, he'd found parking on the street for his truck. He drove me toward where I was meeting a friend for lunch and I asked him about the woman he dated a year or two ago. We talked about online dating, which doesn't go well for him, and Tinder. His phone isn't smart. I said something about fucking outside a relationship and without the expectation for one.

"I don't know why I can't have sex with other women like that," he said.

"What, like . . . for fun?" On a low level I braced, bristled. Of course with me, with a whore, he could do it.

He looked over at me, then back out through the windshield, and still paused. "No. That good."

I didn't know we were allowed to talk about it. If work sex is great, I never say so. I worry it will introduce the specter of insincerity, seem too much like a ploy for rehire. And our time together was in some limbo of not work, not not-work. Talking about almost anything seemed off-limits.

"I don't know why it is either," I admitted.

"I have my theories," he said. "Whether it's mental. Or physical."

"Tell me."

"Some other time."

"I try not to think about it too much, because . . . why look a gift horse in the mouth?" I still can't believe I said that. I started laughing at myself immediately. But I didn't have a language for describing the intensity he could inspire in my body. And I didn't really want to.

When I emailed him to ask if it would be another two years before I saw him again, he replied:

"Elle,

Two years? If so, I would think about it most days until then."

We agreed upon the following week.

Against this and around this, I had paid and unpaid sex with other men. I reached out to him because I thought he might staunch my desire, even if only briefly or locally. He didn't, and the particulars made it hard to wipe off the residue of our transactional beginning. He got a hotel, I showed up; all that was still the same. When I changed the plans for our second meeting a little, truncating it, he replied with, "Be not late."

"Don't boss me around," I replied. "We are doing this as real people now."

He wrote back, "Ok, that was a misunderstanding. I apologize. I meant more along the lines of:

- The sooner the better! I am eager
- No, don't make me wait that long!"

It wasn't his fault. I was overly sensitive and stressed by our circumstances. It's hard enough for me not to think of my time with men in hour increments, even when I'm there uncompensated, and so the second time I came to him, I felt businesslike and brisk.

He booked a room at the new hotel where I'd met the heavily muscled visiting contractor a few weeks before. That man was from Craigslist, not a client, but the fact remained that there are few hotels left in the city without specific memories for me, and few hotels in the world that don't evoke a working mindset and mood. When I walk into one alone with someone else's room number in my head, I turn off more, I turn on more. I dim and shine at the same time. There's hardly any me left in it.

He apologized as he hung up my coat, asking if I saw his email.

"It was a misunderstanding," he repeated. "Misunderstandings. They're more common than you might think."

It was the only time we had sex that felt disconnected. I wasn't there for it. But after, I asked him if he had brought me his book and responded derisively when he said he hadn't.

"I find that, when I gave people the book, it seemed to decrease its value," he said. "They wouldn't even read it. But if someone asks for it . . ."

He drove me to my next destination again. We passed a TGI Friday's I exclaimed over. I'd forgotten it was there—I wasn't usually in this neighborhood—but I'd gone to grad school nearby, for only a year, and I had the fleeting notion I'd met someone there once. An old client who became my best regular, with whom I never had sex? My boyfriend at the time? Someone of some authority at the university? I couldn't remember. It didn't matter.

"It was a long time ago," I told him, since I'd been musing aloud. I would start stitching together a scrap of memory, then reject it for the next. It's possible I'd never met anyone there. I felt knocked stupid by my age, shook my head at myself, and said, "Wow . . . Sunrise, sunset," laughing before I could even get it all out. Now quoting awful, inappropriate clichés to me felt like an inside joke with him. Me, the better writer.

"Is that supposed to be, like . . . time? Or the movies?" he asked. No judgment or disapproval, just trying to understand.

I laughed harder. We were where I needed to be.

"Ok, thank you." I said. "Do you want a kiss goodbye?"

He didn't answer. I leaned across the expanse of his truck's cab, and kissed his cheek. I felt there were so many possibilities hanging between us, and I rejected them all because I didn't want to assume the responsibility to do anything else. Why did they have to be mine to reject? Had he offered me anything? Was I offering him? I felt like he knew this was an ending and he was too passive to do anything other than observe. I was sure he wouldn't email me again unless I wrote to him.

∼

I planned not to, but then I changed my mind. For no concrete reason. Boredom, curiosity. A small nudge could alter everything, I thought. Crack open the egg of whatever weird dynamic rolled between us.

"Are you ok? I worry about you. I also really want to read your book."

"You always surprise me," he replied. "What is your P.O. Box?"

I gave it to him. "You're so laconic for a writer," I said.

"Nice try. That's you, L," he replied. It seemed he was wounded, but maybe I imagined it.

The book arrived two days later. There was no inscription.

It was one strong sentence after the other, sometimes at a detriment to the larger narrative, but compelling. He created a mood; he sustained it. He struggled with self-editing like we all do, but his book built, it accreted power like a good poem. I could give him advice to make it stronger, but that is also praise; it was worth making even better.

He wrote things like, "I glanced up at those dusk-lit faces. I saw no hunger on them. I hoped mine didn't show." And, "I leaned over to kiss her. She pulled away. I felt fine about it—she was way beyond me." There was a short section about almost receiving a hand job from another man: "I didn't like being so controlled. Look at what just happened. I didn't want to need it so badly that I would do any crazy thing."

"I got your (uninscribed!) book," I wrote to him. "I feel the effort you put into it but that's because we know each other. It wouldn't distract me if

I were a regular reader." I told him it was good, and that he knew I wouldn't say that if it weren't.

"You might try talking to me sometime, you know," I added. "We could even become friends."

"I want to be friends," he said. "I want you to want it inscribed."

But he didn't give me anything more, and I was sure I needed more. I felt sick to my center of extending myself for men who didn't seem to appreciate it or be capable of reaching back. My life is so much work, are they all this much work? My problem was minor, I know that, but I'd been beating my head against the wall of male-female failure and I just wanted some relief. I wanted to feel agitated love and connection for someone who could mirror it back to me. The expression was all I wanted. Not dating, not commitment, not a promise. Only a response in kind.

The harder I looked for allegiance with men, the less I turned up. And I didn't think I could do it anymore, walk a man through helping me justify wanting him or becoming bound to him. I couldn't teach him how to be an emotional peer to me. His effort couldn't only come in the form of a tepid response to my initiations.

Or so I told myself. But then I looked at all the strength in my desire. The power in it. My desire was bottomless, so my energy was bottomless. I was inexhaustible no matter how tired I felt. I had a tremendous capacity to persist. And maybe I was only chasing the pain of dissatisfaction but I would rather chase than rest.

"Then/now what?" I asked. We emailed this way, hours and days in between a handful of words.

"Now we hang out, and support each other's dreams and pursuits," he replied.

"Send me your writing," I said. "Any and all of it."

BEGINNING

January 6—September 28

THE INK IN HIS NAIL BEDS

January 6, 2015

The first time was endless and perfect, but in many ways a blur, perhaps because there was hardly a moment when he wasn't hard. After, I would most remember how it felt to be on my stomach, arching my hips to him with his hand on my upper back, and the way he moved making me wonder, *How did you get so good in bed?* But not feeling ready to ask him.

When I used my mouth, I felt spurts of pre-come on my tongue, little gushes like nothing I recall any man doing before. Work makes me forget how easy it is to swallow when I'm with someone I like. How natural. Every time he got up for a condom, he sat on the edge of the bed to roll it on, and I snaked my arms around him and pressed my cheek to his back. There was no moment when we weren't touching.

I'd told myself not to get my hopes up, but, *How are we going to go without fucking each other every day?* was in my head before we even met, and I was right to wonder.

"How do you feel?" I asked him after the fifth time. Meaning: *horny, tired?* I wanted to allow for the possibility that he was ready to leave.

"Like lava," Max replied.

He told me where to go. He found a bar for us and waited there, two blocks from my hotel. I was as excited to see him as I would be for any good friend. No nerves, just happiness. I approached him from behind, swiveled into the seat on his right. I tried his drink, and he ordered another. My eyes kept falling on the mezcal, so he ordered some of that too, for my curiosity. "That smells like . . . the worst thing I've ever put near my nose," I said. I passed it to him.

"It's smooth," he said, nodding as he swallowed. "There's no burn. Like, I don't want to drink it, but I can see why people make it."

"It tastes like ink," I said, my face twisting. "Ballpoint pen ink."

"Tastes like prison tattoos," he laughed. His whole sweet, tall body folded onto a stool. He held his knit hat in his lap. I wore heels and when we stood up together, he was still a head above me.

I'd just finished the first date with a client who pored over my pussy with superlative praise. "You're way too good at that," he said when I went down on him, "even for someone who's supposed to be good." A writer, who marveled at my larger self, "someone so lovely wants to sit alone in a room for hours."

I met Max on Tinder. His pictures were playful, goofy but not contrived. He was participating in the requisite assortment of large life activities: marveling at tropical wildlife, somewhere by a lake, athletic in the water. Not bare or ostentatiously muscled; no mention of height in his bio though he linked to his website for his art. He didn't seem to be trying to appeal to anyone, not strategically or self-consciously at least, but nor was he not trying. This wasn't a thoughtless man.

I showed my friend Fab one of his pictures and she said "I normally hate shirts like that. But I don't mind it on him." He had an air of low-key confidence, like why wouldn't he feel good about who he was?

First we talked about tattoos, then yoga, our back and forth strung out over days. I wasn't in so urgent a mindset that I steered hard toward blunt and explicit, the way I sometimes do. But I liked our banter. It was quirky and cute and charming.

When he stuck to the literal as I tried to edge toward innuendo, I called him "hard to flirt with." He sent me back a single 400-word message, three long sentences about my smile, my body, and how often he wrote and rewrote replies with the concern of seeming weird or creepy.

He's better with words than I am. I read them with shock and slow-spreading delight. It was a discovery, what he said, like we were both in the same secret club, a club I hadn't even known existed.

"What's your number?" I asked. "I want to send you a picture."

It was 2 a.m. on a Thursday. Eighteen hours before I would see him, before the space created by our minds would be filled with our bodies.

All this happened shortly before Christmas. On the 23rd, I was with another client, lingering in the hotel bathroom when I received one of his now-classic huge replies.

I'd written, "I'm thinking about you. Is that a) weird b) irrelevant c) good d) all of the above?"

No one but us will ever understand the night we had, I thought to myself, and then it occurred to me that maybe even he wouldn't, maybe it was an asymmetrical experience that left little impression on him but had carved a wedge out of me.

His response included "d) all of the above if that includes really, like all the possible things, because I feel every nerve in my body is firing when I think about how it felt to be inside you." But there was so much more than that.

I squatted down on my towering heels, nearly weak with joy. I gulped it all like water.

He was on his way to yoga, and I told him, "I'm so jealous of that whole stupid class, what did they do to get to be near you, I don't believe any of them earned it." I knew they hadn't. I hadn't.

I tried hard to hold onto the sensory memory of our perfection. Work sex was extra unpleasant after. One client plunged away the phantom feel of Max's cock as he also shoved his tongue in my mouth and left it there. It felt like something of mine was dying while his penis went sluggish and soft inside me.

Our texts were mostly but not exclusively sexual.

I called myself greedy.

"Can it be greediness if I want to give it to you though?" he asked.

"It's a battle of enthusiasm between us," I said.

"More like a pursuit."

"Two lakes trying to swim in each other," I replied. The best way I could think to describe the night we'd had.

He mentioned an artist he liked. I asked if he knew a particular piece, and he replied with an image of it.

"It's one of the most bittersweet things I've ever seen," I said.

"My favorite flavor," he said.

I want to match Max, who is unmatchable. All I know and imagine of his life puts him in a position that I once projected for myself: entirely devoted to art, surrounded by creative people, living in the rich rim of the city. I want to be a poet for him. A poet again, or for the first time. I gave up so much for such sad reasons. I couldn't have done otherwise; it was the hole of my ego taking precedence because you can't live without an ego, but now I want to be what I once thought I was, that which I still hope to be.

I struggled to write about this because I felt like I needed to explain other things before I could explain myself in this matter—precedents and the background and such. But I didn't want to think about details of the recent past without Max, the things that happened before and in tandem with my meeting him, especially not for long enough to write about them. They bored me and I could not remember the experience of them mattering.

Everything he said and did affirmed our connection, but I needed that affirmation more, or differently, or constantly. I was alternately stricken and elated, maybe because of the high probability he would reject me if he knew about my work, my boyfriend.

The second time we were together, we talked about love. In general, and our history of it. I was terrified I'd given away something that rightly lowered myself in his estimation because I'd said, "I fall in love all the time." It was a lazy, breezy translation of "I want love all the time." It would have been predictable, understandable for him to shy away from a woman who said that. Either thing.

Even in that moment with him, I felt I could see into a possible future of dating him, loving him, still loving our sex months or years later but wanting something different, needing to fuck someone else. Eternally restless. I saw this but it changed nothing about how I felt for him. What type of walking quicksand am I? I am consumed by my emotional greed, my gluttonous heart.

"Too much is still not enough," I joked to a friend in an email when she asked if a poem was too naked. Only, I wasn't joking.

"I don't think there could even be an 'enough' with you, _____," Max said. "The ultimate cosmic qualia: unable to be had too much of." He was talking about our first night, us together, the two lakes. "If I'm going to create work based on the human condition, then I feel, as a human, that I have to be inside that. And that means craving you so hard it hurts, and waking up in my wet dreams, and trying to reach into photos of you, and getting hard in public thinking about you. Because that's all kind of overwhelmingly real and the core of being, and even when I am inside you, it all is still there as part of something larger, not some reward for patience or a means for me getting off."

I want to be a poet for him. I know I already said that. Maybe you don't understand, I don't stop wanting it.

What he says is so beautiful and so purely him, I'm betraying him by sharing it. How dare I? It is unforgivable. But I feel like I couldn't talk about him without doing so, because my words alone would not do him justice. And to not talk about him would be a form of ingratitude, which is also unforgivable.

I tried to pin down the extreme integrity he embodies.

"You're fully integrated," I told him. "That's why you're so compelling."

I can't describe to him his own qualities; I fail in the attempt. Does he see how he can be both incredibly invested, potently present, and yet not pushing or straining? Or rather, does he see how most people live in a lower place where they don't notice this state in others, don't conceive of it as possible, while those who do see it work for decades in aspiration? When he asked me my favorite yoga pose, I told him it was half-moon. I love all the balances but particularly that one for its humbleness, its vulnerability. How lowly it looks compared to showier poses, but how inherently radiant.

"He's sincere," Fab said. That's the best word for it, his balance of intention, action, and restraint. Right effort. Perfectly measured. I have no gauge with him, how he may look to another person, how someone who isn't me might see him, but I desire everything about him.

The ink in his nail beds, I wrote down in my notebook, and nothing else on the page.

I am rattled by the excess between us. I try to regain my footing by looking for more to fill the ground beneath. The ground falls away as it is filled.

I can't remember why, but I told him about almost running away from home when I was 16, almost taking the bus to New York with whatever minor cash I could manage, but not following through because, when I finally told my best friend, she wept and hugged me and begged me not to.

He asked what about my family made me want that, but it wasn't my family. I fought with them, of course, but I was loved; they did nothing wrong. My best friend felt the same sense of rejection. Of course people in your life take it personally. But it's not a deficiency of theirs. A dog doesn't answer a whistle because something is missing. The sound of the whistle just erases everything else.

It's probably not true that I can't not talk about him. Maybe for once in my life I could try not dumping open my heart in front of anyone who will look at me, emptying it like it's a messy purse. Maybe I don't need an audience to watch me sort through every roughly handled, occasionally useful item in my bag until I've figured out why I still carry it around. I have a deep fear that someone who knows him would read this and recognize him, or that he would read this and recognize himself. It's not that I don't experience dread but that I don't alter my behavior for it. Surely that's a maladaptation.

It's possible he wouldn't care. If he doesn't mean what he says, for instance. And especially after George, I try not to forget that option, no matter how authentic he seems. People lie out of meanness, laziness, habit.

"I need to D E T A C H from you," I told him in a fit of weakness. And then to make it less scary, I directed it to sex: "Could you maybe borrow a lamer dick for this week, I would really appreciate it."

"I can give you more and more of many things, but lame dick I cannot do," he said. "At least not for you—seems impossible based on the way your body changes mine."

"I thought you were a biology expert," I said. "Get a pheromone patch or something."

"This is beyond biology," he replied. "New metaphysics."

Does he mean what he says? I don't trust myself to have any perspective. I look at his messages again and again.

That's how to cultivate obsession even if you're only trying for reassurance. Document it. Keep touching it. Make sure it's really there.

"You want moments to be special," my boyfriend said to me. "You want your life to be full of meaning and deep connections. I wouldn't be with you if I didn't admire that about you."

I've thought a lot about something my mother said to me a year or two ago, regarding what a serious child I was. "I thought it was because you expected so much from the world," she said. To think she recognized that before I was bathing myself.

Hearing my boyfriend say it now felt like an observation that could only come from someone who deeply cared for and knew me, someone who paid attention. From family. I almost cried.

"But I won't lie," he said. "You're tough to love."

All my pictures on Tinder are selfies because I spend so much time by myself or in incriminating circumstances that should not be captured. Because all my closest friends live inside devices for me, scattered across the country in pockets I rarely visit or visit frequently but without time of my own. Because I gave my 20s to my neuroses and I don't regret it, but all it left me with was piles of cash. And the powdery ashes of my most acute fears, which only grow again and again out of perpetually fertile soil.

Because I have no large life pictures. Because I keep trying to kick out the walls of my life to let in a largeness that cannot be photographed, or indicated, or contained in any way.

INDIGO
January 14, 2015

Max had to go away for work. He'd be across an ocean for three weeks, back for less than one, then away again for a month. I let this information bounce off me when we first met but as his time to leave approached, it pierced and stuck. From the start we took sleeping together literally, only fucking on occasions when we would spend the night together and only seeing each other when we would have sex. That usually meant 14 or 16 hours of doing nothing but mainlining the good parts of each other, then separating for days. Our encounters were crystals of intimacy; compressed, glittering, flinty.

The only thing that would alleviate my sadness over his incipient absence was fucking. The last time, he pulled out and came on my stomach and then relaxed his weight into it with my arm around his neck.

I felt myself start to beam, joy flooding the pockets where the sorrow's kept. "Again!" I said, bouncing my calves on his back.

"You make me crazy." He shook his head against my collarbone, his smear of semen warm and damp between us. "I can't get enough of you."

"What if I forget what it's like to have you inside me?" I asked. I was trying to expose my fear to him a corner at a time, so he could assuage it. I knew the intensity was irrational but my devastation felt real.

"I'll try to remind you," he said. "We have our mind fingers, remember?" He was referring to the time I texted him about a dream of him walking his fingers over my skin, and he said he dreamt the same.

But that didn't help. "This is like feeling the end of a high, when I'm so anxious just anticipating coming down, and my friend Emma tells me, 'Smoke some weed,' and I'm like, 'I don't want any,' and I go back to feeling nervous, waiting for it to get bad."

"That happened? Or it was a dream?"

"It happened! It's a metaphor. You're like, 'Just sit on my dick, just smoke some weed.'"

"Sit on my dick and smoke this weed," he said. "That would make a good song title. This bed is too full of good ideas."

We went out to dinner and he insisted on paying. When I ordered expensive liquor at a bar, he wouldn't even let me leave the tip. We picked out the best songs on a bad jukebox. He told me about his tattooed father and his spate of brothers and I asked if they were as tall as he was, if they looked like him.

"Sounds sexy," I said, wiggling my eyebrows. "When are you going to introduce me?"

"Oh god, that would kill me," he said. "If you see anyone who looks even a little bit like me, run the other way." Whenever he told me about a male friend, he'd add, "You're never meeting him."

I checked in on him a lot. It's probably a holdover from work.

"Are you comfortable like that?" I asked of our sleeping position. Or in my hotel room: "Is the temperature ok for you?" He never really responded, and I eventually asked why.

"It doesn't seem important," he said. "So I'm too hot, so what? I'll be fine. It's like . . . watching a movie of me being uncomfortable. It feels distant. And it doesn't matter because . . . "

"Comfort is impermanent?"

"Yes," he said, happy I found the word. "It's impermanent."

"Yeah, but what isn't?"

"The self."

I looked up at him like he'd said something immature. "You really believe that?"

"I don't think there's any other alternative."

I remembered my favorite quote on this matter, maybe my favorite quote of all time: "Enlightenment, for a wave in the ocean, is the moment the wave realizes it is water." If we each are waves, we're not quite permanent. But we are enduring.

In the book written by the client I stopped seeing as a client, the man I slept with a few times for free, I found the following: "Even if this feeling fades, I will never have an excuse to forget."

It wasn't always serious; we joked a lot. When he started to talk to me about something frustrating at work, he stopped himself and said he shouldn't complain. "You can complain," I said, taking his face in my hands. "That's awful. No one should ever have to suffer the way you suffer, Max."

"Ah, I love it when you say that to me," he said.

He would talk to me the most after he came in my mouth. Things like, "You pulled that from somewhere deep. That one was raw. That come was like, still being made." And, "You sucked me dry. How do you do that? You're magical. You're a genius. A blow job genius."

"I just go down and talk to it in its own language, since it doesn't have ears. I have to use my mouth in other ways to tell it how much I like it. It's just me and him then. You're out of the picture. I staged a successful dick coup."

"Did you just say 'dick coup?'"

I knew he would have loved to see me squirt, and I can't remember how it came up but I told him how much I am capable of, how I could drench towels, about the huge puddle I left when I did it the first time. The taste so truly good, a sweet ocean.

"It's not fair, men can't just come from some new place when they get really turned on. Or, like, squirt blue come. That's how it feels when you suck me off sometimes, like you're pulling it all the way from under my ribs."

"Mm," I said, grinning. "I'm going to go down right now and get some more indigo."

We went out to get drinks with a friend of his. He kept his hands on me the entire time, rubbing my back and thighs while we laughed at the bar, sipping from each other's glasses. Being together was so natural.

Outside, the minute we parted from his friend, he slipped his arm around me and drew me into his height and said, "Hi, beautiful." Just as he does sometimes when we change positions and find ourselves facing again, and he can see my smile.

I did a bad thing after; I looked at his phone while he was in the bathroom. He wouldn't talk to me about what was going on between us, but maybe he talked to his friend.

"_____'s coming over around 9," Max texted.

"[eight mouth emojis] _____?" his friend replied.

"Haha, yeah," Max said. "I told her she's not allowed to meet any of my straight friends. She's the type of girl who talks about threesomes and I can't tell if she's joking."

"I bet she isn't," his friend said.

I assumed the mouth was a blow job thing, and that made me feel good. I loved going down on him. Before we left for the bar, we sprawled on the bed and I pushed my body down his so I could kiss his stomach and hold his hips, occasionally placing my mouth over the fat swell under his jeans.

"I'm so . . . wet and . . . happy right now," I said in between. "It's so close. It's right there."

"An eighth of an inch, and getting wetter."

'We should see how long it takes to get so wet the fabric just dissolves." I slid up and pressed into him.

He told me about the text conversation later anyway, but he left out the part about the lips. Maybe he wanted me to clarify if I was joking about the threesomes but I didn't comment on it. I played one of my most favorite songs, the first song I ever sent to him.

"I like the things you do, girl," he said, quoting it, with his face near mine.

I started listing my friends to myself as a type of invocation to ward off the aching: Bea, Emma, Melissa, Fab, Annora, Elizabeth. All the women who support me, who make me laugh, who tend to my heart with patience. It's the same way I used to pray as a child, naming everyone I cared for (family, teachers, friends, stuffed animals) until I fell asleep. Every tie branching to another, further and further down a chain of love. My aunt's cats. My friend's mother. A spiritual version of counting sheep.

I knew Max was half man, half fetish, that I was conjuring him the way my clients conjure me, from their own desires, imagination, impressions, intuition. And for all the times he called me "perfect"—when I texted him something he liked, when I told him to feel how wet I was after putting my mouth on him—I was sure it went both ways. I wanted to talk about it with him since I was going through it with him, but I didn't want to be the needy girl, the emotional girl. I went in obliquely—"Does art ever hurt you?" I texted. "Not to make it, but to take it in?"—or tried to bring it more precisely, but without pressing the point.

"Why do you feel so indispensable to me?" I asked him.

"You want an answer or is that a rhetorical question?"

"I want answers when I demand answers," I said. But I wasn't demanding anything from him, only hoping for it.

Getting any explicit statement about his mindset was hard.

"What mood are you in?" I'd ask after an hour or two in bed.

"I don't have moods," he said.

"Then what do you have?"

"Planetary shifts."

"Wow. How often?"

"Every five days or so. With you it resets."

"Oh. Well . . . " I'd rephrase. "What do you want right now?"

"To keep fucking you."

"How nice it must feel," I said, pulling him toward me and wrapping my thighs around his waist, "to know you're going to get what you want."

When I think of him, I think of the way he inhabits his body, how he'll squat down a little in public to draw me to him, how he almost always holds me while he kisses me, folding his frame around mine.

We stayed in bed for too long the last morning and then he said, "I don't think I can do breakfast," which we'd planned on. He had to go finish something at his former home, settle with the landlord.

"Oh! This is . . . such a shock!" I said mockingly, which was unfair. He'd never shied away from being in public with me. He'd held me in the daylight on more than one street. But he couldn't give me everything I wanted, not right now, not ever, and that knowledge was always there, ugly as a cactus.

That same morning, I received an email from a client who'd sent three long letters in the 24 hours before, desperate requests to confirm that our connection was real, not imagined or one-sided. I was too busy getting lost in Max to reply.

"I have considered the possibility that you have the ability to comfortably make serial connections of that intensity, and live that way," the client wrote. "It explains a lot of things."

He also said, "I've never been afraid to look stupid, just afraid to *be* stupid."

"I don't have moods either," I'd said to Max during a lull in our sex.

"Oh really? What do you have?"

"I have emotions."

"I need to unplug from the Max outlet," I told him as I wiped my private tears with the sheet. Every cell of me was begging, *Please affirm our connection so it will be easier to let you go. Say something direct and plain.*

"I'm still getting recharged," he said, strongly hugging me to him. I squeezed him back and we stayed like that, re-hugging when the tension faded.

But I did need to separate, for my own ego and my own sanity. Not merely leave it in the hands of physical distance but make a choice inside myself. Otherwise, my appetite for him was boundless and required drastic intervention. That's why I wanted so much to enlist his help.

I kept hearing those Sharon Van Etten lines in my head: "Break my legs so I won't walk to you/Cut my tongue so I can't talk to you."

I couldn't stop crying, though I tried to hide it by keeping my face still and letting tears roll over the bridge of my nose, down my cheeks into the pillowcase, soundless. I was on my period, and I'd pushed in and pulled out makeup wedges all night to keep my blood from getting on him.

"Why are you leaving?" I asked, his body above, my raw pain below.

"I didn't know this would happen," he said, with genuine regret.

I want to be close to you too much, I wrote down but didn't say. When he was gone, I looked at the words, alone. It was a new year.

A GOOD ONE

January 26, 2015

On one of the remaining nights Max and I were in the city together, I went to see Aaron, a guy I'd found through Craigslist a month before. It was our fourth time seeing each other in a string of impressively drama-free encounters. Our politics and tastes were too aligned for our interaction to be limited to the physical. It was still the primary motivator, but there was an ease and increasing kinship with Aaron that I thought was worthwhile and good for me, not merely as an antidote to the intensity with Max but in and of itself.

Those signs were there even before we met. That first time, on his way over, we texted about veganism and music. I offered to play Sunn O))), the only metal I have on my iPod, since that's what he makes.

"Just don't head bang or do air guitar while you're in me," I told him.

"I don't even think you can do that to Sunn!" he said.

"Oh, I can," I replied.

He was blanketed in tattoos, younger than me, and one of the only men I'd ever met for sex who didn't give away any signs of jittery anticipation. I alluded to my real job and he indicated he understood without it becoming a big deal. I prefaced one story with "not to out myself as a huge slut, but . . . " to which he said, amused, "I think we're probably on equal footing in terms of experience." And like Ethan, he was unbothered by the blood.

"I'm sorry," I said. "It's from my cervix."

"Yeah, I—I kind of figured that out," he said.

"Right, sorry. I'm sure you're used to it. Did it freak you out when you first started having sex?"

"Well you know, it's all scary when you're 15."

"I'm going to come," he told me after 20 minutes or so, in an entirely conversational voice. Not carried away at all, but like we were discussing where to get dinner. It's so funny to me when guys do that.

"Oh. Should we stop? Because it's fine. Do you not want to?"

"I'm going to!" he said, laughing some. "In, like, two seconds."

"Oh, ok! Well, make it a good one." And I pulled his body into mine, trying to spread more, lift more, take more so it would be as strong for him as it could possibly be.

∾

Aaron could not have come at a better time. With lunatic zeal, I'd been searching for a man worth sleeping with, and failing, badly. I kept turning up guys with erection problems, premature ejaculators, and men who lied about salient physical details and/or sent fake pictures. Being with the ex-client was too complicated and he was too passive.

Ari, sweet and good-looking and endowed as he was, still came immediately every time he was inside and once said, while we were rocking and rubbing against each other in a long, sexy, non-penetrative cuddle, "Sometimes I like this part so much I don't even want to do anything else."

There was the mediocre married man and the quaking self-described dominant. The thin-dicked contractor and the comedian who couldn't get it up, who I tried to flee from while he collected pieces of clothing that I was ready to leave behind. Every hookup seemed doomed, my normally strong screening instincts erased by desperation. My intensity changed the task from recreation to burden. I wasn't even sure why I was looking anymore since my libidinal impetus felt long gone or at least buried under unbelieving despair.

The abrupt, effortless joy of fucking Aaron—how relaxed he was, how easy to talk to, how hard and, ok, how big—accounted for my behavior the day after we met, when I proposed I visit him late that night. He was as sleepdeprived as I was, but game for it, and he lived alone in a beautiful home so location wasn't an issue. The sole obstacle was considerable; I'd be with a client, spending the overnight portion of a two-day date together. But not seeing Aaron again, immediately, was unacceptable. The only option was to sneak out.

The client in question is a light sleeper. He always wakes up before me. He claims he's not tired when I'm ready to turn in. We've known each other for years, and if I get up to use the bathroom during the night, he will insist on trying to have a conversation with me when I get back into bed, to kiss and pat and snuggle me with the energy of someone wide awake. I didn't know this was something anyone would do to another sleepy person in the middle of the night, to try to rouse them so fully and so unnecessarily, until I started spending time with him.

I could hardly have selected a more logistically challenging person to escape from but I was propelled by my resentment for him, my lust for Aaron, and my flagging investment in work as a whole. It made for a heady cocktail. I recalled my glory days in high school, night after night of sneaking out when the penalties would have been so much greater, and was emboldened.

While the client was in the bathroom, I wadded an outfit underneath my coat, next to my boots in the first room of our suite. I tucked the only room key—he never gives me one of my own, like most do—into a spot that made it easy to grab on my way out. I waited an hour after we said goodnight and then left the bed in stages, rolling to the floor and crouching by the nightstand, staying still outside the door to the bedroom after I closed it. I wrote a note ("Couldn't sleep, went to get tea. Will be right back!") and dashed outside to a cab.

I hadn't only bled because of Aaron's size. I bled because I was just about to start my period and after being with him, my uterus was on full blast. Upstairs in his room, I told him I wasn't sure I wanted to fuck since it would mean blood all over his bed, and I'd have to try to clean myself up without ruining any of his towels.

"That's no big deal," he said.

"I know. But I don't really want the hassle. Or for you to have to do that laundry."

"I could put down an old sheet and throw it away. Or whatever you're comfortable with," he offered, dealing with it like the deeply sane person I already trusted him to be.

He knew I was "sneaking out" though I had no idea what that might have meant to him. Sneaking away from a boyfriend? A pimp? I received a reply to the Casual Encounters ad I failed to take down since posting it the night before. It was a guy offering me $2,000. I told Aaron about that while we coordinated.

"I'm overwhelmed with options," I said. "Help me."

"The struggle is real," he said. "I can't give you 2k but I can show you a good time. Plus I have cute pets."

"I don't need 2k, to be honest," I said. It felt so sweet to finally admit that, to free myself from the imperative to bite for any money dangled in front of my face. "I pick good dick and animals."

"No, it's ok," I said now, about the sheet. "I was thinking about it and I really just want to go down on you. Is that alright?"

I thought I would come just from sucking him, but I didn't. It wasn't important. His orgasm felt better to me than my own would have.

I rose a little higher on his body and kissed his stomach while he was coming down.

"I don't normally come from getting head," he said.

"Do you like it though?"

"Oh, yeah, it feels great anyway."

"I want to do it again," I said, a dumb grin plastered on my face. I kept going back, ducking down, mouthing him more as his erection subsided. "You feel so good. The head of your cock is . . . perfect. I thought I was going to come."

"Aw, why didn't you?"

"If I was rubbing against something, I would have!"

"You could have used my leg!"

"I know, but . . . "

"You being so into it makes it even better," he said.

I slid up closer to him and pulled my underwear away from my pubic bone, slyly, so both of us could see the transparent strands sewn between my lips and the fabric. "See? It's not blood."

His head fell back. "Yeah, that's so hot."

I left reluctant but elated. "Are you always this happy?" asked the cab driver. It was 3 a.m. I couldn't summon the anxiety to brace myself for a reckoning with my client the way I braced myself to be busted back in high school. I was too pleased with myself.

When I got to the hotel, he was sleeping so soundly his breathing barely changed when I climbed into bed.

～

I was supposed to meet Aaron for the third time immediately after my date with Max—I hedged my bets in case things didn't go well—but once I realized Max and I would be all night, I texted Aaron to ask about the following day instead. I had an outrageously capacious hotel suite to myself then, with a fireplace and a wall of 30-foot windows. I wanted to share it with him, though I was still thinking of Max, wondering what we might become to each other. I worried a little that trying to see Aaron would be a mistake with this other man so fresh in my mind—and my boyfriend in town, on top of it all.

I had to meet Aaron in the lobby since the elevator wouldn't go to the penthouse without a key, and to see him across the public space looking cool and natively so, like he belonged, made me feel suddenly giddy and almost shy. Upstairs, he praised the Christmas tree and talked about some of the semi-obscure liquors from the minibar. I watched him at a distance so I could take in his height and appreciate his sexiness. I noticed we both acted like he hadn't come over to fuck, or that we weren't people who'd met solely for that purpose. We were just acting like friends.

It was after inspecting the spyglass that he finally said, "This is an unwise use of time." I had to leave for a party soon, which he knew, so we only had about an hour. He joined me on the couch by the fire and we began undressing each other.

"I was thinking—I was wondering if I wanted to do it again just like last time, because it was so fun," I said. "I think I do."

"Sure," Aaron said, laughing, making a gesture with his hand. "Hey, whatever you want. But you should come this time."

I love giving blow jobs so ardently and so completely that trying to describe my penchant for it is nearly impossible and verges on humiliating. Most people will read it as desperation, the most basic and debased posturing for male approval, the verbal equivalent of oversized implants and a bad blonde dye job, which is a misogynistic way to put it. But it's a response rooted in misogyny and a judgment I fear more from other women than men. Knowing that doesn't change the fact: going down on a man I want to be with is my surest way to sexual bliss, and that's especially true when the receptive man is built like Aaron.

I regularly got off by thinking about sucking Aaron's cock. Aaron gets so hard but not hard to the point that there's no give anymore. His head stays plush and firm with a slight yield, which is so much nicer to have my tongue against, and because of his size it doesn't take much to draw the insides of my cheeks tight to him. It's easier to suck a big dick than a small one because it already fills your mouth; you just have to keep your teeth out of the way. And Aaron gathers my hair in one hand and rests his other at the base of my skull with the perfect amount of tension and pressure. There's not another man I remember striking that balance—no pain, no pulling or yanking, but still emphatic. And he mutters, "Oh fuck," periodically, but nothing more. So unobtrusive and undemanding yet still present, still participating.

That day, though, kneeling in front of him as he lay back on the couch, I started imagining what we might look like to people who could see in through the endless expanse of bare windows. He with his tattoos and careful haircut, looking like a rock star, and me blowing him like a groupie, someone who primarily wanted to have access to his luxury. I remembered being at a fancy hotel during SXSW years ago and hearing a man in the hall bellowing, venomous, "You cunt, you stupid cunt," over and over. I peeked through the peephole and saw three men and two women pass, the guys obviously in a band and the one who yelled without meeting resistance the obvious star. The others laughed uneasily, even the woman he berated. They didn't know what else to do with his aggression.

Of course a space this spectacular would only belong to a man, be acquired by a man. Of course any woman on her knees is a toy for those with power. I had in my head a recent conversation with a client during which he asked what my family thought I did and I told him my parents thought I was a kept woman. For a long time I've traded on that, relied on that assumption as protection. I've used men as camouflage; I want strangers to overlook what's rightfully mine because it makes me safer. They'll do that when I'm proximate to a man but probably even if I'm not. We're trained to be blind to a woman's power, no matter how conventionally or blatantly it manifests.

These thoughts washed out my joy for a moment, made me feel like I was at work. My own pleasure flexed away from me like a fish. But as Aaron got close the verve came rushing back, and I was there with him when he came.

Before I got up on the couch with him, I did an extra thorough job of cleaning him with my mouth. (The previous time, at his place, he had said, "I'm going to go clean this come off," and I was offended because I'd swallowed most of it.) We talked for a while in the pile of our bodies while the fire blazed.

"You're a whole lot of fun, do you know that?" he said.

"So are you," I said. "I realized when I saw you in the lobby . . . I have a crush on this guy. What with his glasses and his tallness and his veganism . . ."

"This guy," he said conspiratorially, like we were making fun of him together.

"With his . . . David Beckham t-shirt," I said, and we laughed.

I asked if the clock on the wall was right.

"Probably," he said.

"Here, lie on top of me," I said, maneuvering my body under his. "Let me feel you before you go."

We pressed and rolled together for only a moment or so before he looked at the clock again.

"Do you want to be late?" he asked. "Do you want to take off your underwear?"

Part of me was trying to hold onto the feeling of Max inside me. I thought maybe I wouldn't want Aaron changing the physical impression Max left behind. But actually being with Aaron, laughing with him and feeling his weight over me changed my mind.

Again, he told me when he was going to come and I strained against him for it.

"I want you to come in me," I said, meaning it.

"I love it so much," I said after. "Even through the condom. It feels so good. It's so intense. I love it."

"It's hot that you do." His hand rested on my breastbone but above my breast. "I can feel your heartbeat," he said.

I smiled, and placed my hand over his.

I put on "Romance in Durango" while I went to get dressed, and came back to the living room to see Aaron sitting naked on the coffee table, legs spread, facing the fire. His elbows rested on his knees, the Pellegrino I'd given him in one hand, and his eyes on the flames. I told him I thought about bringing mushrooms for us sometime and he said, "I would do that with you!"

"Why do people do tea?" I asked. "It tastes so bad that way. Does it make it get into your system quicker?"

"No," he said. "But orange juice is supposed to enhance it."

"Really?"

"Yeah, some people think it makes your trip harder."

"That's cool that you know that."

"I told you, I used to be really into drugs as a kid."

I thought of the ladder of thin horizontal scars running up the length of his inner forearms underneath the ink and I almost asked if they were intentionally aesthetic, for the look of it, just like his tattoos. But then I told myself not to be an idiot.

He zipped up my dress for me while I lifted my hair.

~

Weeks later, Max cancelled our evening plans because he couldn't get into Manhattan. He was too busy wrapping up his move and housing situation. We'd kissed goodbye outside that morning before I went to get my hair done, and I'd felt anxious and euphoric about him for the entirety of my all-day work date. It didn't surprise me that we wouldn't see each other that night, but it spurred my neuroticism to a new level. So soon, he would be gone.

I went to dinner with a work friend. We talked advertising venues and police, privacy and bad clients. After I hugged her goodbye, I sidled into the restaurant's cold, single stall bathroom and wept shamelessly. I did what I could with my face before I walked the two blocks to Aaron's.

"Would you like a drink?" he asked after he took my coat.

"Yes," I said. "I would."

We finished a low bottle of gin at his kitchen table, listening to Floor and Boris with his sweet dog at our feet. We talked about our karaoke songs, about music in general, about our demeanor while in public. He told me people sometimes try to sneak photos of him while he's on the street, because of his tattoos. We talked about the bullshit clothes that often populate street style blogs, faux vintage concert tees and the like, and I told him about my most recent attempt to wear a tank top along those lines, a raw cotton one that showed off generous amounts of side-boob if I held myself just so, but let an entire tit fall out if I moved the wrong way.

"Ultimately, it looked like I was nursing," I said.

He talked about his friends and I told him a bit about George, mainly my learning about his time in prison. I also told him about Nick, whose texts started showing up as sent from his email account late last year. Because I wasn't sure who it was, I googled the name in the address, and the results displayed a row of pictures of Nick's handsome mug.

"But they were all of him in a button-down collared shirt, and I looked a little closer and he was crying," I said. "He was in a courtroom. Crying. Because he'd just been sentenced to eight years! Another felon. Can you believe it? So now that's the joke, I don't get with anyone who hasn't served hard time. I met them through Craigslist, too. You're the only clean one."

Not without a sense of competition, Aaron shared his many arrest stories, and then we batted back and forth our hatred for cops, the reprehensibility of our white privilege. I didn't get drunk but I got warm. I felt ready to try to forget everything except his body and mine.

Now there was a habit of me sucking him off first, which I was happy to do. I was exhausted enough to fall asleep after but with 10 minutes of holding each other under his sheets, he was hard again. What followed wasn't aggressive or cruel, but it was full of energy and focus. It was his excellent hands in my hair again, on my body, the way he moved against me.

"That has to be one of the most metal fuckings I've ever had!" I told him afterward, impressed with him and happy for myself, and exuberant about the two of us together. I felt compressed by his thrusts, bound up in my own body like a knot, and then the sense of slow release from that once he pulled out felt decadent and diffuse.

"You can 1,000 percent spend the night, you know," he said before we even went upstairs.

"Ok. I would love to. But I understand if you change your mind," I said. I knew he wouldn't say it if he didn't mean it, but old training is hard to break. God forbid any woman be a nuisance to the man she's sleeping with.

It was smart that he'd told me so far in advance, though. It meant after we were through, we could curl into each other's heat and sleep with barely a word more.

$\sim$

Seeing Aaron was a perfect respite from a week of nonstop emotional confusion—"Like shaking an etch-a-sketch," I told Bea—but I still cried when I woke up in Max's bed a day later. It wasn't only about his impending disappearance. It was about how he highlighted all the ways my life was lacking but needn't be. I was crushed by how clearly I saw my mistakes, one of which was staying with my boyfriend, whom I had just texted. I told him I loved him and that I was a mess, I couldn't stop crying. When he asked why, I replied, "My bad heart."

Of all the things I've said to him, that's what he latched onto. He quoted it back to me over and over in the subsequent days. It's the phrase to which he attributed his sleepless nights, his panic attacks. He would do anything to keep us together, but there was nothing to be done. I didn't blame him for being scared since I imagine it would be scary to love someone like me, but his fear made me realize that I wanted that investment for myself. I wanted romantic love that scared me, and I didn't want to keep making him unhappy by being who I need to be.

I called my mom on the day I said goodbye to Max, still crying. I told her I met someone else, I thought my boyfriend and I were finally over, and I was drowning in my guilt because he hadn't done anything wrong and how could I be so monstrous as to refuse someone who loved me so much?

"None of us are bad people," she said. "We're all doing the best we can. I hope you can forgive yourself. The world is tough enough without us creating unnecessary blame."

Maybe it's true that most of us aren't bad, but some of us are better than that. After Aaron and I fucked and snuggled in the morning, he made breakfast for us as his dog played in the backyard snow. He waited for me on the sidewalk at the bottom of his steps while I put on my gloves and closed his door behind me, and then three of us—him, his dog, and me—walked down the block to the corner, where we hugged goodbye.

One of my friends often asks me if I'm not afraid of being alone if I separate from my boyfriend. I think the implication is that it's too hard to find another who would take me as I am, mostly because of what I do. But I know there are many, many men to whom I could make myself precious. More important, there are many men who could become precious to me, and I want to meet them all.

A few days later, I texted Aaron a plain and sincere thank you for having me over. I told him it was just what I needed in the midst of a hard time. He immediately reciprocated in kind: "I'm glad we got to brighten each other's weeks."

It wouldn't be the last time we did. I'd found a good friend in this man.

WIFE
February 10, 2015

It was close to 10 years ago when I met a young, bespectacled, suited man at my agency's massage in-call and straddled his body, laughing, while I told him about the first time I smoked crack. I was in my earliest 20s and new to the work, but not so new that I didn't shake my head at myself as soon as he left: what was I thinking? What came over me? We'd had fun, it all felt exciting and friendly, but surely I ruined any chance of keeping him as a regular.

Soon he was there almost every day I worked. He started my shift with two hours and he tipped me $40 every time, which was more than 20 percent but less than a lot of other guys gave. I made fun of his business's name because I thought he was an employee, not the owner. He always got me off even when I didn't want to, and he lied about liking the same music I did.

Sometimes, later in the afternoon, he brought me a dahl wrap from Whole Foods or some of their lemon capellini. It was not unusual for me to work eight hours straight without a break; I was popular and in love with the money. I could have told my agent to stop scheduling him in favor of another guy who tipped more, but I didn't. The agent finally noticed him walking into the apartment months after he started coming.

"He's cute!" she said. "He's in good shape! I always pictured him as some really skinny guy wearing a trench coat and hunched over like, 'my Charlotte . . . My precious.'"

For Valentine's Day, about six months after we met, he brought me a colossal bunch of roses that were at least three feet tall. I had to carry them with me in a cab, on the train, into a women's studies class, chaperone them like they were juvenile celebrities. Not even strangers let me pass without comment.

"I was going to get you roses like that this year," he told me in the kitchen. "Unless it's too sad."

"That is sa—" I said, my voice breaking off as I nodded out the word. I sealed the tears in by pressing my lips together.

Once, the manager called to tell us a police car was in the parking lot, and we should stay inside until it left, so we got dressed—me, in my jeans and college sweatshirt, he in his business attire—and sat on the couch, breathing the same panicked air in quiet.

"You looked so young," I think he said either then or later.

"What I wanted most in the world was to protect you," I think he said, many days or weeks after.

Ten years is a long time. I've forgotten a lot of what he's said, when he said it.

I wrote this several months after that Valentine's Day:

Today was Rose's birthday. We spent five hours on the clock together, eating, buying sex toys, seeing his house. His house is really nice but also felt a little sad because it wasn't particularly personalized. I mean it was full of expensive, nice things but . . . maybe it just didn't feel lived in. I have a new theory, which is that he was engaged and it only recently broke off. Like, so recently that the woman still has all her clothes in the closet in their bedroom. Or I could be totally wrong and he is married/still engaged and I'm just a sucker. But it didn't feel like a woman lived in the house. Plus he invited me to move in.

We spent a few hours off the clock too, eating at an Asian restaurant where the food portions were tiny, had "nice presentations" and were served with 20 minutes between each dish. It was ok I guess. I learned to eat with chopsticks, or at least managed to get food in my mouth with them most of the time. I had a very strange day because I realized that #1, I might actually date him if I wasn't with someone else, #2 we have a lot in common, more so than I originally thought, and #3 my job is weird and I am bad at being professional but I am sometimes doing my best. #4 is something I already knew; he makes me come all the time, even when I think I'm not in the mood. I could see this getting annoying over time (?)

It was he who taught me how to eat European-style with a fork and knife, something I wanted to learn for work, but didn't even know existed before I watched him do it. I went overseas by myself for school but only to one country; with him, I visited almost 20. He bought me armloads of new clothes, purchased designer handbags on a whim. I wouldn't make the money I make as an escort if it weren't for him. He gave me the costume for my paid class drag. He *Pretty Woman*-ed me, not into a marriage but, to his initial dismay, an upper echelon of sex service.

I always thought we were a bad match. But he was relentlessly generous even when angry. He wouldn't give me up. And there were times when we could have parted, it would have been natural and sensible for us to part, but I begged not to. For instance, when he started to suspect I was seeing someone else, and I was: Ethan.

At some point it felt as inevitable that we'd be together forever as it was inevitable we would break up. Our ability to endure through so many challenges—his marriage, his divorce, a terrorist attack, affairs, lies, the abortion, me working full service—became a self-fulfilling prophecy. We could outlast anything. Wasn't the capacity to push on proof enough that we should?

We spent a lot of the day together. Half of the time I am so irritated with him for no apparent reason, just stupid little things will make me inordinately angry, like his tone deafness or his bad taste in music. Then the other half I feel so tenderly toward him and worry so much that he'll find this blog and what I've written here will hurt him, because he does not deserve to be hurt, especially not by me, when he's done so much for me.

I've never written or talked about what he looks like, what he does for work. For a time, he tried to blame me for ruining any chance of a political career for him. ("You ruined your political career when you hired me," I gradually gained the self-esteem to say.) More recently I've blamed myself, in advance, for ruining his career if I ever tried to live out, to put my face to Charlotte. He tells me that he doesn't care about that, he has enough money for it not to matter and he doesn't care what other people think. That we've been together for so long that even if we separate and I'm public about who I am, he would be identified and smeared. All of which is probably right.

He's praised my vision, called me a genius and brilliant, told me he hated George not out of rivalry but for how he treated me. ("Didn't he realize he was with royalty?") I insisted I would never want children and he said he was prepared to have a childless life if it meant we could stay together. When I told him I needed to move, he offered to buy me a place. He has always been willing to support me financially if I wanted to stop working.

He's offering to be my wife, I realized this time. Meaning he would devote his life to elevating me in whatever ways I chose while he stayed at home, working, loyal, no complaints. It felt sick to accept this offer. It felt sick to turn it down.

"No one will ever love me more than him," I told my mother, my friends. It almost felt like a curse to know this.

"When I look at you, I see forever," he told me when the George situation was at its worst. "That's why I'm still here. When I look at you, I don't see years. I see decades. I see the end."

There's so much love between us now, at the end, that it's hard not to romanticize the past. "What makes me the saddest," I told him a few weeks ago, "is to think of all the time we had together that we wasted not loving each other right." But my regrets go back to drowning as soon as they surface, because you can't retrospectively edit your life.

No one becomes who they are without committing what look like mistakes. Creation is not a perfect process. Destiny isn't clean. And being partnered is a well of strength, even when that partnership is flawed and painful; I believe that now. I feel intimately acquainted with the ways a spouse functions as a lifejacket, just the mere idea of her. We've fortified each other in as many ways as we've damaged each other. The two are directly correlated.

A decade gives you time to play every role, switch every position. First I resisted him, then I was afraid to be without him, then he wanted me to be less dependent on him, and then I was. Now, I'm gone.

"You can do whatever you want. I just want to know you're my girl," he said to me again and again. No matter who else I sleep with, or even if I fall in love with other men, that truth should endure. *But I'm nobody's girl*, I thought to myself, and then I realized that wasn't right either. I'm only my own girl.

I guess what I feel most acutely bad about is our difference in regard for one another, because as much as I like him, I don't think I can match whatever he feels for me. He does really sweet things like spontaneously kisses the crown of my head after I say something weird, and gives me crazy compliments, like saying I'm the most unique person he knows or the most unusual woman in his life, and all his friends know about me and think I am awesome even though we haven't met. We are not entirely in sync. But hopefully I am mostly good to him or making him happy for a little while, at least.

That first meeting is something we both marvel over, still. How charmed he was by me, the clash of the sweet girl paired with the wild one. How comfortable I felt in letting him see the seedier side of me. It was like I told him right away, "I need to live a lot of lives," and he thought that was the best quality a woman could have. Except now I'm on to the life in the wake of him. A life alone. My own girl. My own wife.

THESE FEELINGS
February 16, 2015

With Max gone, I felt as I expected to feel: Forgotten. Abandoned. Before he left, I wanted to see him again but he would only commit to a quick kiss instead of a full night or day together. He said there was too much he had to finish—applications, projects. I told him, reluctantly but sincerely, that it seemed important to him so I wouldn't be a bad influence.

"Your success is good for the whole world," I texted. "I might be selfish but I'm not a monster."

"If I had a choice, I would be monsters with you," he said. "I sure hit the jackpot meeting you, C."

Now there were no iMessages from him, only sporadic emails, usually with links to songs and sometimes nothing more. He was working in a huge urban capital, not hiking somewhere remote, and his silence combined with his absence felt like rug burn on my heart. I thought that might change if I were the first to say a little more, but when I wrote something longer than 50 words, he didn't reply for a few days. The last morning we were together, I'd woken up to two incredibly kind emails from different people. After I murmured something about how touched I was, he said, "I wanna write you nice emails."

"Your nice emails would make everyone else's look like trash," I said.

I found myself in one of the hotels we'd met in, and it hurt to be there, so I left for Aaron's even though I was too listless to enjoy the sex. I thought it might cheer me up to find someone else entirely, so I looked for a guy on Tinder after but ultimately ate dinner with one friend and stayed up late sipping Balvenie with another.

By the time I got back, I was too tired to see the room as anything more than a bed. I tried to convince myself to give up the fantasy of him, me with him. If he felt anything, it must have only been for the idea of me, which would explain why he was content with noncommunication when he could have made an effort to feel closer.

I told myself I wouldn't see him when he got back. I thought the odds were high he wouldn't ask to see me at all.

Then he wrote: "I miss you like thirsting and I want you like burning and the more I imagine the further away you seem."

And he linked to a "Cavity" remix. *The Moon Rang Like a Bell* was the first music played while we were together; I'd chosen it like the eager, reckless fool I am. Like I don't know music is one of the best tools for bonding me to someone.

A few days after that email, he finally messaged: his phone was fixed, the opening was that night, but he was only thinking about me. ("I couldn't text," he said. "Otherwise I would have been bothering you this whole time.")

"New York told me to tell you it misses you," I said. So weak for him.

"Can you tell New York I just miss _____?" he said, using my name.

It wasn't that seamless. The recent past with George left me paranoid and edgy. I even googled Max's "I want you like . . . " lines in case they were copied. I'd been resolute that I couldn't be used for sex, not when I wanted it, but now I wondered. This communication was conveniently timed. I didn't think Max was calculating but that didn't preclude him from being self-involved to the point of cruelty. And once we were back in text contact, he said all the right things unprompted—"I miss everything about you," "I wish you were here"—but I was sensitive to how much he rhapsodized about us fucking.

That's one of the saddest aspects of the double standard, I think; it steals the opportunity for sex to truly be about connection, even if transitory, because it only conceives of sex as a battle the woman almost always loses. We're drilled to be vigilant against a man's presumed lack of integrity so we can't trust, let alone enjoy, our emotions of closeness. They're drowned out by the learned instinct, the voice that only hisses, *He conned you.*

He texted me throughout the opening, sending pictures. He got drunk, his phone died, and then he got it to an outlet and told me, "I'm back, because you're the sexiest being. And I'm the neediest being."

My replies were restrained. I didn't want to give him more room to hurt me.

"Wow, you're having a good time," I said.

"But not as much as if you were here. When I fantasize about possible situations all I can think about is your body in the same moonlight I see."

I realized he was flying back the next day, technically that morning, but he didn't say a word about it.

It was Saturday. I knew he was home, had gotten home hours ago and yet he hadn't said so. Didn't he want to see me? If I had been the one who left, I'd have coordinated well in advance to meet him moments after I landed.

"You're strange," I said finally.

"Why's that?" he replied, adding, "(You're beautiful.)"

He asked if I was in town this week and if I wanted to see him. I said it would be a bad idea.

"For whom?"

"Me." I willed him to say something good and strong. I thought of how I'd respond if he told me what I told him. I would want to know why it would be a bad idea. But most men don't ask why.

"If there is anything I can do to change that opinion I would try to argue/prove the opposite . . . But I don't want to push something if I'm the only one getting pleasure out of it," he said. "It really truly sucks to imagine never seeing you again though."

Then, after a pause, "If you ever have an inkling for our company again I'll be quietly/fervently hoping."

"I'm moving to your neighborhood," I said an hour or so later. I wanted to give myself a dignified ending but not as much as I didn't want it to end at all.

"I wish I could still say how exciting that news is," he replied.

"Why can't you?"

"I really liked being with you and I can only imagine how it will feel wanting you the way I do while knowing that you're physically closer and yet impossibly far away."

"I want to see you so much, I just don't want to be sad afterward," My replies were short, one line after the other. I wanted to lay each thought out so he could hear it on its own. "It's not even about being sad; being sad is one thing, but feeling discarded is another. You have so much going on right now, and I'm not interested in being a burden. I have too much emotional energy all the time. It's my own problem."

"I'm sorry I made you feel discarded. The moments I was with you were rare moments of being confident I was actually doing something generative and fulfilling. Apparently we've both been trying to avoid being burdens to each other."

"I don't want to ask something of someone if they don't want to give it, you know? This would be easier if I cared less."

"Easier isn't always better," he wrote. "I'm still trying to work out the sweet spot between being honest and not being fragile. I like the way you cared, and I liked caring back."

Was he telling the truth? I thought so. But maybe he was placating me because that was easier than finding someone new to fuck. He only had a handful of days in the city before he left again.

"What do you want?" Emma asked when I texted her about our conversation.

"To feel like I matter to him," I said.

I know my friends and I can be quick to advise each other to walk away from a man who isn't perfect from the start because we assume his missteps are intentional or irreparably callous. We have a lot of general evidence to support that cynicism. It didn't sound right to me that his phone was really broken for weeks, or that he couldn't have said something more over email. And he claimed he'd been bumped from his initial departing flight to one the following day, which felt like a lie for a slew of reasons. But never seeing Max again was telling myself a type of story, too, one about how my affections shouldn't be trusted or satisfied.

"I overheard Alex telling his fiancé how beautiful you are," he said, naming the only friend of his I'd yet met, the one he was staying with now that he was back in the city and homeless.

"No way," I said.

"It makes sense . . . "

"It doesn't make sense. Why would that even come up?"

"Because I talk about you all the time."

"You're full of it."

"I'm watching the Empire State Building change colors and they might be all about you," he said.

Why did I resist believing he was thinking about me the way he said he was? Because I thought about him like that, but I didn't tell him so?

He found me as I checked into a quiet hotel, hung back while the woman at the desk gave me a useless litany of amenity details. While he was gone, I imagined how our reunion would look: me literally jumping into his arms while I chanted his name. But instead I kept my distance until we got into the room and even then I felt lifted in my own body, a cat on edge.

I'd vowed not to be surprised if the same thing happened again, if he mostly ignored me when we were apart after. We had two more days together and then I left for a long work appointment, and he'd be gone for another month. But I didn't want to be taken over by that like I was before. I told myself I was doing this for the moment, not for the future. I could only focus on the joy and not anticipate any pain.

So I took off my boots and crawled across the bed to him and let myself dissolve. I realized part of why I'm addicted to him fucking me is that it allows me to forget everything, even him, which means no source of unhappiness. And I didn't want to be sad around him. What a waste of our short time it would be.

I had plans to go to dinner with Melissa and Tommy. He said yes immediately once I invited him along, making sure I was sure I really wanted him there. Of course I did; I wasn't about to be without him if I could help it.

He was quiet but attentive throughout dinner, his leg against mine and his hand mostly on my knee. He asked Melissa to help him with his dessert and he tried to overpay when the bill came.

"What does he know?" Melissa texted while we were on our way.

"We can talk about sex work," I told her. "He just doesn't know I do it."

And talk about sex work we did, liberally, which I hoped was priming him. I'd never cared for someone as much as I already cared for Max without that person knowing about my job.

We said goodbye to Melissa and Tommy outside, then walked holding hands in the unrelenting cold until we found an empty bar where we drank whiskey by a fake fire.

"Being next to you is the only time I feel small," I said. He made some expression of apology and I said, "I love it." I looked down at my hand overwhelmed in his.

"I can't remember the last time I was in a conversation I had so little to contribute to," he said, referring to dinner.

"I'm sorry." I worried he might feel excluded. It seems Melissa and I always have so much to talk about, we can barely spare a breath. "Were you bored?"

"No, it was fascinating. As soon as I thought I recognized someone and I might have something to say, you were on to something else. You're kind of a big deal, huh?"

"No," I said. "Melissa is, though. We have some friends who work in media so it probably seems larger than it is. But it's a small circle."

"It didn't sound small," he said. "There were a lot of names flying around."

He knew some things: I wrote under a pseudonym, I had a Tiny Letter. Weeks ago, I told him how I wanted to go about a book, my ideas on the timing, what I wanted for an advance. He even knew I was doing the NPR interview, and the program's name, but whether he didn't go looking for these things out of respect or disinterest or both, I wasn't sure.

"When do I get to hear your sexy voice on the radio?" he asked before he left, and I ignored it.

I tried to tell him that I'd made a lot of money, which felt like a step toward revealing my real job.

I know I'm a virtual no one when it comes to writing, but sometimes I felt eager and excited for Max to find out what visibility I have, no matter how modest. Because more and more, I am proud of it, optimistic about what I could do further and excited by my larger plan. I wanted to share everything with him though I wasn't sure I could since it meant him sticking with me after finding out about work—if things between us progressed far enough for him to find out.

Back at the hotel, I lit the half-dozen candles I brought and he chose the music, the playlist he had compiled for thinking about me while he was away. He touched every surfaced bone in my spine and let his hand linger at the very base.

"This is where I aim when I'm inside you," he whispered. "I want to reach all the way to the very back."

"You get pretty close, don't you think?" I said.

"Pretty close."

"Keep trying."

It was early in the night when we started and late when we finished. In the morning I woke up to him against me again.

"I like it when you make me feel like I'm taking it," I said. My body felt like warm caramel. "I like taking you."

We were slow to get moving but once we did we ate breakfast in a sunny café and then walked toward the park while he explained the neighborhoods and landmarks. The lawn was a shock of radiant ice and snow, the wind so flinty I could barely think. We dropped hands periodically so he could stuff his, bare, into his pockets. We escaped into a place selling tea and sat down with a pot to share.

"I finally got a chance to really look at your eyes," he said. "They're crazy. Bright green with an . . . orange center. Is that hazel?"

"And yours . . . " I said. I inspected the silvery rim around his melted blue. "Are you wearing contacts? I've never seen you take them out. Are you supposed to sleep in them?"

"People like us couldn't have boring brown eyes."

"Oh no," I said. "We'd gouge them out."

"I'm going to Venice for six weeks in April." He poured me more tea. I absorbed this as gracefully as I've ever absorbed any terrible information. I don't think I even flinched.

"That's great," I said. "That's so exciting."

"Have you been?" he asked.

We didn't dwell on it. I kept learning more and more. Just in the 20 new hours we'd had together, I better understood that he was dreamy and distracted and bad at planning, so details at this point would be useless. But I trusted what I heard around the edges of how he spoke about it: *Would you come see me there?*

We separated so he could work. Emma was in town and I wanted to see her. He said he'd come find me whenever I wanted him to and he did, while she and I were high and had been singing for two hours in a private karaoke room. He brought a friend with him, another man, and I tried to be as kind and accommodating as I could given the circumstances. I struggled to stay focused on anything.

We sang "Go Your Own Way" and "Sweet Child of Mine," and I did "2 On" by myself because no one else knew it. Even in my distracted state, I noticed when Max said something to his friend about my singing, and the friend said, "Yeah, that's really important," joking but not meanly.

"You have a great voice," Max said.

"I'm just loud," I said. "I'm a good shaming alto because I make the harmony loud enough to keep everyone else from joining the melody."

"No, you, like, hit every note dead on," he said.

I spent most of the night crouched down on the floor by his legs, trying to stay near the low table in front of the TV without blocking anyone's view. I was drinking a barrel's worth.

Emma left for the bathroom and Max's friend left to sing in the public bar, and Max, standing, grabbed me and lifted me up so I could latch my legs around his waist.

"Hi, gorgeous," he said.

"Excuse me," Emma said, pretending to be annoyed when she came back in and had to reach around us kissing for her phone.

Back at the hotel, he lit the candles left over from the night before. It was the most I could do to get undressed, though I don't think I did it on my own. The next morning I saw my coat and sweater hung in the closet, and I couldn't imagine having done it myself.

"I wanted to fuck you in that karaoke room," he breathed, wrapping me into him.

"Next time," I said. "Next time, we'll go, just the two of us . . . I should have sung that Alicia Keys song, 'Every time you touch me . . . ' You know that one?"

I was getting to that point in the high that I remembered from the night with George and Emma, where I felt like I was watching my own dreams, not because they appeared convincingly as images before my eyes but because they rose like vapors in my brain, ideas and objects presenting themselves to my attention in unintelligible but not frightening ways. I felt fully absorbed but not concentrating, my mind diffuse and suffused with color.

"I was thinking of a bird's nest," I sighed after he finished, my limbs still draped over him.

"Was it empty?" he asked

"It's . . . empty now." I realized his hair under my hand was thickly wet. "How'd you get come on your head?"

In sober retrospect, I'm sure I reached down to hold him while he pumped it out on my stomach and then immediately reached back to stroke his neck. But I was too high to pay attention to much of anything. All my energy went into resolving over and over again not to be afraid of coming down, from him or the drug, not to be sad, to never be sad with him again. I was allowed to feel anything with him except sad.

I woke still high. He wanted to take me on some art errand he had, but after we fucked again, there wasn't enough time. Downstairs, dressed and packed, I felt like his child as he stood over me on the sidewalk.

"What are you going to do until your train?" he said.

"I don't know," I said. "Find somewhere nicer than the station to wait."

"How about that café nearby?" He kept trying to feed me. He'd been searching on Yelp for a place with options.

"Cafés only interest me if you're in them."

"I'll come with you."

A tea, a coffee, and two vegan banana breads came up the stairs with us as we found the last free table. He asked about what I'd said I was working on, and I took out *Bluets* and *Autobiography of Red*. I told him a little about each, what I wanted to use them to say. I said Maggie Nelson had her heart broken by an artist, and looked at him pointedly.

"Uh oh," he said.

He studied the back of *Red* and set it down with care. I'd told him it was one of the most moving books I'd read.

I reached across the table for his big hand and brought it to my mouth so I could kiss his knuckles.

"You don't want any?" He was picking at the bread on the plate between us, trying to leave some for me.

I smiled and shook my head. "I won't eat anything until dinner." I knew my appetite would be gone until then, if not longer.

"How do you do that?" he asked, like I never eat. I was pretty sure I was still high. Maybe he didn't know, maybe he thought I only drank the night before though I told him I'd brought something for Emma and me, and him if he wanted it.

It was odd to remember how new we were to each other. His strangeness was part of what made him magnetic to me, but it felt surmountable. He felt knowable. Recognizable, or none of this would be happening. Like I were poised to dive into water, like I was hovering above the surface with arms long and hands pressed together, my fingertips wet past the nails. One lake into another. I yearned for that full immersion so badly I wanted to live like it had already happened.

Back on the street, he picked me up and squeezed me and kissed me before he put me in a cab. Thank god it was not as ceaselessly sad as last time. There were no tears at all for me. Feeling connected to him left me strong and clear-hearted for days, believing that at least some light path was laid down, a trail of bread crumbs to lead us back to each other after another month apart.

It's real was the message I left playing in my own head this time, looping loud enough to drown out *he conned you*. I tried to give it an almost physical weight, something that could imprint me softly but steadily. I knew everything between us was so fresh it might not bloom at all, but that didn't mean I had to stomp the buds. And while I tried to train my negative impulses—not to transform them into optimism, but to stop them working against me with premature denials and worst-case scenarios; to let the future be blank instead of carved out either way—I realized there was at least one step I could take toward a truly open field for us. I could quit work.

JACKPOT
February 23, 2015

My sporadic, scattered thinking around revealing my work to Max took different forms. I became a used car salesman of myself, looking at every angle and bargaining chip to convince him to take me. First, there was the money. If I told him how rich I was, would that help? How rich what I did made me—did that make it worse or better? And if being with me meant access to that money, if I explicitly offered to put some of it at his disposal . . . ? That thought disgusted me, not least of all because I couldn't picture him saying yes, and part of me would have wanted him to lose respect for me just by my offering. But it pulsed through my shameful mind anyway.

Preparing to move meant absorbing my financial situation in a way I hadn't done at any point last year, which I thought of as having been a bad one though I made only slightly less than I had in 2013. Sitting down with my bank statements and my cash made me realize I was very close to having an exorbitant sum on hand, four or five months away, in fact, to one easy milestone. Amassing that much could be a natural quitting point. But then, who quits something that proved itself so ludicrously lucrative? So far, I was busier this year than I had been last year. 2015 could be massively profitable. My emotional investment in continually earning more had, like

279

a splinter, not yet fully worked its way out of me. But if I wanted to quit, why keep on at all when what I already had was plenty?

And I truly wanted to quit. I'd been in enough hotels to last five lifetimes, and I didn't need to see the inside of one ever again. I wanted to use my body exclusively for my own enjoyment, however bruised or burned or scratched the result. I wanted tattoos on my hands. I wanted to buy clothes I would be happy to wear any day or every day, and get rid of everything else. When I looked at the dresses and heels in my closet, all those luxe materials intended to be worn in tightly circumscribed circumstances that didn't acknowledge weather or comfort or free physical movement, I remembered feeling like they mattered to me, or like the life they could give me access to mattered. But it was just that, a memory.

In the past, I thought I should put serious effort into being less materially attached, to train myself to like expensive things less. Now it was happening organically and almost violently, with full conviction. I wanted to tear the impeccable fabrics off their hangers and never see them again. Sometimes when I got home from a date, I took off the dress I was wearing and put it directly into my consignment pile.

The urge to leave behind the life of being sexual with clients—that came and went, truthfully, because I didn't have to think about it much. I'd seen many of these men for years and the familiarity of their physicality sometimes made it more palatable or at least less disruptive. The vast majority of our time was without bodily intimacy, and it wasn't unusual for a client to be too tired or otherwise disinclined to bother with sex at the times it would normally be expected. The sex was often short when it did occur. Sometimes I even forgot to bring lingerie or condoms and it didn't matter. The path to my nakedness was no longer novel. We'd undress ourselves cursorily and get in bed to talk; my mouth or hand would be enough if they wanted anything at all.

I thought of telling Max this much. That was another strategy: Minimizing. Dissembling. Emphasizing the clothed portion of the work. Trying to convince him I was very nearly an asexual companion. Would he ask for details, or would I have to shove them at him before he could fill in any blanks?

I thought this tactic might work, but I hated myself for being so ready to employ it. It was true that sometimes there was barely any physical intimacy. Almost always, I was hired for my company more than anything else. Many of my clients now truly felt like my friends. But that core group didn't constitute the only men I saw.

New clients I met during this time became repeats; they were complimentary and seemed happy with me, but I had no gauge for my performance anymore. There was a sexual dullness to work that might have been because of Max or could have been a symptom of doing it for so long without a vacation or break. My motions were disconnected and apathetic, not even backed by the motivation to do a good job. When I didn't check out entirely, I felt confused during it, like a sleepwalker waking up while eating. When it began and I stiffened against the mouth on my nipples, the fingers between my legs, the intensity of my revulsion surprised me.

I'd never been accused of being mechanical, and I was probably too bad at the sex part for that to be the right word. I didn't have a sexy routine the way some women did that I could then run through on habit. I waited to see what would unfold. Now, instead of feeling like I could come up with something suitably engaging, I was too distracted by my horror that the ordeal wasn't already over. Had it always been this way and I'd thought about it less, or differently? Maybe my sexual clumsiness was charming or endearing or inconsequential when I was younger. I think I'd always kept my eyes shut during.

"It's because you so want to be in the moment," one client said, pleased.

The other truth was that work was hardest immediately after seeing Max. Then the sex was unbearable because it was most acutely unwanted. Set against the contact I craved, it made me panicky and resentful. Everything felt worse. I thought of Max when a new client plunged away at me for two hours, when a fellow escort swirled her tongue all over the hairy balls of a different man while I sucked his shaft until we switched. I thought of how my (ex-) boyfriend responded to the threesome with Emma and George, and I wouldn't allow myself to imagine how Max might react to the thought of me licking a woman's pussy just before mounting the man paying us both. For me, it felt mundane. She was my friend, we were at work, I truly liked the guy with us, and having her there made it easier than if I were alone. But I didn't want to do work sex anymore, not even the sex that was mild and unchallenging. I wanted to make extraordinary sex, with Max.

A few months ago, as a client touched me, a startlingly basic thought flitted through my head: I could have a life where I never have to endure someone touching me when I don't want them to. The sheer beauty of this notion was so powerful I couldn't seriously consider it. It was like looking at the sun, and I dropped my gaze. (Lifted it barely, dropped it again. The sun stayed there even when I didn't look.)

While he was away, I sent Max a picture of me naked and smiling with the words, "I miss fucking you so, so much." I wanted him to understand I missed it more than another woman might because I thought I probably did. I suffered non-him penetration with a unique poignancy that made his cock seem like a crucial antidote of which I was being deprived.

Max, meanwhile, was so much more communicative during this month apart than he was during the last, and he gave me a reason to grin almost every day. I believed the future would be very good but sometimes, in the midst of pining for him, moving, and breaking up with my boyfriend, I had to remind myself.

He sent me pictures of his view and his body and said, "What I would give to be sharing this with you right now." He told me he left work early to masturbate over and over to my picture. "Although you'd think my bed would feel larger without you in it, instead it just feels tiny and cold," he said.

Thinking of him was like plugging my tongue into a sore spot in my mouth, or scratching an itch that only became worse with attention. I did it habitually whenever I was bored or in a work situation that allowed me to be passive. The reward was the sweetness that comes with having a magnet for your attention. Once at a show with a client, an actor wore a shirt with a pattern that for the briefest moment looked like it could have been a sleeve of tattoos, and I spent the rest of the performance thinking about Max's arms.

Again with a client, I rode by the High Line and imagined strolling with Max there in the summer while we talked about some unremarkable way our lives had become tangled: a mutual acquaintance, a work challenge for him, a concern of mine about my apartment. I liked trying to project the domestic details of what we could be to each other.

Physically I desired him in a way I didn't always elaborate upon. Occasional flashes were enough, and sometimes I would replay a short imagined clip over and over again: his long fingers moving down his own abdomen to reach for his cock, me straddling him in the karaoke room and guiding that same hand inside the low neck of my dress to cup my breast. I'd worn leg warmers while we fucked once, just for heat in the otherwise frigid apartment, and it drove him crazy. I ordered wool stockings while he was gone; I wanted him to reach up my thigh to discover garters next.

Maybe I was underestimating him and it would be ok right away with no strategy, no appeasement. In some moments I pretended he already knew, that he'd found the podcast after I mentioned it and he'd put the pieces together but was waiting to let me tell him myself. Maybe it made him like me *more*.

"I don't want him to take it in stride," Bea said when I confessed my anxiety to her. "I want him to be impressed by you."

But deep down, I knew better than that.

The last tactic I considered was, what if I made him love me before he found out, if I made myself too dear to let go no matter how repulsed or angry or jealous he might feel about the truth? I doubted he already felt this way, so I imagined the time it'd take to assure this was time that would calcify my lie into unforgivable betrayal. Whichever way he might respond now, I at least had the excuse of our newness and ambiguity. This option may have been the saddest, since it turned the probability of him rejecting me because of my work into a referendum on what our time together meant to him. The truth was that I had no idea what suffering, if any, he thought I was worth.

I remembered what he said once about hitting the jackpot when he found me. It made me happy that he felt so, but I also thought he was right. I knew what qualities I offered anyone who might link their life to mine in some way: Intensity, focus, intelligence, determination, and ambition. The ability to cheerlead honestly and frequently. Sincere support. A good sense of humor, a resolutely ethical sensibility. For him there was also the deep well of my lust and maybe, increasingly, the tenderest cleft of my heart.

I couldn't apologize for my sex work without apologizing for myself, and I liked who I was. Sex work was an important part of my adult development, not because of something superficial and cheap like sexual technique. At this point, of course I had extensive experience in almost every kink and predilection, but in terms of mechanics, I wasn't ever so great at the sex part. I was always better at providing warm mystery, intimacy with enough boundaries to stay interesting.

Even that talent, though, wasn't what I wanted Max to treasure in me. My work, to the extent it influenced who I was, wasn't about the skills it left me with which could benefit someone else. You should appreciate what someone you love does for you, but you love them for something more, for who they are and continue to be when they're not acting in your service. If Max wanted to say yes to me in a meaningful way, he had to say yes to this part of me. That wasn't anything I could convince him to do. He either had that capacity in him already, or he didn't. If he didn't understand it intuitively, he wouldn't understand it at all.

DO YOU WANT ME NOW

March 12, 2015

Sometime last year after every day turned cold, I went to George's apartment in search of something I didn't want to name. My boyfriend encouraged me to for his own ugly reasons, and I didn't begrudge him that. We all sometimes slide into the idle, low-brained trench of ourselves, into the animal ability to enact and observe small cruelties without remorse.

Months had passed since we'd seen each other, and our contact in the meantime was sparse. He sent the occasional email, including one on my birthday saying, "I miss you, love you, and hope you're the middle of some awesome experience," but I rarely responded, and never with more than a few words. I wasn't sure what more could unfold between us. The raw space he'd left in me wasn't fully healed, but it didn't throb the way it used to. I wanted to press the bruise once more to see how much pain was still pooled below the surface. I don't mean I wanted it in the sense of desire. Rather, I intended to do it through force of primal habit.

Nothing was new or unfamiliar about being there. Only his intensity felt different. "How's your writing? How's teaching? How's [your boyfriend]?" he asked almost as soon as I stepped inside. "I missed you so much. Did you miss me?"

I was quiet. I planned to keep myself close. I didn't think I wanted to hurt him, not exactly, but I wanted to leave the option open. I even thought about telling him I was engaged. Maybe that would make him understand he'd lost something.

"It's ok," he said to my silence, cuddling me. "I still missed you." And once we were on his bed: "I love you a little bit."

That same line, the line he used on every woman. I couldn't believe he was saying it to me again.

"I should smack your face," I said. "I really should slap you." I at least wanted him to feel how unimpressed with him I was.

"I would let you," he said, serious. "I've never done that before but if there's anyone I'd try it with, it's you. I'd be honored."

I shook my head.

"You don't understand how I feel about you," he said.

"Yeah, apparently I don't." I kept my voice a little harsh, or maybe just nude. No bedroom tone, no "you're special" inflection. Like I was talking to someone who kept getting my drink order wrong.

I wouldn't be complicit with his pretending our meeting had any reverence or potency. But I wouldn't have been there if it didn't still fascinate me to watch him go through his attempts at creating intimacy.

He fucked me hard.

"I want to make you feel how much I love you. Can you? Do you?" he said to his thrusts. "I need you to feel it. The way I feel about you . . . "

I didn't feel anything, though. Not scared or mad or offended. Fully removed and yet fully aware. Empty and full of echoes.

"Bitch, come on my cock," he said, "squeeze it," and I faked it. It was like I was marking the place where someone else should have been. I could do the bare minimum to maintain the scene, but I wasn't really participating.

"Oh my god, oh my god," he shouted when he came, his body seizing as though someone were striking it out of him.

He slid off me and stood.

"You took too long," he said behind me, panting. He meant the time that had passed since I saw him last. "Why did you take so long?"

I left my face in the pillows until he was out of the room.

~

I couldn't easily remember having sex before, ever, paid or unpaid, that felt so dark. Everything seemed abusive, self-abusive. It wasn't that I felt what he wanted me to feel or that I felt anything, really, besides the force of him hoping to affect me. To whatever extent it was pure manipulation, his behavior was scary. To whatever extent it was true, it still unsettled me. It was desperation without kindness. That's what made it so bleak. Glimpsing the floor of someone's soul. His. My own.

Though I would never trust him again, I still didn't think he was someone unusually malicious, and he didn't scare me. It seemed we were each other's emotional sparring partners, for practicing and exercising love, and the shadows of love, too, the dark parts that come from the same heart. Over the following weeks, I started to feel like I was finally equipped to simply appreciate the good aspects of him that were available to me: his positivity, his responsiveness, his predictability.

"I'm sad," I wrote him once, "tell me something nice."

And he wrote back immediately asking what was wrong.

Picturing him in his apartment, cooking shirtless in his sweatpants, was sometimes a small comfort. I knew I could visit whenever I wanted. I knew he would never reject me or deny me what I wanted if all I wanted was his company.

I told him I'd met Max. I talked about Max to almost everyone in my life, even my mother, who loved my (ex-)boyfriend, and who would tell him, of our breakup, "Charlotte's complicated. Even I don't understand her."

"I feel like this is helping me heal from your father," she said, meaning my affair, which mimicked his. "Because I love you so much, I'm willing to try to empathize with you in a way I couldn't with him."

I cried a lot, and so did she, and so did my ex. I was sorry to be hurting the people closest to me, but those months were like shattering a glass bottle to get to something exquisite held inside. Of a man from my past I'd written, "He was the crowbar prying open my life." And now Max was the same. The hand smashing the glass.

To George, I said I'd found someone about whom I felt so excited I couldn't imagine having sex with anyone else. And then I told him I had big news and I wanted to tell him in person, and then we picked a night for me to come over.

I was living deep in the crater of missing Max, but there was radiance there. He sent me sweet emails from another continent, more diligent about staying in contact since I'd told him it hurt me when he didn't. And best of all, he started planning a week in advance when and how we'd see each other when he got home. He even offered to take a train to me straight after his flight landed.

George's doorman, Tom, called me Sarah, the only name he knew me as, and hugged me. George joked with me in the past that Tom asked about me often and said I was his favorite.

"You left quite an impression," he said. "It's always the same—'Where's my friend? The tall, sweet brunette; I haven't seen her in a while.' I told him we had a misunderstanding but we care for each other and we're trying to work it out. He said we were 'going steady' for a while . . . "

Upstairs, I folded George's laundry to clear a space for myself on the couch while he finished whatever he was doing in the bathroom. We sat on opposite ends and draped our legs over each other. I held one of his feet and said I was moving. I told him about looking at Max's texts and seeing the mouth emojis, which I thought he would find funny. And I told him that Max didn't know about work, and I wasn't sure what would happen once I told him.

"When you tell him, he'll think, '*That's* why she's so good at sucking my dick!'" George seemed to think this was a good thing, like Max would be so appreciative of blow job boot camp.

"Yeah, exactly," I said, emphatically. "That's exactly what he's going to think." And I watched George's face change as he realized that wasn't what I wanted. "I'm going to quit. I mean I almost already have, but . . . I want to be able to tell him it was something I *used* to do, and mean it."

"With me, I'm usually afraid of commitment," he said. "But you don't seem that way at all now. You seem really ready."

"Yeah. I am. It's not like I think it's permanent, but I want to be in it while I'm in it. I've had so many years of nonmonogamy. I don't expect anything from him and won't ask anything of him but for me? I don't want to be with anyone else. I want to know what it's like to only be with him."

We lay on the bed together for a while, but nothing happened. It was a relief in a way to feel the lazy unfurling between my hips when I'd looked at him across from me on the couch. His powers of attraction confirmed, my attraction to him validated. But I didn't want to have sex and he didn't push for it, though he did say, "I didn't think this was how tonight was going to down. I thought we'd have one last passionate . . . " And he couldn't settle on a word for it, which felt right. Our passionate blanks.

"Before you told me you were moving, when you were on your way over here, I was thinking about asking you to be my neighbor," he said. I remember how often he'd talked about that, us living next door to each other. And now he said he wanted to buy some real estate where I'd be, that it was his ultimate dream. And maybe we would be neighbors there, too. His fantasies made me sad, they were so divorced from the most probable reality.

"I can't believe you're going," he said. "You've been such a big part of my life. You know we've known each other for three years?"

"You're right," I said, because he was, though it seemed inconceivable. "You've been a big part of my life, too." I felt no bitterness about that truth. I was there because I wanted to honor it.

"You mean a lot to me. I know we had that misunderstanding, and things were never really the same after, but . . . I think you know I didn't mean anything by it. I hope you know it wasn't . . . "

"I know," I said. I did.

"I hope we'll be friends for the rest of our lives."

"Well," I said, and I felt the full force of a lifetime of being diplomatic with men steering me. "There's no reason we wouldn't be."

"Can I say goodbye to your breasts?"

"Ok." I took off my shirt and bra and he held himself above my chest, looking down. I braced myself for an assault. Clients, my boyfriend—they'd all always been too aggressive with their mouths, even if I protested or moved away or reached up my arms. Even George had left bruises before. But after a moment of simply looking, he placed a soft kiss on each nipple.

"That was so gentle," I said. "I've never had a guy say goodbye to them so nicely."

"I figured," he said. "I wanted to do it that way. I wanted to be the one."

THE CORD
April 8, 2015

I stopped short of greeting Max at the airport, but I was at my hotel a few hours after he landed. I met him in the lobby, found his tall back turned to me as he looked out the high windows and waited. We had a week this time, longer than we'd ever had before. We planned it together upon his initiation well before he got home. This fact still staggered me given the reluctant planner I knew him to be.

"Miss you like mountains," he signed off his emails while he was away. I'd spent so much time telling myself he was a useful mirage, a fantasy of possibility designed to drive me further toward what I needed but not attainable or real. Then he arranged his return travel around me, even offered to come to my city instead of me coming to his, and lived with me in a light-drenched hotel room for seven days.

That time blurs together, though it was only a month ago. It snowed in heavy fits, and it rained. My coat wasn't warm enough, my new gloves fell apart, but my happiness abided. We rode the train to a nearby city and stood in a room full of butterflies that fixed themselves to my chest, his head. We studied each other decorated in their wings, our movements mindful and slow like tai chi.

One evening he didn't want to get out of bed for dinner so he slept off his jet lag while I ate with Emma, and when I got back, he'd lit candles on the windowsills and made the bed and sat waiting for me, showered, in a hotel robe. In the afternoon we worked, he at the table and I in the bed, Natalie Prass playing and sun coming through the windows full force like a waterfall as he periodically glanced over at me in my panties and sweatshirt, and I wriggled coyly until he came to kiss me.

We talked about how it felt to touch and be touched by the other. I told him that when I put my hands on him I tried to communicate reverence and gratitude. After karaoke with Emma, back in bed, I was still rolling when I asked him if there was anything he'd been hoping I would offer, or do.

"Sexually, I mean," I clarified to his silence just as he said, "To visit me in Venice."

Hearing that while high overwhelmed me too much to respond. I went to a part of his body that shocked me by being the sweetest looking I'd ever seen on a man or a woman, and I exclaimed to him aloud about it before I licked him and kissed him there and wet my finger with myself to put it inside.

We went to the *$pread* book party and Emma talked about stripping while we were all out to dinner together. As always, Max made no comment after to indicate he thought my sex-work-centric friendships and activities were unusual or merited further discussion. When he'd been away, I'd suggest deadlines to myself for telling him about work, but once we were together, I couldn't keep them. Whatever was happening between us was so consuming, interrupting that momentum with a dramatic disclosure would have felt arrhythmic and wrong.

Work barely existed while I was with him anyway. I didn't answer emails or talk to any clients. I didn't feel like I was hiding anything, I just wasn't forcing it under a spotlight. We whispered remarkable words to each other every morning and night, and I didn't write any of them down or try to hold onto them. I let them stream over me like water released from someone's cupped hands.

"The story of us now felt like the real plot of my life," writes Miranda July, "which was, terrifyingly, the most incredible, joyful thing that had ever happened to me."

I looked for an apartment and found one. He visited it with me the day after I first viewed it, and the approval on his face meant everything.

"It's really special," he confirmed.

I signed the paperwork that afternoon.

We were already having sex without condoms but then I told him to come inside me. I wasn't sure how long this would last, so I wanted everything while it did.

"Being with you feels like the future," he told me. "It feels like forever."

Maybe he meant it now, before he knew everything there was to know, but I tried to remind myself the sentiment could change.

On our last night I had dinner with Alana and told him after that NPR was interviewing her, too.

"What happened with that, did it already air?" he asked. "I've been checking the website."

I gave him a look outside my control and changed the subject. So he hadn't found out and simply refrained from comment. He still didn't know.

We separated. I had to go home to burn off the loose threads of my old life and he went to visit his parents. He was as expressive and desirous as he'd ever been in the days that followed, counting down the nights before we'd see each other and, when I teased him about him looking for a job outside the city, he swore off being anywhere without me ever again.

I wondered if he had been waiting like I had for permission to care as much as I did. My emotions were too powerful to be fully subdued, but I tried to hide their insistent quality from him at least a little, so I wouldn't seem "crazy." It had been less than 12 weeks since we first met and he'd been gone for over half that time. Now any similar blocks he may have held in place were dissolving.

"My whole chest aches from missing you," he said. "And it's only been one afternoon. It gets harder every time we're apart."

～

The whys or even the exact when of the shift wasn't clear to me but after that week I felt something—us—lock into place. I felt like we were united. I didn't have to trust my intuition alone. It was in everything he said to me and the way he talked about time. That we would travel together. That if we just got through these few upcoming breaks, we would never again be apart. That we were permanent and inevitable. He was fond of saying we were destined to meet, that no matter what else in our lives might have unfolded differently, the fact of us together never would.

Once we were both in the city again, he took me to one of the places he worked and I met even more of his social circle. During a night out, a friend of his asked me what I did and I started to tell her about writing, then stopped when I saw her eyes lift up and over my shoulder.

"Is he making funny gestures behind my head?" I asked.

"He was making expressions of adoration and awe," she said. "Like, 'Can you believe her?'"

Later I overheard her asking him if he'd read any of what I'd written and he said, "I think so," and when a different friend was talking about what a certain Broadway star makes in a week—"I mean, it's not a lot a lot, but to you and us . . ."—Max gave me a conspiratorial, proud look that made me feel like he knew more about my finances than I'd actually told him.

When I shared this with Beatrice as evidence to support my sense he truly did know now, and that my work wasn't a secret, a problem, or something we otherwise had to talk about, I wondered if I sounded delusional. To make that scant exchange the peg on which I hung my hope was so self-servingly optimistic it was ridiculous. But I also knew Max wasn't a liar, not even about small things, so he wouldn't have said he thought he'd read some of my writing if he hadn't. Where else would the uncertainty come from if not my pseudonym?

And when I talked to him about my Tiny Letter again, about my plans for writing and maintaining some anonymity while also becoming more public, he listened with full attention like he always does, with no hint of wishing I was saying something else. This was the characteristic of his that convinced me not talking about work was ok: he focused entirely on what was in front of him and not on what wasn't. He accepted and appreciated everything I gave him, so there were no demands for or unaddressed interest in anything I left out.

In my heart, I believed he knew about my work and that the details of what I had or hadn't done, was still doing or not doing, didn't matter to him, didn't seem relevant. From the start, I was open with him about my willingness to talk sex, sexual histories, fantasies, whatever. He was the more conservative one, not in a way that seemed staid or judgmental but simply more focused and protected.

Sometimes he said it—"Maybe this is very Victorian of me, but …"— and then reiterated his disinterest in props, toys, elaborate scenarios, or third parties. It didn't feel Victorian to me; it felt pure.

"I've seen a lot of sexual desperation," I told him. "and it's contagious and sad and alienating."

I didn't want our sex to be limited and I liked the idea of doing things with him he hadn't done before, but to know he felt we already had a universe to explore just between our two naked bodies was the most beautiful gift I could imagine. And he never lacked for energy or desire or enthusiasm.

He wasn't jealous but he was tender. Once, while we were walking down a block I thought we'd been down before but he said we hadn't, I teased him with, "I definitely walked with some guy here . . . " and he said, "Ow, my heart," and I laughed and hugged him tighter. There was no shaming or opprobrium in his reaction. Just vulnerability.

In my head, though, sometimes, I worried my conviction that he knew about work was utterly naive and foolish.

Without being sure of what he knew, I talked to him as though he knew everything. I told him about the lingerie donation drive and about Lonely Notes, the more reader-tailored letters. I wanted to collaborate with him, have him illustrate them, but he resisted, citing the fact that people buying them wanted my voice but didn't know his.

He was never presumptuous about what I tried to share with him; he paid for dinner and cab rides, or let me split, but always dissuaded me from paying in full. He sometimes recognized and commented on how I spent money in terms of tips, only to say he liked me for my generosity with others and thought it was hot. But it was not something he wanted extended to himself.

His indulgence during my move was boundless. He followed me patiently as I furniture shopped all over Soho, and even pushed a cart around Bed Bath & Beyond for an hour. He brought an electric drill from work so he could put up a magnet for my knives and bolt down the slide out garbage can under the sink.

He took me to an event at his school and everyone there knew him.

"Do you mind that I called you my girlfriend?" he asked me after.

"No, you didn't. When did you do that?"

"About a hundred times."

"You just said, 'I want you to meet my friend, _____.' But, no. I don't mind."

Whatever he called me, whatever we called *it* was moot.

"You're going to Venice," everyone I met said to him, and then turned to me, "and you're going, too?"

"What do you think of Max's girlfriend?" one mentor asked another loudly, teasing us both since we were only steps behind them.

At lunch, Max told me he was only going to rent a studio now, somewhere on the subway that was convenient to me, and not take on an apartment with his friends as he'd once anticipated doing.

We tried to go back to pulling out—or he did, anyway—but it was too good when he stayed inside, and I held him close and urgently told him to do it.

"The way I feel about you is so intense but it's never scary," I said one night while we lay against each other.

"How does it feel?" he asked.

I thought for a moment. "Unrelenting," I said.

"That's the way waves work," he said. "The crash and pull are part of the same motion."

It really was like a wave. At any given moment, I was drawing in as much of him as I could have yet I wanted even more. As we both moved to fulfill my desire, I gathered more desire to me the way hands clutch at fabric. Like Anne Carson writes of erotic desire, "Foiled. Endless."

Later, in the daytime, I tried again to describe it: "Being with you feels like a ray of sunshine. It feels like the truth."

So telling him I loved him became like talking about work. I used all the words to say it except those exact words.

~

I took a morning-after pill on the same day he drank too much to focus on me at night even though I kneeled next to him on the bed, pulsing and mewling for his attention while I waited for him to put away his laptop. He'd told me on more than one occasion that if he had another drink he'd be drunk, and then he wouldn't be able to stop himself from talking about how he really felt about me. But the outpouring of honesty he promised never came when he drank too much, and his misleading disclaimer left behind a cavity of longing that ached for days. This time, on top of that, he wasn't hard and just wanted to go down on me, so I told him it was time to go to sleep. I'd been nearly trembling from how badly I wanted him, and then I didn't get that satiation either.

The next morning, the sex I initiated was disjointed and weird, and when it stopped without either of us coming, I could barely get out the words from behind my crushing sense of sorrow: "I'm sorry. I feel like I made you fool around when you didn't want to."

"I always want to fool around with you," he said. But then he got out of bed and I went into the kitchen and tried to ignore him as he worked on his laptop and checked his phone. When he got in the shower, I went back to bed and curled up with my phone to text Fab and tried not to cry. I told myself he would be gone soon, and I needed to date other people while he was away.

It took him a moment to find me there. "You got back in bed."

"Yeah."

"Can I join you?"

"Of course."

He took off the clothes he'd just put on and drew me to him once underneath the covers.

"You never have to have sex with me if you don't want to," I told him. "But I'm going to keep wanting it with you all the time."

"I always want to have sex with you," he said. "I just had to pee."

"Those hormones are really screwing me up," I said. I lost the battle to keep in my tears and they started sliding down my face vertically, toward the pillow below.

"I'm sorry, Bee." He called me by his nickname for me, and hugged me.

"It's ok. I'm not complaining."

"I know you aren't. But I am. It's not fair. What can I do? Do you want me to stay home from work?"

"No, I'll be ok."

I knew the pressure in me wasn't about the hormones, though, or about him drinking too much now and then. They were exacerbating that edginess in me, not creating it.

I tried to stop crying but I couldn't. I closed my eyes and opened them, looked away and then back at his face on the pillow next to mine, closed them again—and there he was, still looking at me patiently, like he was waiting for me. Like he knew what I wanted to do. He and I already told each other a dozen times in our artists' language, but I wanted it said this particular way.

"I love you," I said. "I'm sorry, I don't think you want to hear it. You don't have to say anything back. I just didn't want to be alone with it anymore."

"Watching that come out was fun," he said, smiling. "I love you, too."

"I'm so glad," I was making fun of myself, laughing as I cried harder. "I feel so much better."

"Now I can say it all the time," he said. In a whisper, against my ear: "I love you."

While he was at work I told Bea about this strange tension I felt, which was that in spite of being completely in love with him, I feared if I ever made any real emotional demands he would shy away from me, and so I should try to disconnect from him while he was gone.

I texted her, "I worry I might have to teach him to communicate with me in the way I need to feel fully loved and happy and safe, and he's worth the investment but I'm still scared to try. I'm afraid he's disinclined to bother or he'll think I'm uncool or needy."

This was what my previous relationship had taught me: I shouldn't lean on the man I was with for emotional support or make my emotional needs his problem. Max was always thoughtful and attentive if I gave him the opportunity to be. But I would rather pretend to choose someone else than to feel him back away.

"Everything you've said about him suggests he deserves the opportunity to meet your needs as fully as you can explain them," Bea said, perfectly, like only she can. And for her to see that about him in spite of never having spoken to him or met him, in spite of how I tried to restrain myself from talking about him too much to her, gave me all the faith I needed to test that theory.

That night Max and I made dinner, and as we sat down to eat I asked him, "If I were to get pregnant, would you want me to tell you?"

He looked at me, caught off guard, and I smiled some, busying myself with the food. "You don't have to answer right now. You can think about it. I just thought, we've never talked about that and it's probably something I should know."

"Would you want to tell me about it?"

"I don't know. I'd have to do it over email or text while you're away, which would be weird. I mean, I'd be ok. I'd be more worried about you and your reaction."

"It's your body, obviously, so . . ." He angled his chair toward me and leaned in. "But I want you to want to tell me things. We're in this together. You shouldn't feel like you have to take care of that expense on your own either. I can help with that. And, if you want me to start pulling out—"

"Oh, I know. I know."

He gathered up his thoughts for a moment. "You're one of the smartest, most capable people I know. I would trust whatever decision you made."

"Ok," I said.

Our bodies had come progressively closer, angled to the side of the table, and we leaned in to kiss, then pulled apart to look into each other's eyes. Then we smiled, and got on with eating, and we talked about how we create and how we think about the world and I loved him and loved him and loved him.

The next morning I woke to him at my back, his arms around me. "I love you," he breathed emphatically into my hair while he was still nearly asleep, and the sweet joy of that moment suffused me like rushing blood.

"I had a dream I had a baby," I told him after we were both fully awake.

"Oh yeah?" he said, amused.

"She was . . . iridescent teal, and not human. And exquisitely beautiful."

"Like an alien!"

I laughed. "Yeah, just like an alien."

"Of course your baby would be exquisitely beautiful," he said.

"But now if I had a human one, I'd be so disappointed. Like, 'Ew, what's up with this gross white skin?'"

There was still one thing we didn't talk about. It wasn't my (former) work. It was that we only had two days left before Max left the country for six weeks, and I would be alone.

~

We got back in bed the afternoon before his flight. I found myself thinking of two people who'd tied themselves together with rope so they'd never be more than 10 feet apart. Wasn't it an art performance? Or was it those disgraced Buddhists? I mused aloud, trying to puzzle out what I thought I remembered.

"I would do that with you," he said sincerely, like I was asking. "It's a beautiful idea. But then once we were actually doing it, I'd be thinking, *What are we trying to prove?* It's more powerful to live that way without the cord.

"When I was at my parents' house, I started writing a speech I could give you before I left today."

"A speech!" I was delighted. "About what?"

"It was going to be about how I was falling in love with you, and it was like I've jumped out of the plane and I'm wearing a parachute . . . and you should tell me now if I should pull the ripcord, but otherwise I'd keep falling. And I was going to beg you to wait for me. I know it's a long time but just please, please wait for me."

"I want to hear it."

"It's better this way, to talk about it with you. I probably would have been too nervous and said all the wrong things. But I needed to think it through for myself anyway."

"Oh," I said. "And what did you find out?"

He really thought before he answered, though it didn't take him long. "That this isn't something I could walk away from. The best part about loving you is that I know how much it can hurt. And I choose to do it anyway, and to do it fully, even knowing that. More fully because of knowing that."

"I'll try to never hurt you," I said.

"It doesn't matter. I'm going to keep loving you anyway."

"But, that's part of my job now," I said. "To protect you."

And the look on his face was like he had never heard that before.

I didn't want to cry but I couldn't stop. It was quiet but very wet, and I tried to ignore it, but when he rolled on top of me and kissed me he said, "Your lips are trembling."

"Big deal," I said. I could barely take a breath. "They do that all the time."

He brought his mouth to the corner of my eye and nibbled at my tears.

"Hey, don't eat those. That's where I keep my strength."

"But I need it. You have to share some."

"When you put it that way . . . " I said. My heart felt like it was fracturing under the pressure, so much pressure from loving him as entirely as I did. I wanted to marry this man. I'd known it weeks ago. I knew how foolish it sounded then and even now, because of how new we were, and I wanted it anyway. I didn't know how I would exist in the world without him for that month and a half. We hadn't even made a plan for me to visit.

~

Max texted me when he arrived in Venice and then sent me an email that night, a gesture I would have been wildly touched by even if his email had not been as long and wonderful as it was. He wrote about my eyes, and the taste of my tears, and about pretending he didn't speak English when a British couple asked him what he was looking for in the canal because he was studying the water and thinking about me.

"I'm looking forward to when these things you make me feel can be inspiring for my heart and soothing for my mind when we're apart—but for now they just tear me up inside."

He signed it, "Too much love."

I wanted to give him something back that made him feel like I felt, reading that. So I sent him this:

Dear _____,

I haven't written a Tiny Letter in a few weeks. Normally I write them about whatever's preoccupying me and lately I haven't been preoccupied but rather absorbed. The more time passes, the less I believe I can keep writing them at all. They were always about some aspect of my life and I can't think of what it would look like to write about my life now without also writing about you. And the only way I could do that would be if I felt separate from you. It's one choice to perforate my own privacy but a different one to do it to ours.

I have the urge to give you something, so here is some (most) of the first (and almost the last) letter I wrote about you. I had to come up with another name for you and it's not as good as yours since you'd already taken the best. I'm sorry. I know I should probably wait to share this until we've known each other a year—or more!—or bury it in a time capsule that I forget the location of, so it can accumulate poignancy or prescience (she said optimistically, omitting the possibility of it accumulating painful irrelevancy) but I want to send it now.

You don't have to react to it to me. I know you know how weird it feels to show someone something you've made when they haven't asked for it. One of my friends who wrote a book told me whenever he gave a copy to someone whom he especially wanted to have it, it was a guarantee they wouldn't read it. That would be ok, too.

I think a lot of people who want wisdom try to train themselves out of how they see the world, or at least to ignore how they see it. But maybe people who are wiser lean into their own perspectives. I know you'll find all sorts of worthwile things in Venice, not because of where you are but because that's the heart you have.

Every place we've been together feels special to me no matter how otherwise unremarkable it is. Part of the reason I'm so willing to go anywhere with you is to spread that magic into the world beyond New York. For now, I'll try to stretch myself out into the echo of you/me/us in this city, and not want for more when there is already so much.

Yours in the most important ways,

_____

And I attached the first letter about him, the one that proved, if I'd ever had any doubt, how in love with him I was from the first time we met.

~

I woke up to many texts from Max, though nothing about the email. I wasn't worried. If I had seen how long it was, I too would have left it for after work.

When he got home that night, his time, he texted that he would respond to everything, but that if he tried to reply now the gist of it would only be, "I'm so in love with you I can't think of what to say."

Sometimes I would start crying almost out of nowhere. I visited my mother for a day, and I saw my ex, and I went back to my old home to collect the many books I'd left behind in my haste, so there were other triggers. But mostly it was missing Max so much that if I let myself experience the full power of it, I felt ready to slump onto the floor and stay still there for days. When I came home and saw the pair of shoes he'd left by the door, the simultaneous flood of love and pain froze me for a beat.

The first early pregnancy test came up negative, and the one I took a few days later did, too. The next day I got my period. I'd felt nothing but panic and remorse when I thought of being pregnant, but part of me was disappointed by the results, the same part that hoped every part of my body might reflect the yearning for connection, and the conviction in the rightness of connection, that my heart felt for Max.

His reply three days later was even longer than mine, so I skimmed it even as I told myself to slow down and not hurry. But it was like I knew what I was looking for.

He told me he had no words for how my email made him feel. He said he trusted me more than some people he'd known his whole life and however I might write about us would be "genuine and beautiful and full of you, which is something the world needs more of."

He added, "You are a writer, I am part of your life, you write about your life, and I love you truly madly deeply, so in that sense the way my life appears in your writing is as much (if not more) yours than mine."

Then he wrote, "I really believe that being creative and expressive is how we create our own character, and seeing as how it's your character that makes me so attracted to you […] I would be a complete fool to discourage you from accessing the medium and context for your go-to mode of expression/creative exploration."

There was more, much more, but then I came to this: "I thought a lot about whether I wanted to sign up for your Tiny Letter weeks ago when I was at my parents' house—"

"Oh," I said aloud to the empty room, and then immediately I wept. He did know, he really had known for weeks, just as I thought he did. He knew about what I'd done and he still loved me. And I don't know that I'll ever again feel as overwhelmed by joy and relief and gratitude as I was in that moment. My love for him was so right. It was the truth, it had always been the truth. I still cry thinking about it now.

I knew what happened without having to puzzle it out: that look I'd given him when we were talking about Alana's NPR interview made him go back to the show's archives and listen to what he'd previously overlooked. But in the following days, I reinterpreted everything that had happened between us within this new timeline, and, impossibly, it made the revelation more powerful. It wasn't just that he told me he loved me after, it was that he'd folded me into his life so completely in the wake of knowing. That he introduced me to even more people who were important to him, that he spoke so assuredly about our future together, that he'd planned that "wait for me" speech. Everything he'd already done that was precious and dear and valuable to me was amplified.

I remembered what Bea said a long time ago when I fretted to her about telling him.

"I don't want him to take it in stride," she said, "I want him to be impressed."

And he had been. He'd been the man who loved me more because I was Charlotte. The man who made expressions of adoration and awe behind my back when we were together in public, who put away the clothes I left puddled on the floor, who woke me up in the morning by telling me he loved me, and all of this without ever making me answer for who I was or what I'd done, but only praising it, over and over. *No one gets this lucky*, I thought to myself. *No one is given something this good so easily*.

~

But in the kitchen a few days later, a thought was delivered to me. Even calling it a thought makes my mind sound too participatory in it. It felt like something truly impressed upon me, dropped into my consciousness like a stone in water. *I am that good at getting what I want; I am that lucky. And within a year I will be married to this man.*

PAST LIVES
April 27, 2015

Intellectually, I believed the weeks without Max were a good thing. It made sense to be alone in the wake of my breakup, the move, all the changes. I needed to pitch the articles I had in mind, to circulate in the city on my own, to establish some patterns not dependent on him.

But it didn't feel good. I tried to excite myself by thinking I was preparing the apartment for his return, but my errand running had no energy. I sat to write and instead stared out the window, blanker than usual. My vague ideas of connecting and reconnecting with acquaintances and friends guttered out almost instantly.

I had no desire for anyone else but the idea of sleeping with other men swelled up in me like a minor wave. I knew why; I wanted something to rupture the airlessness. It would be like kicking a can down an empty street. He was right to implore me to wait for him.

We never talked about work—was I or wasn't I, how recently I had been—and we never talked about monogamy. So maybe sex with someone else wouldn't have been outright deception, but it was a corroded, weak-hearted notion from the start. I told myself I could do it and never write about it, never tell a friend. It would never hurt him because he would never know. It would be my test for how well I could keep my own secrets, which I've never succeeded in doing.

I was inspecting my loneliness, my listlessness. What would it feel like to . . . ? There was no true benefit in it nor, mercifully, any motivation.

"I don't understand why I even have a body without you," I texted. "It's just one hand clapping over here."

He didn't talk about me visiting because he believed it would be a hassle, financially burdensome, and inconvenient, and he could not do enough to help. I didn't want to intrude when he needed to work, but gradually I became convinced he only held back from planning out of some sense of chivalry.

"Well, let me see what I can do," I told him after he admitted for the first and only time that he felt bad about the expense.

"I know what that means," he said.

"Oh, really?"

"Yeah. Baby's got it covered."

And I did.

~

On the flight, I thought about what it would be like if the plane crashed. Not with fear, and no vivid details. Simply curious. What if the energy between us were wiped out? Death seemed like the only thing that could interrupt it. Or maybe it was my disbelief something this good could endure.

Everyone in my life seemed happy for me, but I read skepticism into their positivity. Was that cynicism or sensitivity? I tried to explain, even if I were told that marrying him would end in a bitter, ruinous divorce, I would still want to do it. I would offer part of my future as a sacrifice to honor what existed now. I finally understood the appeal of the ceremony, the ritual. It was a seal. Not to bind him to me, because we were already bound, but to crimp the edges, to contain what would otherwise overflow.

I sat on the courtyard stones next to my backpack and duffle while I waited for him to get out for his lunch break. I'd woken up from my four hours of sleep on the plane full of electricity, sporadically grinning for the few hours it took to navigate the airport, the ferry, the streets to him. It took me less than 20 minutes from the gate to hit fresh air. The bus left moments after I bought my ticket; I sat in the window against the light and the spray. I had everything on my side. I half envisioned our reunion as tearful or incredulous, but when I saw him loping toward me I felt the way I always do, like a freshly filled balloon. I reached my arms for his neck and he lifted me with his hug and there was nothing to cry or marvel about, this was simply the way the world was supposed to be.

∼

During the day while he worked, I wrote and ate and shopped for more food. I opened the windows even though it meant mosquitos and peeled tiny oranges and bananas alone in the sunshine, or broke open another package of crackers with my laptop watching from the table like a cat. I soaked dried grains and beans. I assembled a daylong playlist one afternoon when my jet lag had me too drowsy to order words. I made soup at night, or pasta, and once a millet risotto that took hours, listening to music we hummed when we moved through the streets later: "Beast of Burden," "Land of 1000 Dances," "Sixty Minute Man." He sang the harmony on almost every song, flawlessly.

"I can't believe you're you," I said.

"Yeah, what are the odds?" He was teasing me.

"One in infinity," I replied, resolutely sincere.

His face was impossibly beautiful to me. I could imagine others not understanding its elegance, but I was mesmerized. I got lost in tracing his planes with my eyes, the high cheekbones and the rise around his lips, while reminding myself that he kept this out in the open all the time. He looked like this all the time, in front of everyone! "Your face," I said now and then, and reached out my hands like I needed to block it from my view.

"I'm sorry," I told him one night over dinner. I was genuinely embarrassed, not least of all because I was sure I'd said it before. "Sometimes I love you too much to listen to what you're saying."

I walked with him to work in the mornings and I met him there at nights when he was done. I hadn't looked up any landmarks. I didn't do any sightseeing. He was the sight.

On his day off, we hit our stride and it finally felt like we were us again. Hours and hours in bed. Hermetic intimacy. It was then that we started talking about youthful wildness. For him, bridge jumping and egging houses and other types of petty property damage. He felt guilty about it, the latter things.

"Ok, what have you done that you're most ashamed of?" I asked.

"Oh, no. No. I don't think we're ready for that yet."

"What?!" I pushed him with my body. "Now you have to tell me."

"I think that's for later. Let's wait a year."

"It's not even that bad. I already know, it's something you feel really bad about, but when you tell me I'm going to say, 'That's nothing.'"

"Well, yeah," he said. Like, of course he feels awful about it: that's its defining feature, and my impression of it wouldn't alleviate his vulnerability.

"Apparently you don't understand what love means," I said in mock offense. "Apparently you think love means you can just decide to back out anytime you find out about one thing you don't like."

"I couldn't back out if I wanted to," he said, finally deflecting. "What about you? Your stories?"

"The worst thing I ever did as a kid? Or . . . "

"Wait, let me think about how I want to say it."

"Yeah. Think about it. Anything. I will tell you anything you want to know." I had complete confidence. I was excited to think of what he would ask me, looking forward to whatever reminiscence it might trigger and his reaction to it. My high school memories are fond and vibrant.

"What's the riskiest thing you've ever done?" he asked.

My brain skated off toward an answer, and as different possibilities presented themselves only to be replaced with others, I had the emotional sensation of the moment you lose control of your car on ice. I can't imagine what my face looked like, how many seconds it took me to answer. But I thought of my very first attempt at selling sex, which is a story I don't think I've ever written down, and so many incidents thereafter, too many to be distinct. Too many motels, too many men, too many high-end hotels, and still always me and a man. Is it risky if you get away with it? Is it still risky if the bad thing happens, or does it then become simply dangerous, stupid? One part of my mind kept holding up potential answers while the larger part of me sunk into total dread.

"I think you may not want to hear about that," I said.

"You're probably right," he said without hesitation. Like he'd been thinking about it too as soon as he asked, and realized what a mistake it was.

"And it's not about keeping secrets from you, because—" I felt like he knew this, I wasn't even sure what I wanted to say. Our bubble had burst and I was grabbing handfuls of air to try to repair it—"I'd tell you anything. But it's about not wanting you to be uncomfortable."

"You're right." He wasn't looking at me. There was quiet. Wherever our bodies touched suddenly felt accidental. "I'm going to go get some water."

And he left the bed.

It was as though the luminosity that gives my love for him volume, that fills me up inside with light, drained away to leave dregs that were no less intense or true but full of fear and desperation. I had a complete and immediate sense of the irrevocable; there was nothing I could do about my past.

Just as immediately and completely, I understood the desire to wipe it out, which was something I never imagined I would or even could want. At one time, the mere suggestion would have been deeply offensive to me. But if I could have excised that part of my life then, on my back in the bed without him, I would have. Not out of sexual shame or general propriety but because any part of me that hurt him, that couldn't be shared with him, might as well be gone for me, too.

When he came back, I thought of changing the subject, saying something goofy. To show my belly, to manage the mood toward something less scary. Which is what I would have done if I were at work. But I remembered some of the best advice I've ever read, from Thich Nhat Hanh, about not closing off from your partner when you're hurt but being honest with them about your pain.

"I feel really bad," I said.

"Why?"

"I feel like I did something wrong."

"No." He put his arms around me but he was in his own head.

"I never want to take you for granted," I said. I was thinking about it a lot even before that moment, but with everything suddenly tenuous, it seemed even more relevant. Being with him was so easy, so intended. It had the quality of something designed but that didn't mean it was invincible.

"I love you, _____," he said a little later. "I love everything about you."

He hadn't done anything wrong. He had a right to protect himself, a right to be honest with me about what that looked like. We'd never acknowledged my work before while face-to-face—I suppose we still hadn't. He asked me later if I had any Advil; he had a headache and his eye was irritated from his sleeping in contacts, so the circumstances were bad on top of it all.

The desire to erase my past was as meaningless as it was impossible. What would I be like, who would I look like, how would I have met him? But that didn't change how badly I wished to. Once, pursuing sex work felt like the decision that would define my life. Now, I believed that about giving myself over to this love.

What was the riskiest thing I'd ever done? I couldn't have answered that question even if he'd let me.

~

On my last night, he said he knew a good place where we could watch the sunset, so we walked for 30 minutes to sit there. It was a series of benches lining the boundary of the park, and the one with the best view was unoccupied, as if reserved for us. There was little of it left for us to watch since, as usual, we'd been slow to leave the apartment.

"Look how fast it's going," I said. "Are we always going that fast? What kind of maniac is driving this thing?"

The sun was wreathed in fog with pinks and purples haunting the sky above as it descended, but the water was the more beautiful view. It lilted with a slightly yellowed white sheen riding over the silvery blue. I wasn't looking at Max's face for once, only feeling the nap of his heavy sweater and long arms underneath.

Back in the apartment he would say, "Can you believe you're here? It doesn't make any sense. Imagine telling yourself this would happen six months ago." And that was close to my own thoughts in the moment there with him. I was trying to take in that I was with him now at all, let alone in another country. I thought of how much I cried the afternoon I said goodbye to him in DUMBO, only four months ago. All the anguish. Would it have comforted me then to know what I knew now? Or would I have howled inside that he had left, anyway? I still would have had those weeks without him.

After the sun was done and I sat up to face him, he leaned into me.

"I'm crazy in love with you," he said low, in the emphatic way he has, like his whole body is clenched tight around the words. A deep and necessary breath. And then he added, "I like it. It feels good."

"I'm not sure if it feels good," I said. My love for him exposed me to terror. And just when I thought I loved him as much as I could, and it was already too much, there came more. "But I don't think I have a choice." I paused. "I think it will be bearable as long as you keep loving me back."

~

"It feels like you've been gone a week," he texted me after I'd been home for less than 24 hours. He was right. My trip seemed as though it were ages ago. What would living with him be like? We'd never been together for more than 10 days at a time. I imagined myself starting to panic inexplicably after two weeks of him home, my subtle physical systems all preparing for the drop of another departure.

I thought again of the skepticism I'd perceived from some of my friends. Maybe it was my own paranoia, my own inability to understand. I kept returning to something I said in my last letter, about how much I loved him from the start. I wondered if I were allowed to say that, if I would someday look back and be embarrassed by how much I'd inflated the truth, how wildly I'd played with the scope. How humiliating it would be if after a solid month together, we grated on each other's nerves so much we severed ties entirely.

But I still felt like my love for him had been in me since birth like a vein of gold ore. During my visit, we talked about how we met. I'd been so eager to start telling each other the story of us. To hear him talk about the circumstances around that long text he'd sent me on Tinder before we met, was pure sustenance.

It was 2 a.m. and he'd been up late working on a project—that much I knew. The pressure of replying to me was hanging over him, my comment that he was hard to flirt with, he wrote the message on his computer, then sent it to his phone. He pasted it to me just as he was about to go to bed, thinking he would never hear from me again because he wasn't used to those types of messages getting a response in any context: work, personal life. I couldn't believe that long, perfect paragraph he'd written me was supposed to be a sign off, but at the same time, it was entirely him to put that much time and effort into telling someone he barely knew what he had hoped and intended and been thinking during their brief exchange.

"When I read it," I told him, "I felt like . . . I recognized you. Even though I didn't know you yet. And that part was easy to fix."

While he was visiting his family in March, when he found out I was a prostitute, he'd sent me a link to "Past Lives." It was just silly pop music but he played it some nights in the Venice apartment while we made dinner and the lyrics moved me deeply now: "Don't you remember, you were meant to be my queen, meant to be my love."

I wasn't waiting for him; I hadn't conceived of him. I didn't know that ore was there or that it was for him. Sometimes I wondered if all the pain of the past years was me seeing the light glint off it but not knowing how to touch it. I imagine many of us suffer inarticulately with these deep reserves inside us, a capacity for connection we don't know how to tap.

How could I love him before I knew him? It's like asking how I could have known him before I knew him—it's a nonsense riddle. And yet I had.

POISON

June 9, 2015

When Max came back, he lived with me. He had so few belongings I cleared just one dresser drawer, and left space for hanging clothes in the closet.

"Is he like . . . an art vagabond?" one of my friends asked, and at the moment he indisputably was, though he was quick to point out this was only true since the spate of international work, and not a habitual way of being.

When we were at parties and people asked where he was living now, he'd say, "I'm staying with Charlotte for a while," with faint reluctance. This hurt me every time, though I assumed he was careful about the wording to acknowledge my sovereignty as well as to be gentle on his ego.

"Does this feel like your home?" I asked him once, too early.

"It feels like your home," he replied in his considered way. "I think when we have our home, we'll know it."

The weeks without him had been hard on me, a fact I attributed to my fluctuating chemical state. I'd taken the morning-after pill two months in a row, then started on hormonal birth control again after a year without it. I hated my body as much as I ever had, maybe even more. For a week I was overcome by the threat of breaking down in public, the very real possibility of panicked, frenzied tears over how intolerable it was to be inside my own skin, how shameful to be seen by others. I texted my ex about it while sobbing at the kitchen table. In the moment, I'd felt completely out of control and incoherent but when I read the conversation later, it was dramatically mild:

"Something's really wrong, I'm not thinking right."

"Maybe you should go see a doctor."

"I'm too scared. I don't want to take anything to make my brain feel even stranger, and I know they'll try to give me drugs."

He offered to pay for a therapist; he said it scared him, too, because loss of control was so out of character for me. I walked by a condo building he and I had talked about moving into years ago. I recognized its unusual facade when I passed even though we'd only seen an artist's rendering back then. I took a picture and sent it to him: "Is this the place I think it is?" We were both at the stage in the breakup where we sporadically, communally marveled at the years of being so close in comparison to where we were now, so abruptly far apart. This may be a stage that never ends.

My mental/emotional state sawed an edge into every moment of my day, but for Max I remained ardent. Our love was like a conspiracy, a twinship. Coming back to consciousness in the mornings, I felt drunker on him than on the lingering leadenness of sleep. There was no vocabulary for how singular our connection was but we talked about it all the time. We were particularly amazed at how underdeveloped our imaginations were in comparison to this reality, at the impossibility of conceiving of one another without having already been presented with the fact. And we teased each other about our marriage, our inevitable wedding, creating a running joke about hijacking the ceremonies we'd attend later this year.

"The whole speech is going to be about you," Max said of his best man's duties in one.

I immediately channeled what he would say. "'I know you thought I was going to talk about Alex and Dylan today, and I'm sure they're very attached to each other . . .'"

"'But marriage is supposed to be about the ultimate,'" he said. "Like, cosmic love."

I admitted to some peers I wanted to write a book but never without clarifying my insistence that it not have the trite ending of almost every sex worker memoir. (Meet a Good Guy, fall in love, quit the work, know that whoring is entirely in the past forever, period, goodbye.) For years, I'd chafed against the suggestion of anything in the shape of a memoir because of that prescribed narrative. Now, I wondered how I could avoid the truth that Max was the final act.

I was so inspired by him I even wanted to write stand-alone articles about the beauty of monogamy and my realization of the freedom in this pact. How ironic to, for years, not want that style of partnering, to not seek it, to actively reject the sheer notion of it all—stopping work, "settling down"—only to then do it without hesitation. And yet it was not ironic at all but rather a symptom of believing myself immune to engagement in the most consistent, normalized social practices. Too special to be human.

Max had been back for about a week when I woke one morning from an impressively bad dream. In it, he and I were together but then I disappeared, leaving him alone at night in a car that malfunctioned. When he called for service, he found himself in the home of a woman posing as someone who could help but who wasn't who she claimed to be. He discovered extensive notes about himself, information culled from surveillance of his online presence and possibly more nefarious means. I didn't even know you could dream that way, without yourself. It was like watching a film.

"If something is poisoned, add more poison," the woman told Max over the phone, before he got to her house. Maybe the woman was me, me somehow in the third person.

I'd read *Unmastered* and *Her 37th Year: An Index*, and become paranoid about our sex. Was it as good as the sex sketched out in those books, as good as the sex in the life-defining love affairs of other women? If our sex wasn't flawless, what did that say about our connection at every other level? This was an irrational and unfair train of thought but I dwelt on it anyway. I didn't want to be with anyone but him, yet sometimes I was frustrated he wasn't better at getting me off. I already felt like I came for him more than I came for myself, because my orgasms mattered more to him than they mattered to me. It was easy to resent him for not helping me more with something I felt I did for him.

But then, making him happy *was* for me. And it wasn't as if coming didn't matter to me at all. Usually, in the aftermath of a failed attempt, I became irritated with myself for being irritated, for letting anything negative puncture our cocoon of bliss, but also irritated with him for applying too much pressure, moving too fast, not stopping sooner, for starting at all. I'd be too physically agitated to finish even by myself, worked into that place where the desire to come dead-ends in the discomfort of too much wrong sensation.

He was aware of this, and occasionally made bitter, self-critical remarks. Mostly, instead, he promised to get better. "I know it's not sexy to be asked to say what you want, to have to tell it," he said, and I loved him for knowing this—which I too believe to be true—even as the diligent sex education-reading part of me felt obligated to say otherwise.

"It's not sexy to hear I want you to fuck me again and again?" I asked, smiling, pressing myself to him. "That I want your cock infinitely?"

I wasn't lying; I continued to desire everything about him. The only part of our sex I didn't like was when he focused on me too vigorously. And the worst part about the disconnect around my orgasms was that it overshadowed the otherwise wondrous quality of our sex.

"I feel every wild and tender thing when you come in me," I told him once after he had. I felt full of the softest fire then. I tried to name the states that arose: "Powerful. Devoted. Claimed."

The doubt and anger were nonsense. My brain still wasn't working. *I* was the poison. Our love wasn't like anyone else's so why should our sex be? I'm aware of how much confessional writers self-edit. I know better than to confuse the fan dance of artful personal revelation with transcribing, creating a literal account. Even in *Unmastered*, Angel writes, "Sometimes I needed to goad my desire along." For everyone, pleasure swims away at inconvenient times, and the intensity rises and falls and plateaus for each party across many encounters and within a single one. There were moments when I'd wanted Max to come and he hadn't, but I didn't doubt his desire for me. We were so new. We'd figure it out.

I brooded anyway. I didn't know what my own body meant anymore, why it responded the way it did or didn't, and what it was trying to tell me. I wanted effortless orgasms if I was going to have them at all. I wanted to be upended into pure physical pleasure, not pushed through it by concentrated or sustained work in my mind or hips or hand. I wanted neither he nor I to labor. I wanted someone to intuitively tip me over so I could be poured out.

My anxiety built to a fever pitch on a night when we fucked, he came, and then I wanted him hard again almost immediately. At least I think that's how it happened, because I found myself scowlingly asking, in my head, if the very first night when I met him was false advertising.

When he left to use the bathroom, I picked up my phone with the intention of activating my Tinder profile again. I knew this was lunacy but I was too upset to care. I was slowly convincing myself that Max was keeping me from something I could have had with someone else, though when I thought of Nick fucking me in the public bathroom months ago—Nick being the hookup I was probably most reliably hot for—I had no idea what I would get out of another encounter like that, let alone one that came at the expense of damaging what I had with Max. No man carried me away like I sometimes hoped for, at least not consistently. And Max's track record for giving me sunny orgasms—the ones that well up to the surface with ease and break like a wave you thought might hurt you but instead just thrill—was as good as anyone's had ever been.

Too incensed to do much else, I announced I was going to yoga and he asked if he could join. He knew I was fitful and bound up in my own head, so he asked in an unimposing way. My instinct was to be alone but I didn't want him to know that, and regardless of my temper, my curiosity about him was too insatiable to say no to more time together, ever.

We started out walking the mile to the studio holding hands, but I was listless and withdrawn. I considered the idea that Max isn't the last man I'll ever have sex with, whether we're married or not, even if we stay together forever. This possibility—that there would be others for me, that I would choose them, invite them, arrange them—seemed inevitable and hopeless, the bleakest truth. My instinct toward casual sex felt like a fact, like destiny. Not a choice. A sentence.

What a fool I was, to think my restlessness could ever be quelled. No one stays loyal to someone else that way. You can't have an active sex drive and be monogamous, wasn't that what every prolonged attempt at fidelity taught us? In *Her 37th Year*, the narrator cheats on her husband, the man with whom she seems to mostly share a sense of emptiness. I couldn't tell if the affair sex is really supposed to be that good, but I was willing to use it as fuel for my neurotic fire, to make it a commentary on Max and me in the one arena where I worried we were ordinary.

We angled our bodies around others, the sidewalk crammed with construction partitions, newspaper boxes, trashcans, and slow tourists. Max spoke to me but I barely responded. It was dark out. Through a window, I glimpsed a message tee: *You were my cup of tea but I drink champagne now.*

We passed through a narrow area and moved single file to accommodate other pedestrians. Though Max kept his arm stretched out behind for me, I almost dropped his hand. It was that moment, the sensation of my skin almost slipping from his, that seized me, and instead of letting go I grabbed his palm tighter. We moved into a space wide enough to stride side by side, and I took hold of his forearm with my other hand and made a noise from deep in my throat. On the other side of the crosswalk, he stopped and turned his body to mine and squatted down some to take my face in his hands and we kissed and kissed.

"I love you," he said, and it sounded like he meant it more than anyone else who's ever said it to me. His devotion landed on me like streetlight. It would have been madness to not keep holding onto this man.

This man. My man. Mine because of how completely I was his. I'd never belonged to anyone the way I belonged to him. Or belonged with. To say I needed him was wrong, too base. To say I wanted him meant nothing, because "want" sounds like a whim, a passing fancy.

All verbs were too flimsy. There is no word to describe being tethered to him the way I was, but I had absolute faith in our connection, complete conviction in the strength of the filaments that held us together. The problem was, I had less than absolute faith in myself. It's as if each of us held the end of an impossibly strong cord. The cord would never break but I could drop my end.

Max was my happy ending, the ending that's happy because it's the beginning of a thoroughly joyous adventure. After that night, I never stopped believing that. But even if it held true, the cliché sex worker conclusion couldn't be mine. I still hadn't quit working.

OTHER LIFE
July 13, 2015

On a weekend when Max would be away at a wedding, I traveled to LA for a client. Max knew I was making the trip though I may not have mentioned it at all if I weren't leaving a day before him—if I thought I could be gone unnoticed. When he asked what I would do there, I said, "see a friend." When he asked if that friend was Emma I said no, and pretended to be reflective about where in the world Emma would be that weekend.

I murmured distractions in response to his questions about where I was staying; I would stay in my client's home. He—the client—had already booked me a flight out and back.

Before Max returned from Venice, I dyed my hair teal. It was something I wanted to do, and I reasoned it would deter me from trying to work, or at least from taking appointments with anyone new or uptight. I couldn't expect a man to pay thousands of dollars for his dinner date to show up with the head of a sea witch.

LA client was a regular. He wouldn't like the change, but I thought he would forgive it, or at least tolerate it. I didn't want to jeopardize him by standing out too much while we were in public spaces, so I went to buy a wig. The day I'd designated for this outing happened to be the same day my financial domination client suggested we go shopping. I wore the wig out of one store and into another. It was long, with bangs—every cheap wig has to have bangs.

"What's going on with your hair?" he asked me. "It looks great."

"Oh, just trying something new," I said, and he, overcome, kissed the wig's crown.

Max knew about the wig. I didn't make an effort to hide it from him but I tried to keep other evidence from calling attention to itself. This limit of covertness, tact, obfuscation—whatever it should be called, and to whatever extent it existed—kept wiggling. When I came home with bags of new shoes and handbags from the financial submissive, I hastily found a place for everything new so it wouldn't be left out when Max got back. But when my LA client sent me a check in advance of our weekend together, I pinned it on the bulletin board in the kitchen. (Folded in half, with only one side pinned down.)

I'd called clients "friends" around Max before, and I continued to give them that descriptor if I described them at all. Sometimes if I was inspired to share a story about someone I knew (a famous inventor, a director) a pall fell over our exchange.

"How did you meet _____?" Max would ask, impressed, even interrupting me in his surprise.

"You know," I said, smiling, self-conscious, making some goofy motion with my hands or head or both. And he would look at me for a beat before he understood. Once, he turned over a piece of scrap paper I'd been using and read aloud "Condom Depot" from the back.

I wasn't working a lot. Since he'd come home, I hadn't worked at all—until I saw the shopping sub. This was mostly a function of me not being willing to sacrifice any time I could spend with Max. But when I left for LA, he hadn't even been home for two full weeks. So I was not exactly proving my stamina for restraint.

The LA client collected art and his home was filthy with it. I snuck a few pictures to send Max; I could not be in the presence of art without thinking of him. The household was obviously worth millions, first for the property itself and then for the furniture and custom fixtures, and finally (most of all, probably) for the art.

The client told me to use his wife's bathroom and closet for my own things. When I looked at her shoe wall as I unpacked my roller bag, I realized I had double her collection in heels alone, and remembered what a tight rein he kept on her spending.

He was easygoing and gave me plenty of personal time, which meant I could text Max regularly and I did. From galleries, from restaurants, from bed. Missing him was a constant ache and I almost cried about it one night looking out over Beverly Hills in the absent wife's bathroom. I used to be an interloper in the homes and hotels of these men. They snuck me into their world and I was happy to crash the party. But now I had to leave my life to insert myself into theirs. That was the part that hurt. Now, I had a life to leave.

I don't think I was good company for those few days, but I may have been saved by how much I genuinely liked the man I was with. Also, even after all this time purporting to understand and supply what men want, I often misinterpret them as desiring lively engagement and mental stimulation when really they just want a sentient ornament, someone who doesn't inconvenience or complain but only smiles occasionally, or compliments them.

A week from the day I'd left for LA, Max and I went to a crowded opening he'd bought tickets for on a whim. He was frustrated by the long wait in spite of the time on our reservation and disappointed by the end result, and my eagerness to cheer him up translated into clumsy stupidity. Apropos of something I can't remember, I started to joke-brag about the coolest place I'd ever had sex in my prior hometown. I tried to cut myself off at the last minute as I remembered this type of storytelling had always tended to go badly, temporarily draining all the joy between us — but it was too late. He'd slipped into the shuttered space where no tender words or physical affection could move him, though I did my best anyway: holding his hand in the cab on the way to dinner, leaning in and kissing his shoulder, telling him how good he looked in the streetlight.

We sat outside at the restaurant, and I said how moronic I felt when I let myself go like that. I hated the distance it created between us. No part of my urge to share the sexual aspects of my past was worth feeling separate from him. He told me it was a physical reaction more than a mental one, his stomach dropping so dramatically he couldn't help but respond to it. He regretted it, he wanted to be beyond it.

The waiter brought Max his whiskey and Max drank it immediately. Then he told me that on the night I flew to LA, he ate mushrooms and walked around Chinatown alone for hours to clear his head, his heart. To gain some insight.

It didn't work; he'd not been able to get to a different place even with the help of drugs. I had trouble understanding the impetus behind this but he made it clear it was a diffuse pain, the same suffering that made him seal up inside himself when I mentioned my sex life before him. The fact of me or at least his being with me troubled him, and that would have been true even if I hadn't made the clumsy mistake of occasionally calling attention to it.

For the first time since meeting him, it occurred to me that I might be bad for him. That his romanticism, and his commitment to romanticism, meant I'd always be a source of sadness. That this dissonance might be fundamental to who I was and who he was. That being with me up until this point had been conflicting for him instead of the surest decision he'd ever made in his life, like it had been for me.

I looked at the ground and kept my face still while the tears ran out. I was too crumpled by that possibility to speak, too overwhelmed to look at him. Even if I'd had something worth saying, my throat was too constricted to do it.

He apologized, he implored me to talk to him, look at him. He excoriated himself. He told me lowly, our entrees in front of us now (untouched), that I meant everything to him, that clearly he'd not said anything the way he intended to if I reacted to it this way.

Finally, I risked turning my wet mouth to his and we kissed one perfect, fitted kiss and it felt like the truest, most complete kiss of my life. The charge went direct to the deepest part of my body and my pussy throbbed in a strong pulse that seized and released like a sob.

We walked home and paused to look at the moon and hold each other but it didn't help. I just wanted to crawl into bed with the lights out and listen to music, so once we got inside I told him I was going to lie down.

He asked if he could join me and I said yes. I curled on my side and tried to dissolve into the dark and the sound.

After a few minutes, Max spoke. He was scared.

"Can I ask you a question?"

"Sure, you can try." I felt choked, worthless. I thought he'd ask what I was feeling, thinking. If I had doubts about being with him or if had complaints about our sex, or he'd want me to tell him what exactly he said at dinner that sliced through me.

Instead he asked, "Are you still working?"

"Yes," I said. I said it right away to force any thought of hesitating out of me, to preclude the possibility of even considering lying. "But not a lot. And in a very limited capacity."

I heard him breathing and then he said, "Could you . . . give me some way to think about that so it doesn't hurt so much?"

I rolled over and took his face in my hands and said, "I can stop. If you want me to, I'll stop. You're worth so much more to me—it's not even a sacrifice. It's not—it's not even something . . . You mean so much more, there's not even a measure for how little it . . . "

He had been carrying this fear and knowingness for so long. I hated myself for not realizing it, for not even suspecting. For thinking him unobservant enough to make up stories for the spaces I left, for him to do the work of a lie so I wouldn't have to. I wondered how many times, while we were fucking, he asked himself if I'd already been with someone earlier that day.

"It's not my place to do that," he said. "I can't tell you what to do."

"But I don't want you to be in pain. I need to stop anyway. I need to write. You'd be helping me. I know I need to quit because I can't write the way I need to if I'm still doing that. It's just hard to turn down the money. But I don't even need the money, that's an excuse. It comes from this anxiety . . . It's not a good thing for me anymore."

He said he knew I was with a client in LA, that's what the mushrooms were about. He told me he thought I'd get back from the trip and break up with him, though I'm still not sure why—something about glamour? Money? A lifestyle he couldn't provide but suspected was inherently desirable?

"The drop," he said. "It would happen because I hadn't asked. That's why I would go quiet. I knew I needed to ask, but I couldn't. And now that I have . . . I'm not going to pretend it's not hard. I'll feel it in every part of me, but I can take it. I'll just drink a lot on the nights you're gone."

"No," I said. "No. Fine, you don't have to ask me. That's not fair to you. I'm just telling you. I'm not going to work, ok? Let's leave it at that for now."

"But if you change your mind. If you ever feel like you need to—I mean for reasons other than money . . . "

And when he said that, I knew Max saw me in a way very few people in my life ever had, or would.

"No. I need you to trust me. I need you to believe I can do this." I heard my own desperation. I knew he probably shouldn't trust me. I didn't trust myself.

The next day, we left to stay with one of Max's college friends in another city. The friend's wife was ebullient and sweet, another artist. We visited her studio and then sat in a bar eating pretzels. We snuck vegan ice cream into a different bar where we ate dinner, and the wife got adorably drunk.

"These two are going to do such amazing things together," she told her husband, almost indignant, like he disagreed with her.

It was hot, so Max and I left the windows open at night and slept under only the thin sheet on the air mattress, otherwise naked in their living room. On our second night, in a candle-lit church, Max wrote "I love you" with his finger on my right palm, one large letter after another.

Back at the apartment, just before sleep, Max's friend laid down on the couch next to the mattress, all of us on the same horizontal plane while we laughed and talked about silly things. His wife had left that morning for a trip with her friends, and the home had the altered air of having half its normal animation missing, then replaced: the unfamiliar inside the familiar, the foreign within the private.

But it fostered low-level excitement instead of discomfort. It'd been a long, long time since I had that communal feeling of being in a pile of boys. I first experienced it in high school when my group of friends allowed themselves puppy physicality, the unselfconscious seeking of automatic tenderness and affection—three and four of us in bed at a time, or sleeping on a floor, girls and boys together in whatever formation we fell, which was usually one girl amid several boys, because the boys had less strict curfews and faced less severe punishments. The closeness was always more charged because of the possibility of sex, but the primary mood was one of camaraderie, pure and warm and loose. It was good to giggle with two guys, fear-free and without needing to satisfy their expectations. Hating men so much had exhausted me.

In the following weeks, the days started to open. Without the distraction of planning work or doing work (sex work, I mean) I gained the ability to focus on other things. I could turn my attention toward writing. I could write for a day and then another day, each right after the other. I woke up to Max. I went to bed to Max. Daily routine was remarkable. I thought, I could get used to this. I thought I was getting used to it.

Max was at his studio when the submissive client asked to meet again. He was always impulsive, infuriatingly so, and he only gave me an hour's notice. I was supposed to meet Max a little later, so I stuck to my geographical demands, refusing to go as far uptown as he wanted me. We failed to make a plan for shopping. At the last moment, he proposed, "Meet me at an ATM?"

I put on makeup and the wig, and a pair of heels he bought when we were last together. Then I got into a cab.

Did this count as working? How could I turn down $1,000 that came virtually free of effort, that would make both my and Max's life better? I posited it this way—money for me was money for Max—which was both true and disingenuous. Anything I had was his, but Max lived so frugally, he didn't need me to support him. And while he would never have tried to shame me about the source of my money, or act disgusted by where it came from, there was no circumstance under which he would encourage me to spend or earn for him. That went for straight work, creative work, any work. He would only defer to me and what I wanted.

"Want" was where it broke down, though. I couldn't think about this in terms of "need" or "want" because work was habitual, compulsive. I don't mean I wasn't responsible for my actions, only that the motivations felt so mindless, there was barely any mental process in me when I acted upon them.

327

This was what I knew Max didn't understand when he talked about not being able to provide for me financially at the rate I was used to; even if he'd been in a position to give me $1,000, if he'd had a limitless family inheritance that I could draw from at will, it wouldn't be the same. That $1,000, the submissive's $1,000, would still be there, glistening like raw meat in a bear trap.

And it never goes away. Doing sex work is like having a chip installed in your head that gives you money radar. Suddenly you see, everywhere you go, no matter what else you do, how much money men are willing to part with if you know what to offer them and are willing to offer it. I felt like I was collecting, not quite working. I was claiming what was already rightfully mine. So maybe the money wasn't the meat—maybe the money was the bear, and I the one who set the trap.

When I'd seen the submissive last time, we went to an ATM, and then a bank. That afternoon, I made as much in two hours as I used to make for a date that lasted a full 24.

I met him on the corner.

"Where's the ATM?" I asked after we exchanged greetings.

"I already went," he said. "My next appointment's uptown, so I thought we could get a cab and talk on the way there, and then you can just take it to wherever you need to be."

"Oh. Ok," I said. I hadn't planned for this but immediately I understood: he wanted a semiprivate space where I could pet his dick through his pants, and this was the best option his limited time would allow.

I asked for the bank envelope first, scanned the contents, and then demanded his wallet and took the 20s from inside. Traffic was awful; we were going crosstown. I couldn't concentrate on his questions, which were as maddening as ever. He asked me why I hadn't responded to his emails from over the weekend when Max and I were away, emails that consisted of only a few lines each, all trying to arrange last-minute dates. In one after the other, he'd altered his range of what time and place might be possible, then pressed to get an immediate response. I'd read them all at once, days after they'd been sent.

Then he switched to manic inquiries about the present. ("What are you doing tonight? What if we got together again later? What if I got a hotel room?") He'd done this before, always when I had plans with another client. He made escalating offers to get me to free my evening for him—more shopping, $10,000 in cash.

All I could think about was Max in his studio, expecting me, and I saw the cab's dashboard clock and realized if I rode all the way uptown, I'd never make it into Brooklyn when I'd promised I would. Not if I went home first to change out of the outfit that would otherwise give everything away.

"I have to get out here," I said finally. "I'm going to be late if I don't."

"You're just using me, aren't you?" the submissive said, his upper lip wet with sweat. He was always sweaty. He shaved his head, which was big and pink, but ignored the handful of white whiskers that curled out of his face at irregular intervals. He stiffened and fanned out his lips when he went to kiss as if they were the fluttery rims of a cartoon clamshell. Kissing him was the worst part, much worse than teasing his negligible erection under the low overhang of his belly.

In boots and a tank top, I followed the corridors of floor around Max's pieces. His work was still new to me because I hadn't had many opportunities to see it. The way he spoke about his decisions, the decisions that were in evidence, revealed something about him I wouldn't have learned any other way. I didn't know how to turn this into a reaction, so I didn't say much, only looked.

We walked to the subway holding hands, which I can say not because I remember the walk—though I do; he recognized someone crossing in the other direction, and raised his free arm and said hello—but because we walk everywhere holding hands. When we came home, I'm sure we had sex because we did it constantly though not obsessively. It wasn't frenzied, it was inevitable. Our lives were full of time and desire.

I had a dream about living with a client. I couldn't believe I'd put myself in such a stupid position.

"I'm in love with Max," I said, trying to appeal to the man's decent side. "I want to live with him. I want to be with him forever."

The client laughed at me, cruelly; he would not leave the home we shared and he wouldn't allow me to, either. I had no power to influence his behavior.

"No one will help you," he said, taunting me. Daring me to try to enlist anyone's aid. "You're a felon." I knew what he meant: a whore. It's all the same.

Max was in every dream now. If not in body than in my dreamself's interior thoughts. Over and over, sleeping, my subconscious recited a variation on the mantra of wanting him definitively, loving him conclusively.

It's more than I dared to hope for, I'd written down in my notes from my visit to Venice, while recording some memory scraps from when we sat on the bench at sunset. I kept trying to place where it fell relative to the other bits of dialogue, but I still wasn't sure which of us had said it.

Several days later, I received an email from the submissive saying he was giving up on seeing me again because my schedule was too full. That ATM visit was the only appointment I had for the entire month of June. I cancelled three others with my best regular, all of which would have meant easy, good money.

I woke up to Max, I went to bed to Max. The other life lapped at the edges of the world outside our bed, rhythmic and patient as the ocean landing on the sand.

COMMITTED

August 17, 2015

I didn't tell Max about my occasional urge to sleep with other people until I was high. The night of renewed connection, when I'd looked at Tinder in despair and then felt the magnitude of how destructive it would be to pursue that to an end, was momentary wisdom but did nothing to extinguish the impulse longer term. The instinct surfaced whenever I felt slighted, even when it was surely unintentional— when he fell asleep while I wanted to keep touching me; when he left for his studio and I wanted him (to want) to be with me instead; when I didn't come the way I wanted to.

Anytime I felt a sense of abandonment or loneliness or separation, I considered it.

Sometimes I thought about calling Aaron, or an Australian man I sexted with before Max and I told each other we were in love. Sometimes I relied on friends to keep me company or feed me drugs to distract from it.

Max always knew something was wrong. He's sensitive anyway, but how I withdrew made it obvious. And sometimes he made his subsequent panic transparent, nearly begging me to meet him somewhere or let him come get me while I encouraged him to keep working, or to spend time with friends instead of worrying. I didn't want to hurt him or hamper him.

Half of the time my reaction felt legitimate, the other half unreasonable. Either way, I wanted to protect him from myself. But eventually, giddy and unedited on Adderall, our conversation led me to confess.

He was crushed, not angry but self-critical. He'd suspected, he told me. His worst nightmare was the truth; he couldn't satisfy me. He vowed to be harder more often, to last longer, and I shook my head and even laughed and told him he already performed in this department as well as any man could, better than most.

Trying to change our sex, I said, would be like trying to cure someone who touched every doorknob 12 times by replacing all of a home's doorknobs.

Intellectually, I still believed long-term monogamy was irrational and counterintuitive but I also had the sense to recognize this wasn't about physical desire or overfamiliarity. It was a negative habit, not an addiction but akin, maybe, to ultimately unhealthy self-medication. It sprang out of my anxiety, my insecurity, as a desperate bid for distraction and ego-inflation. I never felt elated or excited by the idea, only hopeless. I didn't want anyone else besides him, but I tried to reassure myself I had other options than this consuming love.

In spite of my explaining this, Max had trouble believing it wasn't an indication of his failings. He vowed to do better without insults or threats, nor demanding my fidelity.

I realized I was the only person threatening our relationship. In the metaphor of us each holding an end of cord, he would never let go of his end. But I might let go of mine.

The next day, I deleted Tinder.

~

We visited my childhood home and slept in my old room. I told him I'd been here on Christmas morning, in my teenage bed, heating myself with thoughts about my mouth between his legs.

"I imagined you in a fancy hotel on Christmas," he said sincerely, and I laughed, surprised. In conversations about our earliest days together, I only slowly started to see myself as Max had: impossibly sophisticated, in control, direct. We only met in hotels when I summoned him during my trips to the city. I was always blown out and glossy, wearing work makeup even if I hadn't been working.

Of that first meeting in the bar, he said: "You were like, 'Ok, I'm ready to go back to my hotel now.' And I was like ' . . . Ok. Can I come?' You were so in charge. I loved it. Then we got into the hotel room and you just started taking off your clothes."

"Really?" This was highly plausible, but not something I recalled specifically. "Did I at least help you take off yours?"

"Oh, yeah. I was just lying on the bed totally stunned."

I remembered that then, him laying back on the bed and me arranging my body over him.

"And eventually you said, 'Are you planning on going home anytime or . . . I mean, you can stay if you want.' And I realized I was just one name on a list." He didn't say this in a self-pitying or judgmental way, but it still hit me in a vulnerable place.

I had to spend time thinking about how I knew him now and what I assumed of him then. I'd thought he, like every man on Tinder, like me, wanted a casual hook up and had done it before. I forgot how blasé and assured work made me, how nonchalant. I wanted to attribute my boldness to work too, until I joked with Max that all I did in high school was get hickeys and get stoned.

"I would have been so intimidated by you," he said.

I started to protest, but remembered who I was in high school and realized I may have propositioned him just as I did some other male friends then. (Artlessly.)

The continuity of my teen self and adult self was almost staggering. How had I never seen it before? But thank god for that consistency, not only because I liked who I was and what my life was like but because these qualities were what made me the complement to Max. My curiosity, my persistence, my brazenness would have never worked in our favor if it weren't for his intelligence, his openness, his sweetness. But similarly his hesitancy, his shyness, would have been our downfall if I weren't able to offset it. Neither of us accommodated the one more than the other.

Sometimes I was uncomfortable with how much I felt I'd had to pursue him. But these revelations about who we both are, small and constant, helped. My ardency wasn't indiscriminate, so it was nothing to be ashamed of. And it wouldn't have been so insistent if he weren't who he was. He'd been struck by me; in awe, he told some of his friends what happened. But he didn't have faith there'd be a second time for us, and he was so impressed by my hotel rooms, my seemingly important job, my lack of nerves, he didn't trust he'd made the same impression on me.

"I've never seen you look so happy," he told me his best friend from college said while we were all out with Alana, celebrating the sale of her book. This from a man who's known him for more than 10 years.

"I know why he said that," Max added. "I've never *been* so happy."

The odds of us finding each other at all, we decided, were very low. But once we'd found each other, it was certain we'd love the way we did. So I held these two convictions in my heart at the same time: the vast improbability of us being together and the impossibility of us not being together. How unlikely. How inevitable.

~

We drove north so Max could DJ at his friends' wedding. It took at least six hours, probably more with the detour to collect the equipment, and we were a little late for the rehearsal but nobody minded. In this milieu, people immediately treated us as a professional team.

"What's the gig?" the bearded man at the music store asked after he flattered me with a lingo-filled spiel about the sound system. "You're a duo?"

The morning of the ceremony, we set up in the barn where dinner and dancing would be. Tables sprawled everywhere and the intended floor plan didn't quite match up with the current layout. While Max unloaded the heavy pieces, I walked down the hill to a tent where six people stood preparing food.

"Have any of you seen Judith?" I asked, naming the wedding planner.

The only man looked up. "Are you the one getting married?"

"No," I said. I was in dirty white corduroys and an oversized tank top, my green hair pinned lopsided near the top of my head.

He put down his carrots.

After the ceremony, while most guests mingled outside drinking, Max set up the dinner music as I found our table. Before I could sit, the caterer, now dressed in a black, ironed apron with his dark hair smoothed back, stopped to talk. He mistook me for a fellow worker there, I think. He asked questions about the night's timing, and what distance I'd come from. I took his friendliness for camaraderie among behind-the-scenes people until I noticed how long we held our eye contact, and then, with a slight panic, I wished Max were by my side.

He was soon, and when he appeared I grabbed his hand, and the waiter bowed out with a smile to us both.

"Don't leave me alone for long again," I said, trying to sound like I was teasing, "or the caterer will be on it."

So then any time the man passed near our table with food for another, Max turned his face toward mine and showily kissed me.

The next morning while we had sex, I kept thinking about him. Not in a purposeful way, not because it turned me on, but because Max and I were disconnected and I was distracting myself from the disconnect. (At 2 a.m., while he kissed down my body, I giggled and lovingly but unwisely answered, "Whiskey dick," when he asked why I was laughing.)

When I let myself wonder what sex with the waiter might have been like, I realized I only had to use my intuition, which is pretty sterling in this department, and was suddenly certain he'd be emphatic and physically commanding at first but come very quickly and then not again. I tried to imagine some sexual style for him that would have been more satisfying for me but I couldn't. No fantasies could ensue; the first impression was unalterable.

I didn't have any interest in sex with anyone else anymore. The impulse was exorcised, not painlessly but through pain that came with tenderness, and there wasn't any self-control required, no effort to keep it out of my mind. Understanding the instinct let me release it, which calmed me in a way I hadn't expected or even thought possible. And not working meant that when I was with Max, I could be with Max. I wasn't reminded that sex for myself is akin enough to sex for work, at least in its physical details, to justify—or necessitate—the paranoid, hair-trigger response in my head. ("Is this just like work?" "This is just like work.") I don't think I'd been free of this inquiry since I started working as an escort.

Once, immediately after he came, I cried.

"My love," he whispered, kissing my face from above me, smiling slightly. "Why are you crying?"

"They're happy tears," I said. It was stupid and shallow, ridiculous to put into words, but I'd been overwhelmed with gratitude for how much I adored his body, how thoroughly I loved his cock. To think I would have access to this type of pleasure, this degree of fulfillment, for the rest of my life was beyond fathoming.

"I worship you," I told him while we were in bed together, to which he laughed.

I could imagine how someone might miss his beauty, but I was not that someone. I adored his face. Occasionally I couldn't focus when he talked because I became so absorbed in its perfection. When I looked at him from a distance, I sometimes experienced the full force of my attraction to him and almost panicked, stricken with a vague plea of "No, don't take it from me . . . " "It" being anyone's guess: his body, our love, him.

"She remembers the first night she knew she loved him," writes Jenny Offill, "the way the fear came rushing in. She laid her head on his chest and listened to his heart. One day this too will stop, she thought."

In the early days, my ex excoriated me for bringing up my desire to work in the ways he'd forbidden: full service, overnights, travel.

"You know I don't want you to!" he'd cry. "Why do you have to ask?"

His incomprehension is, of course, part of why we couldn't stay together.

Max refused to make these same mistakes.

"I'm not [your ex]," he would say before disavowing his ability or willingness to tell me "no."

He said what he'd said before about not wanting to force changes into my life, about not expecting me to conform to his discomfort by stopping. He said he could withstand as much pain as required to be with me, and he would never stop loving me unless I told him to get out my life.

I tried to frame it all hypothetically: What if I needed to go back because I got too anxious about money without it? I was trying to abide by my promise to him, made only two weeks before, that I wouldn't work for a while, not until we could discuss it properly. I don't think he or I realized this discussion would count as that.

∾

I don't know why I woke up to the memory of Hot Client a few days later, but once he was in my head I also recalled my fantasy of a life with him involving private jets, executive-only picnics, a general air of casual and delighted affluence. I knew this was a level of wealth I'd probably forfeited access to forever, not because Hot Client and I had any future together but because work allowed me to touch such luxury through other men, too. This was something Max cited regarding his fear about me giving up work while with him. He thought I was sacrificing a lifestyle I might want more than I realized, or resent him for keeping me from.

I didn't have that concern because Max was the most important part of what I wanted. Vacationing in others' richness had been fun, but I was aware I was a poseur and not a permanent fixture. Max meant more to me than anything I could imagine or recall caring about, certainly more than comfortable travel or frequent shopping sprees or spa days. I believed we would have a good, happy life together. I'd have a career as a writer, however modest—though I believe in my tenacity to make it grand—and he would continue to be devoted to art in ways that allowed for survival if not financial thriving.

But I also knew money matters. It's fine and true to say it can't buy love, but it can provide time and resources with which to fully enjoy your love, to live with the person you love for more hours than you work away from them in a job you hate.

By the end of June, I'd turned down many requests from my best regular, a man who often said he was too tired to have sex and who demanded little else during our time. This was someone who loved me, or thought he loved me, and I felt loyalty toward him that rivaled if not surpassed my allegiance to the money.

"The window is closing," I'd told Max some time ago. I could feel my willingness to work evaporating. All of it would soon be too much of an interruption in my life with him regardless of how much money was on the line. But I wasn't quite there yet.

Max went away on a bachelor weekend. When he got back, I told him that in a few days, I was leaving town for work.

THE ONES WHO CAN PAY

September 21, 2015

Starting work again while being with Max was an easy decision in that I felt too compelled toward it to refuse any longer. I believed my instincts wouldn't so directly oppose my happiness with him unless there were good reason. But I hadn't parsed those reasons yet, and so I wondered if I was jeopardizing the greatest love I'd ever known from a place of greed or neuroticism: asserting myself like a child, testing him, pathologically, unnecessarily insecure about money, unwilling to give up the idea of buying whatever I want when I want it. Was I driving a wedge between us out of habit and weakness?

I needed to understand more for myself and for Max. Even I, who try to say everything, hadn't yet found the words to describe what work means to me. And explaining it to him felt especially impossible, insurmountable— no obvious place to start given his resistance and panic, and my own.

"It's not like you're thinking," I said over and over. I didn't know what he was thinking, only that it had to be wrong.

~

When I told Max I was leaving for two nights to see a client, it plunged each of us into fear and isolation. I felt myself struggling to stay connected and I knew he tried the same but I realized that when it came to my work, we'd each said things we wanted to mean but didn't, or couldn't—at least not yet—and we'd spoken from inside the hope that the other wouldn't call on us to prove it.

He cocooned himself in his doubts and ignorance while I circled and pleaded, hesitant to break through with force but afraid to see him seal off. He hurt me deeply when he aired his fears that my clients offered me things he couldn't. It came out like an accusation that I was inextricably drawn to excess and luxury and monetary validation.

"You think I'm a greedy narcissist."

"Don't put those words in my mouth, _____."

"Why do you think I want to be with you, if I care so much about those things?"

"You like the image of yourself that's reflected back?"

This landed as violently as a slap. "Is that why you're with me?"

"Sometimes. But mostly I just love being around everything you are."

"So why don't you think I feel the same way about you?"

What sliced deepest in these moments was my sense he didn't believe in our love the way I did. For me, our bond was absolute.

"This is not a trial run," I reassured him when he was frustrated with himself, convinced he'd done something to break our stride. "I never worry about us. There are no contingencies."

But his personal insecurities manifested as insecurities about us.

I tried to articulate it for him, guessing at the source. "You think I'm making fools of my clients and I could do the same to you?"

"Maybe. It's more that, I know how it feels to want to be close to you, to see you smile at me, and to be inside you and feel connected to you. I know there are parts of you I don't see. I worry that's a separate you altogether and the other you—if you switch over like that—the other you doesn't know you love me. Maybe you won't be able to switch back."

He was good at listening. I'd told him I myself worried that there were parts of me he'd never know or see, because work was so entirely off limits for discussion. And not just work but all my sexual and romantic history. His attention backfired sometimes, though, when it became fodder for misinterpretations like this.

"But I'm a column of loving you, all the time," I said. "It's like my central nervous system."

"It's not fear that you'll leave me for someone else but that you'll leave me for a lifestyle. That you'll decide you want something other than love."

"You don't think I've tried to live that way already?"

"It's familiar." More proof he listened, but twisted again. I talked a lot about needing time to shake the familiar, to create a new normal.

"That's true," I said. I didn't know what else to say. His concerns were all intelligent, almost founded. They were consistent with my behavior in the past; they were decisions I was capable of making. But to become reality, they'd require my love for him to be weaker than it was. They required someone other than him on the other end of the choice.

"I can imagine both of us still loving each other but you deciding that I just don't fit into your goals and needs." He was quiet, then said softly, "It makes me hate people."

"Makes you hate who?"

"The ones who can pay."

~

I wanted to want to quit work more than I did. I wanted to quit it some, but not enough. The most obvious motivation to stay—money— was, on one hand, right and true. I didn't want to deplete my savings while I figured out how to make writing financially supportive, and I assumed I'd be responsible for both of us when it came to maintaining the cushion that allowed comfortable travel, a beautiful apartment, stress-free emergency expenditures.

The notion of being the primary provider, even outside of continuing sex work, filled me with pride more than trepidation. I trusted I could do it even if I knew Max might not like that I was doing it, or might disapprove of my means. It all came out of my (pleasurable) impulse to provide for him, for us, simply because I could do it so well. Whatever form it took—planning travel or covering an expense or addressing bureaucratic inconveniences with authority and alacrity—I felt energized when I flexed into my competence, fluid and strong, an animal using its muscle memory. Continuing to earn at a high level was a piece of this.

But the pull was more than money, and this gave me the most pause. I was through with the vast majority of appointments, that much was clear, and it felt like a blessing. I wouldn't see men with whom I had a cordial, lacquered dynamic. I wouldn't meet anyone new. I stopped reading pop psychology and science books, shunted *Fortune* and *Fast Company* straight to the recycling bin, consigned a slew of cocktail dresses.

The guys I'd seen a handful of times, who were fine (tolerable, amiable) and mostly forgettable, were easy to let go without explanation. But my most regular clients were men I cared for, whose company I enjoyed because it was familiar and relaxed. Our relationships were not uncomplicated but they were warm and authentic. I wasn't faking it with Drunk Client, or the man in LA, or Roger, my longest standing and most devoted patron—not when "it" was sincere affection.

So many aspects of my life changed immediately after meeting Max. I didn't resent that, but it couldn't all be immediate. I was figuring out how to be finished with this. I needed it resolved inside myself, on the pre-intellectual emotional level, before I could make the termination complete.

Most challenging in all this was Roger, a man who, with self-control, made it clear he was in love with me. When I met him, Roger had seen at least a hundred escorts, probably more, over the span of more than 20 years. He'd even booked Ashley Dupré long before she became notorious for her date with Spitzer. A year or so after our first appointment, he stopped hiring other women. He told me he'd never see another escort again; after I retired, he was done. And for months he talked about preparing himself mentally for me to quit, because he assumed my quitting was inevitable.

I believed him. He was a sober, self-reflective man with no inclinations toward deception or manipulation, and recently, he'd begun to age noticeably: his walk slowed, his hearing diminished, he fell asleep easily and often. He wasn't as old as these changes suggest, but their result was to render me more aware of his mortality than I've ever been of anyone's, including clients much older than he. My impression was that he and his wife had no physical intimacy, probably not even casual affection. The notion of leaving him celibate and worse, lonely, for the remaining decades of his life weighed on me. That force alone would not have kept me working, but it was a factor.

~

"I would love to tell you about it," I told Max while we were in bed together. This time the "it" was everything, all the pained and conflicted thoughts that jousted for precedence at any given moment. I wanted to reassure him of how little sexual contact there was anymore. I wanted to tell him about my sense of obligation to Roger so I could feel at least slightly unburdened.

But he gave a clear, brief shake of his head, and we settled back into silence. (One night, I made the mistake of saying to Max, about Roger, "He would be really happy for me if he knew about you."

"Don't say a word about me," Max replied, with a vehemence so cold and immediate that I almost lost my breath.)

"It's not like you imagine," I said now, repeating myself. "And I don't know if it's better to tell you what it's like, even if you don't want to hear it, or respect what you want. But I think about it all the time."

"I trust you," Max said, meaning there was nothing he needed to be told. "I don't think you make decisions that would hurt me or us."

"I couldn't. I can't make any decision without taking into account your being in my life." But I knew part of Max wanted more information. Sometimes he'd ask questions—"Do you look forward to it?" "How many people are you seeing?"—and then cut himself off with, "Don't answer that."

This time, he said, "I keep what I imagine it is like, or was like, or could be like, in a separate place from how I feel about you. The anger and sadness is at the system, not at you. I'd rather understand this as pain from loving you so much than to have you tell me what happens and be forced to admit that my pain is unreasonable, or for you to see it as unreasonable. For it to be revealed as jealousy and pettiness.

"But the truth is, I want to be the only person whose hand you hold. The only person you smile at. The only person who gets to kiss you. The only person you tell jokes to. The only person who makes you wet. And I know how unfair and irrational that is, but I still want it.

"I also know that if I could pay to hold your hand, I would. If I could pay you to seem interested in me, it would be worth it. I know I talk a lot about how sexy you are and how hot I am for you, and it's true. But there are many more other things that make me love you, and want to be with you forever. And I know I'm not the only person who wants that."

I held very still while he said all this, gripped by the intense pressure inside me. He was so right about it—how badly I'd been hoping that telling him would alleviate the stress between us. And he was right about my clients, too. When I'd last been with Roger, he said, "I would marry you if I could figure out a way to do it."

During a particularly raucous lunch with Drunk Client, he suddenly became serious and said, "What if you were my best friend?"

"I think that's ok," I said. He was not the first client to tell me this.

"No, but I mean, even better than my wife?" He glanced into his drink, altered by what he'd spoken aloud. "I don't want to talk about this."

~

The greatest struggle was reconciling my anxiety about Max's sadness with my gratitude for Roger's participation in my life. Max's hard drive died and it cost over a thousand dollars to fix, which I paid for. My freelance income barely made a dent in rent for the apartment where we both lived, but my income from Roger alone covered it easily.

"I'm grateful for Roger," I blurted out during one exchange. "His money helps us live the life we have."

"I don't think I'll ever be grateful to him."

"You don't have to be!" That wasn't my point, of course. I was trying to indicate my conflicting allegiances. That one man allowed me to be with the other.

"The imagination that hurts the most is how I'll afford to compete with all the others who want time with you," Max said.

"Am I competing with _____?" I asked, naming the artist who hires him. Knowing the irrationality of his framing made me desperate, sporadically angry.

"I worry I'm incapable of filling the shoes of the character you're in love with now," he said. "I want to live up to Max, but I don't know if I can."

"You're not a character to me."

"I know you love me for me. I get pangs of genuine inadequacy though—I assume from this feeling that you deserve more."

Ultimately I understood his reactions and my own. I understood why we each acted as we did and I wasn't sure how it could be different or even if it should be. I knew what would hurt him to hear. But he was my best friend. I wanted to tell him everything as strongly as I knew I shouldn't.

≈

Max had a dream in which he kept calling me on the phone, and I told him that I couldn't see him again for a long time, years maybe, because some men were paying me a huge sum to stay away from him. Paying me to keep us separated, but nothing more.

"There's not enough money in the world," I said to him after he recounted it. "You think I could really be that mean?"

"You weren't mean," he said. "Just practical."

≈

Max and I were in the park together on a Friday night. I'd returned home earlier that day from a work trip, one that—characteristically, now—consisted of me lying awake until early in the morning, furtively texting him because he wouldn't sleep while I was gone. I'd begun to think the best course of action might be hitting him with his worst fears, to confirm I'd received every lavish service he could conjure. So I told him about the private plane. It happened years ago: I missed a connecting flight in Texas, and the client I was supposed to meet chartered a plane to take me to him. It was a pragmatic, albeit grand, move. We didn't have much time together, and the next commercial flight was hours away.

"It was cool. It was fun. And I know if I had heard of someone doing that for an escort when I was younger, I would have been really jealous and felt like it was so glamorous and that it was an important thing to make happen in my life but . . . it didn't matter. I mean, how much can you feel about it? It's not important. It's not relevant for living a good life."

Max was quiet, brooding. He'd laughed once when I started, when I said the words "chartered a plane," but then nothing. It was the vaguely angry laugh of someone hearing something ridiculous. I kept going.

"I remember thinking, a long time ago, about what a huge compliment it is for an escort to date a man for free. Because she gets treated well by men for a living, and those men make efforts a lot of boyfriends don't. She's seen all the rich guys, had every type of sex, been gifted expensive things, and now this is the man who she wants to fuck and spend time with without making any money at all. But I knew a guy wouldn't be able to understand, to see it that way."

Max was still thinking. Then he said, "I think talking about what's going on inside me makes it worse. Naming the shadow, trying to give shape, only creates something new. It doesn't take away the original idea. And then there's another dark thing hovering nearby."

The most hurtful thing he'd ever said to me came during one of these many discussions about work: "Words don't matter to me." I couldn't concentrate on what followed. It felt like the most personal way he could have injured me, even though I didn't think it was intentional.

Naming what was in me always soothed me, but I knew that effect was temporary. I could make one sensation dissipate but another would appear. And I swung back and forth between feeling righteous and justified about working, and feeling disappointed in myself.

I broke while we sat at the kitchen table one raw morning. I cried. Why couldn't I feel more coherent inside? Why didn't I just stop working? Was it that I couldn't, or that I wouldn't?

"I wish I could be a different person for you," I said, and he pulled my body into his.

"No, no, no, no. Never say that. Don't you ever say that. That is not how this works. I love everything about you. I love every day you've been you. I love all the yous you've been."

"I hate to think about you getting calloused to this." As much as I wanted work not to cause rifts, his resolutions to be "cooler, better" worried me. I didn't want him pretending he wasn't bothered or teaching himself to be inured from the outside in.

"I don't think it's a bad thing."

"But I love everything about you, too. And I don't want to change any of it. I want to protect it."

"Maybe you could let go of your worry for me the way I let go of the pain," he said. "I'm happy once you're back."

And that was true. He never tried to punish me when we were together again. He never held a grudge.

The sense of separation was real though, while we were apart. I felt it changing us. I worried I wouldn't be able to keep loving him as I had been. I worried he would convince me to see him as unworthy as he believed himself.

FOREVER BEGINNING

September 28, 2015

I'd imagined retirement as a slow slope into civilian-hood. I figured I had at least a year—if not two or three—of maintaining my most pleasant and generous regulars before stopping altogether in an official, announced exit. But as I grew away from the emotional and mental states that made sex work possible, so did those former intimates withdraw from me. The vibrant, consuming pursuit that animated my 20s shrank to the size of a pebble in just a few months. My website was offline, my public online presence dark, and I no longer sent chatty emails asking clients about work and hobbies and pets. Had my efforts been the only engine keeping our professional relationships going? Or had the men simply grown tired of me as I grew tired of them?

I told the client in LA my real name. Roger already knew, but now I granted him permission to call me that, to text me on my primary number and write me at my personal email address. It was my concession to the impending jump. These two people I thought I wanted to know for a long time, in an integrated way. Our connections seemed sincere and worth preserving. But nearly everyone else simply disappeared from my life as abruptly as they'd entered it. We had nothing to bind us without the transaction.

I might have been more bothered by this evaporation if I were inclined to think about work at all anymore. But instead, my world with Max occupied all energies.

I liked having my attention honed to him. It was grounding, it gave me direction, and yet it wasn't limiting because he was—he and I together were—limitless. "The joy lasts limitlessly for as long as it lasts," writes Hélène Cixous of love.

My mission now wasn't to make more money or instigate massive situational change, as it had been a year and a half ago, but to understand the way I loved Max, to abide inside who I became by loving him.

"You're the most interesting thing in my life," I told him one afternoon, realizing the truth of it as I said it. "I would give up books for you."

"Whoa," he said.

I nodded, then shrugged. "My curiosity about you is much more urgent."

And it was wild curiosity, not jealousy. I was dying to know how he'd lost his virginity, but afraid asking would make him uncomfortable. And I was desperate to understand more about his last girlfriend, a woman who broke his heart and of whom he would only make cryptic, vague pronouncements like: "She's the type of woman who doesn't need anything."

I finally met her at a brunch party in Soho. We could hardly have been more dissimilar: she, petite and ethereal with a spacey, blasé vibe that rendered her somehow more barefoot than the barefoot rest of us. And me, with my height and alertness and nosey intelligence like a dog's. She was not at all my enemy, but I managed to elicit a spark of surprise when I looked into her eyes while shaking her hand. At least I think I did, and I took it as a compliment.

"I envy your confidence," Max said, "that you can hear stories about who I was with in the past and not turn it into a comment on how much I want to be with you now." In contrast, he remained as cautious as ever about treading near my extensive intimate history.

"I love thinking about pre-me you having sex," I said. "I like to think about you walking around college with this big, beautiful, secret dick that nobody knows about."

"Not even me. I never looked down."

"That's right. I was the first to discover it."

Which didn't mean it was easy for me to hear about Max's high school or college years. I missed him retroactively, I felt pangs of denial and exclusion about not knowing him then. That sense of separation juxtaposed with our current sense of closeness confused me as it suffused me, and then I felt silly for being so emotional about something so ordinary. Of course he had a life before me, as I'd had mine before him. But the intensity of my love for him made me feel yoked to his past self, even if only in the sense of looking through a temporal window, holding my love for him like a clutch of flowers not yet given away.

This space and time-traveling notion first arose while he was gone in Venice for so long. I felt him next to me sometimes when I sat down on my yoga mat or paused in my reading at home, not because I was conjuring him in my imagination but because my retention of his presence was clear enough to render him there without effort or imperative.

This impression became stronger and more fully formed when I started working again—I had incorporeal Max by my side whenever I had time to myself—and I pictured him accompanied by a disembodied me, too, as if a lane ran parallel between our lives, where two ghostly incarnations conspired and kept our physical forms company when we couldn't share the same 3D space.

~

With so few clients requesting my time, I sometimes went weeks without leaving. Max and I could have bliss then, freed from the work of filling in the pit that opened under us when I went away to be with another man. But the ground still fell away when I left, and before I left, too. Simply telling him about an upcoming trip would start the crumble.

We didn't fight or fling insults, but we could be unintentionally vicious with our clumsy suffering. On the worst occasion, I left our bed mid-night for the couch, sleepless. I felt like an alien; everything in the apartment and street below, even my own body, was foreign and meaningless. I finally felt convinced I was wrong about the mutuality of our devotion. He couldn't be so destroyed by my work if he trusted that I loved him like I did. If he understood how I loved him, he'd know nothing could threaten or corrupt that. But I was incapable of reassuring him, and his need for reassurance felt like a failure. It meant I'd misunderstood our complete connection, the lucidity and coherence of our dynamic.

In the early light, he left the bedroom and showered, moved around the apartment without speaking to me or looking at me. I hoped he'd wake and comfort me, say something kind. Instead, when he finally sat on the edge of the couch, he asked, in the voice of man betrayed, why I'd left the bed.

"So you could sleep, I didn't want to keep you up," I said. I wanted to touch him, or for him to touch me.

"Was it because I said waking up to you was my favorite part of the day?" He nearly trembled, and I realized this was the closest I'd ever seen him to rage.

"No. I was restless, I didn't want to bother you."

"Was it because of how I fucked you last night?" His voice even quieter now. I knew he wouldn't hit me but his body radiated excess energy badly in need of discharge. I wanted to touch him but it seemed reckless. I didn't know this person. Myself, or him.

"No!" Anguished, I saw that he could only interpret my being on the couch as an attack meant to punish him, not a request that he come after me or a protective move to keep my crying and shifting from ruining his sleep. I could barely believe we could be like this with each other. Was it all a misunderstanding? I needed to find my way back to trusting that he was my Max, that I knew what this was and who we were. I finally reached out and put my hand on his skin.

"I don't know why it's been so hard for us lately," I said two days after, hollow inside from things still not being right. That crumbling situation, it wasn't only external, between us. It was internal, too. Small pieces breaking and falling away from my heart. Feeling this way didn't make any sense, not given how much we said we loved each other.

In less fraught times, I'd told Max, "You'll never know how I love you. But it doesn't feel lonely. It's like an exciting secret; it gives me a sense of pride, like I've been entrusted with an important job. There's honor in being asked."

But the first aspect took on a more ominous cast on days when our ruptured attachment refused to be fully mended. You'll never know how I love you, you'll never believe how I love you. You'll never understand how I love you, and so the resulting insecurities will swarm and hover over us until they obscure us from each other.

My ex sent me messages more regularly now. In one, he quoted an email he'd written to his cousin about me, on the first day we met.

"I'll always love you," he told me after.

I wondered if I'd made a mistake in leaving him. I wondered if any coupling that stretched to a decade and beyond would resemble every other no matter how it began. Perhaps all aged romances are alike, with resignation and pragmatic accommodation haunting a sincere, scarred commitment.

Only once did I miss my old city and former life, and I recognized what I really missed at that moment was the stability and predictability it gave me. I didn't seriously doubt that breaking up was the right choice or that moving was the right choice. Even if Max and I only lasted a few years, being with him would have been worth it.

But that was the worst development: I started allowing the possibility that Max and I might not be forever. When I left for my first long work appointment, I'd given Max an envelope. "In case of emotional emergency," I wrote on the front, and inside was a print out of "The Cord," the Tiny Letter in which I described telling him I loved him for the first time and learning he knew I was Charlotte. I handwrote a short explanation to go with it, to reiterate that I was his entirely, with him permanently.

I included the lines, "I already am your wife. Sometimes I'm impatient for everyone else to know it, but no one else matters."

Those two days while I worked were exhausting. I texted Max constantly, trying to ward off his despair, but failing. I assumed he'd open the letter since his mood could hardly have been bleaker, and I was hurt that nothing in it moved him to respond. In one particularly hopeless moment, I cited the letter's inability to reach him, my continuing inability to reach him, and said how bereft that left me.

"I haven't opened it yet," he replied as he rushed to calm me down.

But months later, he admitted he had, he'd opened it just hours after I left for that trip. He didn't mention a word about the sentiments inside, ever.

I could no longer tell him I never doubted us, and mean it.

~

Gradually, our perfunctory conversations around work became less strained, and our subsequent time apart a little less intense. I knew Max was making an effort to be more accepting, which I appreciated. For my part, I now only saw Roger, no one else, usually only twice a month at most.

But nothing was fully resolved. It was a sunny morning the day after I'd gotten home from a work trip when Max declined to have breakfast with me as we usually did, and I felt so trampled by pain that I fled outside while he was in the bathroom, and cried on a bench nearby in my pajamas, my face wedged into the crook of my elbow.

"Where are you?" he texted a few minutes after.

"Outside."

"Can I come join you?"

"Sure."

When he came down, I pulled my knees in closer to my chest to make space for him.

"I wasn't trying to be mean about breakfast," he said.

"I know."

"It's just hard to have an appetite."

"I know."

It was hot, uncomfortably hot even before noon with my legs and arms bare, but the sun helps everything to feel a little less dire. I wasn't angry. I was depleted, alone. There were so many things I couldn't tell him because he didn't want to know—about my ex, about Roger, about huge swaths of my past. And apparently I wasn't capable of telling him about my present, which was him, and how I loved him—how I love him. Maybe I would never be intelligible to him, and I should stop trying to make myself so.

"I feel like I'm the only dog pulling a sled," I told him. "Every time I stop and start again, the sled gets heavier. But I have to keep pulling."

He leaned his face into mine. "There's no reason anyone on earth should feel like a lonely dog when they have someone who loves them as much as I love you."

Through it all, he hadn't lost his ability to move me with his tenderness. I remembered the morning he left for Venice, when he ran an errand and then came back to the apartment. I looked for him out the window when I was expecting him back, as soon as I put my face near the glass I almost pulled away in surprise. Because as I glanced down from the apartment that would become our home, he was striding down the street, already gazing up at me.

≈

"I think the strangest things during sex with you," I told him.

"Sometimes I have flashes of color and abstract thoughts," he said. "It's like every door is open. Like my own mind is flooded with itself. I realized that the fifth or sixth night we were together."

"I'm afraid to afraid to tell you mine, it seems presumptuous and invasive. Too greedy."

"I think you already started so you have to finish."

"Ok. Well . . . it's the feeling of you sliding inside me at the start. I think about the first time you had sex and what it was like for the girl you were with. If she realized how special it was, how important." I was crying because saying this ached but with the clean throb of purging, the pain that follows removing a thorn.

Surely, she must have understood with physical intelligence the goodness of it. The grand luck beyond luck of him, that his body was this way, that he was this way, that he was.

("Every single moment that we were together was miraculous," Anne Druyan says of her dead partner. "We knew we were the beneficiaries of chance. . . . That pure chance could be so generous and so kind. . . . I don't think I'll ever see Carl again. But I saw him. We saw each other. We found each other in the cosmos, and that was wonderful.")

"And the person after that too, what did it feel like for her? It's not jealousy, not really. It's about . . . feeling connected to her, to them. I'm too greedy with my desire for you, for knowing you. My sense of being tied to you can't be extended into the future, so it moves into the past."

"It's already filled up the present."

"Yes, so it has to go somewhere."

I wondered what he felt with them, too, though I didn't say that then. I trusted I would have time to ask. Even if I didn't know exactly how much time we had together, I believed we had more. How many nights we'd laid together in the dark trying to describe the joy we took in the other. How many more nights did we have ahead of us?

"I love you forever, _____," he said. "All the way forward. All the way backward." The love lasts limitlessly for as long as it lasts.

~

When thinking about Max's college years, I vividly remembered my own, and how once I started at university, I was in an urgent hurry to finish. My fundamental impatience makes me feel that way about many stages of life. It's as if I live in a permanent interim. I see evidence of that in my eagerness to marry Max, and in my idea of the loyal ghosts.

I wanted Max and I to only know perfect love. Not painless love but seamless love. The doubts, the disconnects—they were intolerable to me. They were proof, I thought, of something fundamentally wrong. If ours was as special a union as I thought, wouldn't our communication be flawless?

The saner part of me knows that temporarily losing each other doesn't make our affinity less precious or real. I want to trust that our love isn't changing, not exactly, but rather it's being turned over in our hands. We keep examining it from a fresh angle, like a crystal that never catches or refracts the same light twice. As long as we're looking together, it's still ours.

Shouldn't that make the occasional uncertainty bearable? Because change is constant, because instability is the world's only guarantee, commitment can only look like the determination to start over and over again. Or so I tell myself.

"Such is life," Roland Barthes says, quoting a Japanese proverb, "falling down seven times, and getting up eight."

~

"I am the finite that wants the infinite," Cixous writes. "Loves infinites me."

All the way forward. All the way backward. Each of us beginning again and again against the fabric of forever.

BIBLIOGRAPHY

Katherine Angel, Unmastered: *A Book on Desire, Most Difficult to Tell*

Roland Barthes, *A Lover's Discourse*

Anne Carson, *Autobiography of Red*

Hélène Cixous, *Stigmata*

Miranda July, *It Chooses You*

Thich Nhat Hanh, *True Love*

Jenny Offill, *Dept. of Speculation*

E Rekstein, *On Moon Square*

Suzanne Scanlon, *Her 37th Year, An Index*

ACKNOWLEDGEMENTS

Thanks to Melissa Gira Grant for leading by example: the value of your work cannot be overstated. Massive love to Beatrice for granting me access to her intimidating intellect and wise heart, and to Catherine Plato for giving me one of my most enduring and important adult friendships. Janette Park, I'm nothing without you. Snaps to Lux Alptraum for her suggestion that I use Kickstarter, and to Ruth Curry and Emily Gould for sage recommendations on all things publishing. Praise to any and all higher beings that Meaghan O'Connell's number is in my phone and that she's so responsive to texts in spite of the many other demands for her time.

To the glamorous and whip-smart sisterhood of Bardot Smith, Annora, Kat, Susan Shepard, Johanna Freeman, Josephine, Caty Simon, Bettie, Molly Smith, Eithne, Fornicatrix, Amelie, Lori Adorable, Peech, and the many other sex workers I've met online and off: you are everything.